Alma Calder Johnston

Miriam's Heritage

A Story of the Delaware River

Alma Calder Johnston

Miriam's Heritage
A Story of the Delaware River

ISBN/EAN: 9783744666602

Printed in Europe, USA, Canada, Australia, Japan

Cover: Foto ©ninafisch / pixelio.de

More available books at **www.hansebooks.com**

MIRIAM'S HERITAGE

A Story of the Delaware River

By ALMA CALDER

NEW YORK
HARPER & BROTHERS, PUBLISHERS
FRANKLIN SQUARE
1878

Entered according to Act of Congress, in the year 1878, by
HARPER & BROTHERS,
In the Office of the Librarian of Congress, at Washington.

MIRIAM'S HERITAGE.

CHAPTER I.

"Fresh come to a new world, indeed, yet long prepared,
I see the genius of a modern child, of the real and ideal,
Clearing the ground for broad humanity, the true America;
Heir of the past, to build a grander future."
                                    WALT WHITMAN.

MIRIAM MORGAN'S home is nestled among the mountains of the Delaware: a long narrow valley, hedged by hemlock-crowned hills sloping eastward to the river. A brook, after miles of wandering in the forest, finds an outlet here; leaping merrily down the southern hillside; resting quietly in the pond above the mill; dashed to glittering fragments on the wheel; then rushes foaming across the valley to join the beautiful river, which sweeps unheeding by, until, lingering at a rocky cliff, its current is divided: part hurries onward, and part returns to welcome the noisy little brook, and reflect again the grassy bank, the white cottage, and the green hills; forming one of the prettiest scenes to the eye of an artist, and the best rafting eddy to the eye of a lumberman, to be found in the country.

Here millions of feet of logs and lumber are each year rafted by hardy men, who brave heat and cold, fire and flood, to cut, haul, rescue, and raft the lumber, which is their only source of revenue.

Sometimes a storm overflows the mountain streams, fills the mill-ponds, bursts the dams, and sweeps away buildings, bridges, roads, trees, and lumber. Sometimes a traveller empties the hot ashes from his pipe by the roadside, or a deserted camp-fire will be fanned by the breeze into a flame, and cords of bark and acres of timber are destroyed.

But oftener the lumber which has escaped these perils, been piled upon the river's bank, withstood the crashing ice and roaring flood, been formed into rafts, and started hopefully on its way to market, its oars well manned, its steersman well chosen, its provision-box well filled, and a good freshet to carry it to tide-water, will strike against a bridge-pier, collide with another raft, or be blown by the wind out of the channel, and become a wreck, scarcely worth the labor and expense of rerafting.

The men who encounter and overcome these perils, wresting a living from out the hands of Nature, while all her powers seem arrayed against them, develop the hardy, reckless part of their characters rapidly.

Their faces are keener than the farmer's, coarser than the tradesman's, lighted by a social, shrewd expression; while their rollicking, reckless manners have stamped the name of *raftsman*, in town and city, as a synonyme for *rowdy;* few aware of the brave, unselfish impulses lying beneath the rude exterior.

To these wilds, and these associates, came John Morgan, almost forty years ago, bringing his wife, and two boys, aged five and seven years.

A wealthy farmer's daughter, reared with little knowledge of life beyond the quiet village, where the dominie, the doctor, and the dress-maker were each alike infallible, where the lowest forms of vice were never seen and poverty unknown, Mrs. Morgan found it difficult to reconcile herself to the privations of her new home, harder still to accept those loud-voiced, queerly clad people as neighbors and friends, and was inexpressibly grieved to witness the ease with which her husband and sons adapted themselves to the customs of their associates.

John Morgan was a man of more than ordinary ability and self-appreciation; having a singular mixture of qualities common to opposite temperaments.

Usually reticent, undemonstrative, unsympathetic, he was always sensitive, impetuous, intense. Haughty, selfish, dictatorial, sarcastic, he made many bitter enemies; but those yielding implicit obedience to his will, and doing homage to his judgment, found him a wise counsellor and a generous friend. Proud of a lineage unstained by vice, he exhibited no fondness for the culture which had made them famous. Though ambitious to regain the wealth lost by his ancestors, he insisted that a life of ascetic frugality was the noblest and happiest; social alike to his equals and inferiors, he considered any expression of regard or sympathy to his family or employés as undignified and injurious: lavish to a fault at times, he was often penurious and apparently unscrupulous.

Adopting the profession of his father, a lawyer of some prominence, he studied with him for several years; but upon marrying a farmer's daughter, and receiving with her a well-stocked farm, he abandoned his profession, to till his wife's inheritance.

Here ten quiet, prosperous years passed. Absorbed in the same occupations, members of the same church, interested in the same people and pursuits, John and Mary Morgan were similar in tastes, harmonious in opinions: as two mountains crowned with the same verdure, cultivated with the same care, none could suspect one was filled with veins of gold, the other a latent volcano.

The monotonous calm of their lives was broken by a fire of religious enthusiasm, which, kindled by an "evangelist" in an adjoining village, swept the entire country.

During the heat of the excitement, John Morgan publicly declared his intention of becoming a missionary to India. The entreaties of his wife and the expostulations of his friends were alike insufficient to deter him. Each obstacle added to his zeal.

The farm was sold; a house in the village rented for his wife and two boys; arrangements made for their maintenance until he should return, or send for them to join him; and with perfect confidence in the purity of his motives and his fitness for the work, he presented himself to the Board of Foreign Missions. But here new difficulties arose. No company was ready to start for India, and the treasury was not in funds. Some knowledge of the language and customs was also necessary; and the zealous young man was advised to spend a half-year in study. Cheap lodgings were found, and days of wearisome study and impatient waiting lengthened into months before the time of their departure came.

Then some detention occurred; and the hasty spirit of John Morgan could endure no more. Angry words followed, and the young man left the presence of the assembled Board in a towering passion, renouncing the idea of sacrificing himself for the benefit of the heathen. Mortified, but not humbled, he resolved to find another home before returning to his friends. The purchase of these timber lands was recommended by their owner's agent, and highly praised by the man who had them in charge.

"Tell ye what, mister," he said, "thar hain't no purtier-layin' land 'long the Del'ware, nor no better timber nowhar. Easy to git at, an' cuts up *prime* lumber. Thar's a good house, an' a fust-rate mill put up this year, an' a sort o' barn an' a storehouse; but them'll want fixin' some. Ef ye conclude to buy, *an' yer woman'll cum,* you'd better make yer plans to git along in April. Ye kin bring yer traps on a raft from Beaverkill ef thar's a fresh; an' ef thar hain't, ye' kin git along with an ark, and maybe a canoe or a float. 'Twon't cost ye much to move, an' ye'll be hard to please ef the place don't suit ye. Why, I tried livin' in Jarsey, but I couldn't stan' it. Tol' 'em I got to git whar I could smell hemlock an' see maountains, or I should die. I'd ruther hav' the fun o' gettin' out an' runnin' a raft o' toggle timber than the hull crop o' the best Jarsey farm, *ef I had to raise it.* No sir-ee! Thar's nothin' in the State fit to hol' a candle to the upper Del'ware; 'nless it's the gals—an' they're a contrary lot; thinkin' more o' thar ol' Jarsey sandhills an' mud flats than anybody or anything else. But now I tell ye, mister, that thar lot o' lan's offered ye dog-cheap; an' ef ye take it, ye'll git a bargain; that's so!"

The agent also assured him that the country was healthy, beautiful, fertile, well watered, abounding in fish and game, covered with valuable timber, and on the line of the New York and Erie Railroad, now being constructed.

Captivated by the description, he only waited to assure himself of their location and title; when, without seeking the advice of any, he became the possessor of five thousand acres of hemlock forest in the unbroken wilderness, with their overseer, Bill Morris, engaged as foreman.

A few weeks later, he, with his wife and sons, and all their household goods, were floating down the Delaware. At twilight of the second day they were landed on the pebbly beach before the log-cabin, now their only home.

Exhausted by the wearisome journey, Mary Morgan dragged herself listlessly up the pathway, entered the bare, rude cabin, and waited until the workmen who accompanied them had brought the goods from the raft, cut boughs of fragrant hemlock, scattered them in heaps across the two ends of the room, and kindled a bright blaze in the big fireplace.

Then she spread some blankets over the evergreens, called the boys to her side, bidding them kneel and repeat, as usual, their evening prayers. The men hushed their laughter and jesting, gazing with surprise and awe upon the unusual scene. Their "good-nights" were said, and soon all slept.

The sunlight, streaming through the uncurtained windows, awoke Mrs. Morgan to a strange sense of old things having passed away. The men had risen and gone out an hour before, carrying their boots in their hands, lest they should disturb her slumbers.

Her boys were still sleeping soundly, when, rising, she wrapped a shawl around her, and went out to take a first look at their new home.

The thickly wooded hills, where evergreen and deciduous trees intermingled, wore a wintry look; patches of snow covered the fields, and the river was rippled by the chilling wind. A saw-mill beside the brook, piles of lumber around it, a storehouse of hewn logs with heavily shuttered windows, and a slab barn: these were all the signs of human habitation.

A spring bubbled out from a huge rock a few steps from the door; a stump garlanded by leafless vines was beside the pathway, and a pile of uncut wood and scattered chips lay near the door. A shout of delight from the boys, Jamie and Davy, as they ran from the house, chasing a squirrel up the hillside and scaring a rabbit to its hole, aroused the mother from sad memories, to suggest new fears. Visions of wild beasts upon the mountains, snakes among the rocks, and the dangers of river and mill-pond to her venturesome boys, sent a chill of terror to her heart.

"Well, how do you like it?" said her husband's voice beside her.

"It is rougher, wilder, than I expected, John. But if it is to be our home, of course I'll try to make the best of it: yet what will become of our boys?"

"The boys! why, it's just the place for them. They'll grow up with the country, and become hearty men; able to assist me in the management of this immense estate, and become leading men in the community."

"But they are children now; and I am afraid they will get hurt, or lost, or drowned."

"Oh, nonsense! I expect them to be able to hunt, fish, and swim, like the natives."

"Oh, John, do forbid their going

into the woods alone, or near the water till they can swim. I mean until they learn to—"

John Morgan's loud laugh silenced her. "Keep them out of the water till they know how to swim! Well, if that isn't a woman's idea! No, I don't intend to do anything of the kind. I mean my boys to grow up fearless, independent men, with no sickly sentimentalism about them. I intend they shall learn to shoot a squirrel in the eye, hunt down a bear or a panther, ride a log, steer a raft, swim a mile, or run a saw-mill, as well or better than any one in the country."

The boys, attracted by their father's laughter, had come up unperceived, and, catching a glimpse of the astonishment and anguish in their mother's face, understood her terror.

Jamie slipped his little brown hand in hers, as his father walked away.

"You needn't be one bit afraid 'bout me, mother dear," he said, pulling her arm around his neck; "I won't go into the mill, or river, 'thout asking: and Big Bill (that's what he told me to call him, mother, said it made him feel's if he had on a starched shirt to be called Mister Morris); he's going to teach Dave and me to swim: and he's a real good fellow, Bill is; he won't let us get hurt a mite. You'll see."

The mother stooped and kissed him. "My blessing!" she said, as her eyes filled with tears.

"Well, *I*'m going to learn to shoot a gun; and then noffin' won't hurt *me*, for I'll kill it. And I kin learn to swim by watching the frogs; Bill said so," added Davy.

"Here, Mary," called her husband, returning with a panful of fish; "see what Sanders caught for breakfast. This is the place to live! Here's fifty speckled trout, caught in an hour, and the woods are full of game. No nobleman has a park like ours—nor an appetite like mine. Come, here's a dozen men ready to praise the cook by eating everything she sets before them. Just give me a tin, and I'll have one of the men clean these fish. Now see what you can get for us to eat."

"But the stove isn't set up yet," she said; "and the lunch is all eaten."

"Well, can't you cook a meal over the fireplace? I've seen my mother get as good meals over a fireplace as I ever tasted."

Mary Morgan turned from the sight of the struggling, gasping fish with a shudder, and entered the house. Two men were piling up the blankets, heaping the hemlock in one corner, and stirring the fire.

"If one of you will open a barrel of flour," she said, timidly, "I will try to make some biscuit; but I don't know how to bake them. There's no tin oven, and it will take so long to heat that outside oven."

"Guess you hain't never cooked over a fireplace much, hev ye?" inquired one of the men.

"No."

"Wall, now, yeou jist stir up a johnny-cake—that there is a bag o' Injun, I guess, an' the milk in that jug is sour'n swill—an' I'll bake it for ye. An' yeou jist let Big Bill fry them fish. He's so tarnal conceity, Bill is, he thinks nobody can't cook fish 'longside o' him. Here's the coffee-kittle. Neow I'll jist step out an' split up a slab for this ere fire. 'Spose you never eat no wood-sorrel, did ye? Wall, neow, I allers like suthin' kindy sour 'long o' fish-an'-meat vittels; an' we hain't got no gardin'-sass started yit. Guess I kin git a han'ful or two, an' them 'at don't like it needn't eat it. Found your saleratus? I've seen my woman burn a corn-cob 'fore now, an' use the ashes to lighten her johnny-cake. May as well be gittin' the table an' cheers up here too. Don't see what them fellers is all doin' over to the mill: might 'a had everythin' moved and settled by this time."

CHAPTER II.

"'The meal unshared is food unblest:
Thou hoardest in vain what love should spend.
Self-care is pain; thy only rest
Is labor for a worthy end.
Then do thy work; it shall succeed,
In thine or in another's day:
And if denied the victor's meed,
Thou shalt not lack the toiler's pay."
WHITTIER.

THE spring days lengthened into early summer. Diligent hands had united with nature's efforts to improve their surroundings; and the Morgans were settled in their new home. An addition to the rear, and a veranda to the front of the house, repeated coats of whitewash to both inside and outside, with woodbine and grape-vines twining over the doorway and windows, had transformed the brown cabin to a cosy cottage.

The old store had also been rebuilt, and the saw-mill was kept busy night and day cutting up the logs with which the pond was filled into scantling to be rafted for the fall freshet. The few acres of wild meadow-land had been ploughed, and planted with corn, and the garden beside the house gave a supply of vegetables.

The hills were covered with raspberries, whortleberries, and blackberries in their turn, and barefooted children clambered over the fallen trees of the "clearings," and among the half-burned stumps of the "fallows" to pick them, carrying the fruit of their toil, in well-filled pails, to the store, to exchange for sugar and tea, calico and trinkets; and Mrs. Morgan's ingenuity was taxed to the utmost to devise ways and means to preserve the berries, their only fruit, for the coming winter.

All business ceased at "Morgan's Settlement" every Saturday night; and, various as were the excuses of the settlers coming on Sundays to purchase tobacco, or shot and powder, the store was never opened. The workmen spent the day in visiting their friends; and the family in rereading the books brought from home. There were no churches or schools.

A circuit-rider held monthly meetings at a farm-house ten miles away, and colporters sometimes preached at the same place; but no efforts had ever been made to attend their meetings.

"If there were only a school!" the

mother exclaimed, daily, as her sunburnt lads ran from the breakfast-table to examine rabbit-traps, hunt for fish-lines, or play about the mill and store.

"Why don't you teach them, Mary? You haven't forgotten all you learned at the academy yet, have you?"

"But who would do the cooking and cleaning, and bake, and wash, and iron, John? We number ten in family, now, since the night sawyer and the clerk came; and I work eighteen hours a day to get the housework done."

"Well, there's Jane Rodgers: you might get her to come and help you."

"No, that wouldn't do; it is as easy to do it all as to instruct and oversee her."

"Well, then, do as you've a mind to! If you'd rather the boys would grow up as ignorant as the natives, as wild as hawks and rough as bears, *I* can't help it." And the father walked off to superintend the measurement of some piles of bark and attend the burning of a "follow," as the land was called when, the valuable timber having been removed, the remainder of the trees were reduced to charcoal and ashes.

The mother began the day's labors with a heavy heart; but as one task after another was accomplished, the germ of a resolve grew up in her heart, and blossomed in a song.

"Jamie, Jamie! come here; mother's a-singing!" shouted Davy, from the wood pile, to his older brother at the spring.

Their mother heard, and smiled. "I do believe it is the first time I have sung since we left home," she thought; "and my boys have noticed it. This is all wrong! I may be harming another life by my discontent. The little one God is giving me must have a sunny spirit for her dower, and strong nerves and intense vitality. Ah! I must make a change in some way."

The scraping of feet on the doorstone announced a guest, and Mrs. Rodgers walked in.

"How-de-do! how-de-do!" she exclaimed, rather than inquired. "Dreadful glad your getting kindy chirked up. Jane said as how you's powerful hum'sick; but I guessed you was a gittin' over 't when I heerd you a-singin'. Camp-meetin' tune, wa'n't it? Tell yeou! nothin' so kindy raises me up, an' goes all through me, like a good ol'-fashion' camp-meetin' tune! An' neow I'll tell yeou right off what I cum fur. It's a burnin' shame the way things is goin' on here! We've hed fishin' an' huntin' on Sabba'-day all along; seemed like we couldn't help it, cause the men-folks 'ud git powerful tired o' salt pork, and kindy hanker arter suthin' fresh. Then the raftin', an' runnin', an' bark-peelin', an' farmin' all cumin' in right along on top o' one another, so's thar don't seem to be no time for workin' in the gardin, or gittin' any game, 'less it's on Sunday. So I don't say nothin' 'bout that, no more. But las' time Jack was down the river, he got him a *fiddle;* walked the hull way hum carryin' that thing in his arms. An' next time, like 's not, he'll git him a pack o' keards! an' finally—his day o' grace will be clean run out—an' oh-dear-me-suz! seem's ef I couldn't stan' it! But las' night, 's I was a-layin' in bed, seems to me 's ef the Lord he jis' spoke an' said, 'Go to Mis' Morgan!' An' sez I, Lord, I will, soon 's ever I git the cows milked an' the breakfast work done up. An' so I jis' left Jane to tend the bakin', an' I cum right over. An' neow I want you should tell me what we're goin' to do."

And the good old woman leaned back in the cushioned rocker and fanned herself with her sun-bonnet.

"Well, Mrs. Rodgers, I think we are living like a set of heathen; and I know we ought to have preaching here every Sabbath. There's the store Mr. Morgan has fitted up; he had two wings built while the carpenters were here, rather than have them come again; but they only use one; and I know the other could be made quite a comfortable meeting-house."

"Wall, I dew declare! you're a fustrate hand at plannin'. But who'll we git to preach?"

"I have thought of that too. Maybe we can get a congregation large enough to bring Elder Smith over here. But for the present we have some of Wesley's and Calvin's sermons, and my husband can read them to us—he's a very good reader—and I will teach my boys to sing the hymns, and—"

"The Lord bless you! You dew beat all I ever see fur pickin' up a body's thoughts an' carryin' them right along. Your David's got a v'ice like a bobolink; an' I never heerd nobody tune up sweeter than yeou did 'fore I cum in. My Jack's got a powerful nice v'ice tew. Mebbe yeou could git him int' the notion of singin' suthin' 'side them silly songs o' his'n.

And yeou tell Brother Morgan," lowering her voice and wiping her face with her blue checked apron, "that I wouldn't mind makin' the prayers myself, ef he feels anyways back'ard about it."

"Oh, I don't think he would mind," Mrs. Morgan said, hurriedly: "we always used to have family prayers, and he often prayed in the conference meetings at our old home. You stay to dinner, and after the men have gone out ask him what he thinks of our plan. We have veal pot-pie for dinner; and I think that will be a treat. Mr. Morgan sent Jenkins way up to Cole's with the canoe after it."

"Fur the land's sake! Sent ten mile to git fresh meat! Well, I hain't hed a bit o' fresh meat sence Jack broke his gun; an', somehow, I don't stomac' wild meat as I used to, anyhow. Yes, I guess I'll stay. Our men-folks takes their dinners in the woods with them long 's bark-peelin' lasts, and Jane 'll tend to the chores."

The shadows were creeping up the hillsides when Mrs. Rodgers walked homeward. Her strong face was quivering with emotion, and great tears rolled down the brown, wrinkled cheeks.

When a turn in the road hid her from view, she knelt beside a mossy log and poured out her thanks to the All Father who had sent these Christians to her help.

The simple, earnest, tender-hearted woman had long been pained and perplexed by the increasing levity and lawlessness of her neighbors. Believing that all alcoholic drinks were made by the "Enemy of Souls," and cards "devices of the devil to entrap the unwary," the calm peacefulness of her nature had been stirred to its depths at hearing of the social glass and games of chance too frequently indulged in by her neighbors; and many fervent prayers had been poured out from the mother-heart for her boy, that he might shun "them devil's drinks, an' pasteboard traps, marked with the black of Satan's fingers, and painted with the heart's-blood of his victims," often wondering why the Lord did not rise in his wrath and strike down the evil-doers who tempted the innocent into sin.

To Mrs. Rodgers's consciousness of being the only "professor" in the settlement was added a feeling of personal responsibility for the souls of her neighbors, which would have been overwhelming to a more sensitive nature, but which, in her, caused frequent and frantic efforts to save the sinners, *nolens volens*, and induced public and pointed exhortations, wherein more zeal than wisdom was manifested.

These efforts for their good, united with generous deeds and gracious hospitality, had not been received nor rewarded with that consideration she felt was her due.

Then, too, her convictions had sometimes yielded to circumstances; and it was with a vague hope of a definite standard of morality being established that she welcomed these Christians to the wilderness; and as she knelt by the roadside, desires and hopes united with her thanksgiving.

Before the Sabbath came the long, low room had been swept, and garnished with hemlock boughs and laurel blossoms. Plank seats were supported by blocks of wood. A large dry-goods box, with a smaller one placed upon it, and covered with a large dark-green shawl, formed the pulpit. On the smaller box the family Bible was laid, and on the projecting ends of the larger one Jamie and Davy had placed their china mugs, filled with wild-roses.

"It's jest as purty as a picter!" exclaimed the Saturday customers to the store, peeping into the room; and each one readily promised "to come to meetin'" the following day, and bring their friends with them.

CHAPTER III.

"Think ye that sic as you and I—
Wha' drudge an' delve through wet and dry
Wi' never-ceasing toil—
Think ye, are we less blest than they
Wha' scarcely tent us on their way,
As hardly worth their while?"
BURNS.

SUNDAY morning dawned bright and clear. Jamie and Davy were up with the birds to welcome the fair day; but the shouts were louder than the songs as the boys ran to the barn, hallooing to Big Bill the glad news that this was "goin' to be a real sure enough Sunday, like we used to have home"—*home* being still their birthplace, the village farm.

The shadows had passed the noon mark, when along the new road, and down the mountain paths, came groups of men, women, and barefooted children. The men clad in homespun, their "wamusses" of butternut-colored flannel tied down the front with brilliant-hued strings; knitted caps on their heads, running up to a peak, and terminating in a gay tassel; while one or two possessed coats brought from "down the river," and hats of straw braided by the fingers of sister or sweetheart.

The women wore sun-bonnets or handkerchiefs tied over their ears, with homespun or calico frocks: here and there a brilliant pink or blue gingham adorned a girlish form, cut to reveal the plump white shoulders and round sunburnt arms.

Shyly, and with surprised gladness, they met and greeted each other, "goin' to meetin'" being an unusual event, and each having wondered if the other would be there.

The men talked of "crops," the "price of lumber," and the prospect of a "June fresh;" while the women chatted about the last quilting and logging bee, of deaths and marriages; and not one word was spoken of the subject uppermost in their minds, until across the meadow Mrs. Rodgers came.

Her cheery face gleamed with gladness as she shook hands with her neighbors, exclaiming,

"I'm powerful glad to see you all a-comin' out to meetin'. I've been a prayin' an' prayin' that some on ye'd flee from the wrath to come. But I'm feard some of ye's jest come to show off your store-clothes. I see

Lucy Jones has got on that string o' blue an' yaller beads o' hearn. Oh-dear-me-suz! When I think what poor dyin' worms we be! But the Lord is pitiful an' gracious, slow to anger, and plentiful in mercy! An' ef Brother Morgan 'vites you to come to the mourner's bench, I dew hope some on ye will git convarted, and come out on the Lord's side, to-day."

Big sobs choked her voice, and tears rolled down her quivering face, as she pulled her sun-bonnet over her eyes and hurried into the temporary chapel.

"Neow, I'm beat holler, ef Auntie Rodgers ain't a powerful preacher! Stew me fur apple-sass of I wa'nt jest reddy to shout Amen!"

"You're sassy enuff neow, an' you'll git stewed hereafter probably," said a tall, lank man, sneeringly, as he walked by.

"Land's sake!" exclaimed the boy, grinning, "Long John can't go by ye in the road 'thout hittin' ye a slap."

"Mebbe *you* never felt 's ef ye had a soul, Sam Jenkins," said a clear-voiced, bright-eyed girl, turning to face him; "an' ef you've forgot the bowls o' gruel Mis' Rodgers made fur ye when you's sick, I guess ye hain't got one's worth savin'.."

"Laws-a-massy, Susan! heow yeou dew flare up at nothin'! Hain't I always sed, and stuck tew it, thar hain't no better nuss than Auntie Rodgers 'n the hull Yankee nation, hey? nor a cleverer woman nuther! But then it's my 'pinion she is kinder out o' the current in her ideas 'bout gittin' religin. Neow look at this yer 'arth, all trees, an' purty posies, an' nice gals, an' birds, an' sunshine. Stands tew reason, don't it? the Lord wants his critters to have a good time, else he'd a made everythin' humbly as I be. Neow there's Big Bill: dew you 'spose the Lord likes him any better sence he took to mopin' 'roun' than when he was a jokin' an' laughin', an' singin' all day? He done his work jist as good, and helped t'other fellers do theirn, just by keepin' their sperits up. Tell yeou! that time we stove up in Wellses, guess we'd lost both rafts, an' gone to Davy Jones's locker, ef it hadn't a' ben for Bill! But sence he's got religin down in Jarsey—don't know's 'twas religin altogether, though—but I don't b'leve the Lord wants anybody to go groanin', an' snivolin', an' mopin', an'—"

"Neow, Sam, you jest shet up! Much you know 'bout what the Lord wants. Mis' Rodgers 's 'bout as well acquainted 'ith him 's you be! Thar hain't none of us but what's done things we orter be ashamed of an' sorry fur, an' ask furgiveness fur, too, I 'spose! Thar, neow, you'll be a-tellin' what a smart preacher *I* be too! Well, I don't care. Come, Lucy, thar goes Mis' Morgan an' her boys. Les us go in."

The girls entered the wide door and seated themselves on a bench near it. Several young men followed, with much sideway glancing to see who were watching them, and a ready sneer to exchange with a companion, or transform into a serious smile if meeting the reproving glance of a "professor."

The seats were already half filled; and the whispered admonitions to restless children, the flutter of the partridge-tail fans, and the undertoned talk of the men gathered about the steps suddenly ceased as John Morgan, with a flushed face, entered and walked hurriedly to the extemporized pulpit, opened the black morocco hymn-book, and read the old familiar hymn,

"Come, thou Fount of every blessing!
Tune my heart to grateful lays."

Mary Morgan arose; her boys, one each side of her, looked eagerly over the book she held, and joined their childish voices with her sweet treble. Here and there a grumbling bass and a quivering soprano joined in the old-fashioned tune.

From the garden fence, from the store steps, the curious loungers came, hushing their noisy footsteps as they entered, unwilling to lose one word of the fervent hymn. One by one had risen, until all joined in the attitude of song; and the late-comers were forced to walk to the bench before the pulpit to find an unoccupied seat.

Close beside Davy came Big Bill, and next to him stood Jack Rodgers.

Jamie pushed the hymn-book toward them; his mother took the gentle hint and placed the open book in Big Bill's hands, with a nod which said "We know it," then sang on,

"Teach me some melodious measure,
Sung by raptured saints above;"

The amateur preacher had been fumbling the leaves of a leather-bound volume, with nervous fingers; now, his heavy bass voice joined them in singing,

"Praise the mount, I'm fixed upon it;
Mount of Thy redeeming love."

At the close of the second stanza, Big Bill's voice united with his—

"Jesus sought me when a stranger,
Wandering from the fold of God;"

And as the final verse was begun, the flute-like voice of Jack Rodgers soared, sweet and clear, above them all, inspiring each to unite in the melody as they shouted,

"Here's my heart, oh take and seal it,
Seal it from thy courts above."

The hymn ended, John Morgan knelt upon the floor, and, one by one, the "professors" followed his example, the rest of the congregation bowing their heads upon their hands.

Briefly, but fervently, he implored "Divine assistance, that light might be disseminated, truth be promulgated, and righteousness cover the face of the earth as the waters cover the great deep," asking also that "God would bless this portion of his moral vineyard, making it to bring forth fruit to his glory."

Another familiar hymn was sang, and then John Morgan's voice announced "A sermon preached before the University, at St. Mary's, Oxford, by John Wesley, June 18th, 1738. Text, 'By grace are ye saved through faith.' Ephesians II., second chapter, eighteenth verse."

In a deep, distinct voice he began to read. The novelty kept the attention of all until the first five divisions of the three-headed discourse had been logically considered. Then the bare feet of the children began reaching for the floor, their eyes wandering to the squirrels chattering a defiance at them through the open window, to the trees nodding and beckoning in the sunlight. Sprigs of caraway, doughnuts and cookies, frowns and whispered commands to "set still," were all unavailing. One after another broke from the guardian hands, and ran out into the sunshine.

Then the younger ones cried, and would not be pacified. Passed from the arms of one to another, they refused to be comforted, and were carried out as Mr. Morgan reached the concluding paragraph, and sat down with a sigh of relief that the seven pages of fine print were finished.

His wife arose, singing,

"Praise God from whom all blessings flow;"

several voices joined; and as the final word of the grand old Doxology was uttered, the handshaking of friends and neighbors began.

Amidst the greetings and inquiries, Mrs. Morgan stood watching her husband until he passed by an inner door into the store.

The sermon had not been a successful venture; the interruptions confused, the inattention annoyed him. He had anticipated congratulations and requests to read for them every Sunday; but no such requests came.

Evidently the rural congregation had had enough of sermons addressed to universities.

Well, he had done his duty. No one could say he had not tried as a Christian to establish the worship of God among these people: now, if they went hunting, fishing, and visiting on the Sabbath, the fault was not his!

Mary Morgan read these thoughts in his face; and as he turned away, closing and bolting the door behind him, she sighed heavily.

"He is right in the first thought," she said, mentally: "reading Wesley's sermons will not do; but these people ought to know about God and Christ: they want to know! There is Polly Sanders and Sam Jenkins; how eagerly they listened at first. Poor Auntie Rodgers, how disappointed she looked, too! Well, there *is* a way to lead these people, and we must find it. Maybe it is a Sunday-school; but we have no teachers nor books."

"Mother, mother," called Davy's eager voice, "there's a woman to our house, an' she talks the queerest! A woman from way off, mother!"

A blue-eyed, golden-haired girl met her as she entered the rustic gate.

"Wad ye mind cf I bide wi' ye the day, mistress? I'm ower-tired; an' I ken I'm at deith's door wi' hunger."

"Come in, come in. Jamie dear, run to the cellar and get a pitcher of milk. Davy, can you pick up a basket of chips to build a fire? Father will want some tea. And you, little children"—to the flock of curious urchins gathering—"run away to your mammas: maybe they have some more cookies for you."

She drew her strange guest into the house; and the group of wondering children ran away to claim the remains of their lunch, proclaiming the news of the arrival.

"A yaller-headed gal talkin' the queerest stuff. Guess she's crazy."

Mrs. Rodgers was earnestly exhorting Big Bill to "come out boldly on the Lord's side," when the foremost urchin overtook them, shouting the news.

"What's that yer sayin'?" he asked; "who's come? what's her name?"

"I don't know; guess she's some furrin critter. She talks outlandish-like. Mis' Morgan, she took her int' the house and sot her down in the big rockin'-cheer; an'—"

"Yes, sir," panted another runner, coming up; "an' she giv' her some breen-milk, an' she's a layin' down on Mis' Morgan's bes' bed this ere minnit!"

Many were the wonders and guesses of the neighbors; but a sense of propriety kept the most curious from intruding upon the family, and no more was seen of the strange woman until, after a refreshing sleep and quiet dinner, she told Mary Morgan her history.

Then she walked across the meadow, and stood leaning upon the bars opening into the pastures, awaiting the large comely man who was coming down the hillside, driving the cows before him.

"I ken it wad be better sae," she said to her sympathizing hostess; "my een greit wi' th' thocht o' seein' his bonny face agen. I dinna ken the words I'll whisper in his lug, but he'll forgie his lassie, an' n'er fash o' me agen. Eh me! the lang, lang day sin syne! Forgive me, lady, I maun greit, tho' I dinna want to do 't."

The cattle came up and stopped at the fence; the man stepped forward to let down the bars, gave a long stare at the woman standing beside them, then bounded over the fence, and caught her in his arms.

"Bess, my bonny lassie! my little wife! so ye changed yer mind, did ye? You've come into the backwoods, after all, hain't you? An' here I'd jest made up my mind to give up lumberin' and go back to Jarsey, and work the farm. I swan! ef that hain't cur'us now. Jest as I give up *my* way, you give up *your* way; an' here you be! *I* couldn't stan' it no longer 'thout you, an' you couldn't stan' it no longer 'thout me—an' you're jest as purty as a picter, Bess," holding her at arm's-length, while happy tears trickled down his cheek and over his bronzed beard. "Thar hain't a gal 'roun' yere ken hol' a candle to ye, lassie, an' *yer my wife, too!* an' ye come all the way from Jarsey to git to me. I swan! an' I a-thinkin' mebbe ye'd got to hatin' me fur leavin' yer so!" And he clasped her to his heart again. "But how did yer come? not walked from Pleasant Point! For the land's sake! Oh! why couldn't I know'd ye's comin'! Seems like I kinder felt it too. Auntie Rodgers, she thought I was under conviction; guess I was, too. Lord knows I've enough to repent of to *you*, comin' 's I did to yer hum an' promisin' the ol' folks I'd stay an' work the farm, ef they'd let me hev ye. Jehoshaphat! I'd a' promised anything! But I sorter hankered fur the hills an' the woods; seemed like I couldn't stand them Jarsey flats another year! An' I r'ally thought, Bess, ye ought to leave yer hum an' come to mine. I couldn't bear ye should think more of the ol' folks 'an me; that's what made me madder 'n anything. But I see differ'nt now, Bess. I read in the Good Book t'other day—jest happened to cum across it—how 't the husban' must leave his father an' mother fur his wife; but it don't say nothin' 'bout her leavin' t' ol' folks fur *him*. By jimminy! I liked to holler'd when I see that; an' I says, says I, I'll go back to Bessie, ef she'll hev me agen, an' I'll work them Jarsey flats etarnally ef she wants me to. I swan I will, Bess, ef ye don't like it here an' 'll jest say the word."

"Ah, Willy, me braw bonny laddie!" cried the Scotch girl, clasping both his brown hands in her own, "wad ye do sic a thing as that fur luve o' me? Wad ye be leavin' the heelands, an' the work yer sae fond o', an' bide wi' my kin in the lowlands? Eh, Willy! I ken ye luv me weel noo. But I wad na' hae ye mak' sic a sacrifees. Our gran'sire cam' an' he brocht Marian to bide wi' my mither. An' 'twas jes ruggin' an' reevin' at my he'rt the thocht o' ye; maybe sair-he'rted, or may be waur than that—gacin muckle wrang, wi' nane to hand ye oot th' ill gait! an' I cud na' reist, but whan th' winter gang awa', an' I see the rafts a gaein by, an' some stoppin', I hoped ye wad cum agen. Many lads cam' fur metheglin, an' buttered sconces (as ye did first, Willy), an' my faither speired o' ye, an' they tellt him ye staid at hame an' waur douce an' dourie. Willy! I cud beir na mair. I did nathing but greit, an' then—well I cam' awa' an' I foun' my ain luv! I winna leave ye noo; sin ye canna bide i' th' braw lowlan's, we'll mak' a bonny hame i' th' wildwood t'gither.

"'Where thou bidest, I will bide.'"

The reunited pair walked hand-in-hand to the cottage door, where John and Mary Morgan, with their boys, were seated.

"Mis' Morgan," said Big Bill, his face radiant with delight, "this is my wife, as I s'pose she's tol' ye. Mister Morgan, this here young woman is Missis William Morris. Came all the way from Jarsey to hunt up a good-fur-nothin' lummux of a husban', that never knowd what a rale treasure he'd got till he thought he'd lost her, and jest by his own sheer contrariness, too. Ain't she the purtiest little lassie ye ever sot yer eyes on? Wall, I swan! I don't see what sech a piece of pink-an'-white china ken fin' in *me* that's worth comin' nigh unto a hundered an' fifty miles after, anyhow!"

And he threw himself on the doorsteps, and gazed admiringly into his wife's face; while she, laughing, blushing, with eyes brimful of tears, sat in the big rocker, and told of her home, her friends, her wearisome journey, and her new-found, sweet content.

"Can't ye give us a song, Bessie? Not one of yer genuine Scotch, ye know; but one that a feller can understan'."

Bessie smiled. "Hae ye forgot all the Scotch I taught ye, Willy? 'Tis Sabbath night, ye ken, an'—"

"Oh, call it Thanksgivin'. We don't either of us feel like chantin' a psalm to-night; besides, Bessie, the sun's gone down."

"Weel, I'll sing ye a ballad ye ne'er heard, but needna' speer the meanin' o'."

And, slipping her hand in his, her sweet, clear voice warbled,

"The lowland lads think they are fine,
But O they're vain an' wondrous gawdy.
How much unlike the graceful mein
An' manly looks o' me Highlan' laddie!

"O'er Benty hill wi' him I'll run,
An' leave me hame an' lowlan' daddy,
Frae winter's cauld an' summer's sun
He'll screen me wi' his Highlan' plaidie.

"Nae greater joy I'll e'er pretend
Than that his love prove true and steady,
Like mine to him, which ne'er shall end
While Heaven preserves my Highlan' laddie."

A silence fell on the little group, and the husband moved closer to the singer and laid his head against her arm. He would not lose one instant of this delicious stillness for the sweetest speech.

The rippling waters, the insects' chirr, and whippoorwill's plaintive notes harmonized with the twilight hush. The thoughts of each were busy with the past. It is the alternating joy and grief that make histories, as pictures are formed of varying light and shade.

Mary Morgan's voice dispelled the silence.

"Your song was very sweet. I hope you have come to stay. Did you say you left your chest at the end of the stage route, and walked the rest of the way?"

"Ah weel, I didna' tire."

And she looked at the head which rested against her knee, as a loving, faithful dog's might have done.

"Bessie, little wife"—and the big head raised slowly, as though roused from slumber—"I've got to git that chist here 'fore to-morrow night! Mebbe 'twill seem 's though 'twant all a dream then, an' ye'd come to stay. Guess likely Mis' Morgan can keep us a spell, till we can knock up a cabin of our own. Wall, I dew say! ef thar ain't them cows a-waitin' thar by the bars yit! Git me the milk-pails, Jamie. Jehoshaphat! ef thar's a happier feller 'n I be 'long this here river, I'd like to shake hands with him."

CHAPTER IV.

"Have I not said that womanhood involves all?
Have I not told how the universe has nothing better than the best woman?"
WALT WHITMAN.

In a week's time the domestic arrangements in John Morgan's home had undergone a change, Bessie Morris taking entire charge of household affairs, leaving Mrs. Morgan free to begin the promised school.

A score of rosy-cheeked, bright-eyed girls and boys entered the long bare room one Monday morning, where Mrs. Morgan, in cushioned rocking-chair, sat awaiting them, and with much whispering and giggling, seated themselves on the high, hard benches, their shoeless feet dangling several inches from the floor.

"Children, haven't any of you a book?" inquired their teacher.

There was more whispering and giggling.

"Mar said I better bring 'long a Testamunt," one of the largest girls answered, "but par said 'twant no use."

"But has no one brought a Reader or a Speller? I didn't expect geographies or arithmetics, but I hoped you had spelling-books of some kind. Well, when there's a freshet, we can send down the river and get books. Until then, we must get along with these two which I have. But I want you all to go up the creek to the stone-quarry and get smooth flat stones to mark on. Get them as big as this book when it is open—*so*, and as thin and smooth as you can. Then get some small pieces of soft stone to mark with. They will do for slates and pencils until we can do better. Polly Brown, can you read?"

"I guess I kin a little: pop learnt me; but I hain't no book but a Testament: t'other's all wore out."

"All who have Testaments, please hold them up," said the amateur and much perplexed school-ma'am.

Four much-soiled volumes were exhibited; and a voice announced,

"Mar has got one in her chist; an' Bob guesses his folks'll let him bring theirn."

"Very well; bring them to-morrow, and any school-books you can find. And now, Sammy Brown, you and Dicky come here, and tell me the names of these letters."

A little urging from older sisters brought them to her side; and after wriggling and giggling a moment, staring hard at the pictured page, both muttered, "I don' know."

"That is A, Sammy; say it—'A.'"

"A what?" inquired the boy; and the other children, big and little, laughed outright.

"The letter A, Sammy: there, there, children, stop laughing! Letter A, and letter B. Here they are on this page too."

"Oh, I know now; that's what pop says when he's a-milkin', and I'm a-helpin': 'Let 'er be—let 'er be!'"

At this the boys and girls broke into another peal of laughter, in which their teacher was forced to join.

Just then came a rap at the half-open door: the laughing ceased as suddenly as it had begun; and as Mrs. Morgan arose, the form of a tall dark-eyed youth appeared in the door-way, and hesitatingly entered.

"How-de-do, Mis' Morgan: I thought as how, seein' I was out of a job, mebbe you'd let a feller uf my size cum to your school fur a spell," he stammered. "I hain't never hed no chance fur larnin' nohow. An' I thought I'd like to know a little suthin', ef I hain't too dumb to git at it."

"I am glad you've come, Jack," said Mrs. Morgan, encouragingly; "you can help me teach the children to sing, and I can help you study. What do you wish to learn most? Can you read a chapter in the Bible?"

"Wall, I guess I cud git the sense out of 't; but figgers is what I'm after neow. I should like to larn cipherin' uncommon well. You see, fellers gits the tallest kind o' pay fur countin' lumber and measurin' off land, an' sich work. An' ef you can larn me to calculate how many foot o' lumber there is in a tree, an' how many acres there is in a lot o' land, why, I tell ye what! I'd be powerful 'bliged to ye, and wouldn't mind payin' ye suthin' middlin' handsome fur it, tew! Guess 'twouldn't take more 'n a week or so, would it? For I'm goin' off the Fourth, an' I'll hev to pitch into the work soon's ever I git back."

"How far have you ever studied arithmetic? Have you ciphered through the 'four rules?' And do you know all the tables?"

"Tables? Don't know nothin' 't all 'bout it, Mis' Morgan. Never seed no figgerin'-book, as I know on."

"Why, Jack Rodgers! to learn all you wish to know of arithmetic will take a year at least. But I want you to try, and I'll help you all I can."

"A hull year! well, I dew say! I can't go to school an' work tew, I s'pose. An' there's the foller to burn; an' it ought to be got into buckwheat right along. An' there's the bark-peelin' an' hayin' an' raftin', an' mebbe three or four chances to go down the river. Bill Morgan said he'd trust me to steer a toggle-timber raft next spring, ef I'd go down with him a couple o' times this season. I tell ye I hate to think o' bucklin' right down to a book. But ef I go at it, I'm bound to go through; blamed ef I won't! 'n ef you'll kinder help me along, I'll jest set right down an' go at it now. Ef you want any o' these young uns thrashed, or anything else done that's in my line, why, jest call on me."

Jamie's slate and pencil were

brought, and the numerals copied from a page of his arithmetic again and again, until the uncouth characters began to stand erect and resemble the Arabic numbers.

By this time Mrs. Morgan had organized the little school into three distinct classes. The A B C scholars; the Primer class, which included Davy; and the Testament readers, of which Jamie, though least in age and stature, stood first.

The whole school received instructions in arithmetic and geography, with daily information regarding theology, history, and etiquette.

A few rules were laid down for the government of the school, and the circulation of the two spelling-books among seven pupils. Then they were dismissed, one by one, each turning at the door to bow or courtesy to their teacher, which ceremony at first nearly convulsed the school with suppressed laughter; but a few days sufficed to give more ease and grace to the queer "bobs" of the boys and the comical "curcheys" of the girls, as they imitated the oft-repeated example of their teacher; and soon a whispered command from the older girls to the smaller children to "make your manners," as they left their seats to start homeward, was a sufficient reminder for all.

The introduction of the simple words "Please" and "Thank you" was also a strange innovation; but as no request was granted unless prefixed by the first, and withdrawn unless followed by the second, the custom soon became a common one, in the school-room at least.

The singing, however, was the chief charm and the greatest incentive to study.

"If every word of these two lines is spelled correctly, children," Mrs. Morgan would say, holding up the Webster's Elementary before them, " we will sing 'There's Much Good Cheer,' and the 'Happy Land' before we go home; but whoever misses will have to stay and study; and that will take up all the time."

Very eager were the faces as they hurried to their positions in the spelling-class and placed their bare toes in line with the designated crack in the floor.

Very happy were they when word after word was correctly pronounced and spelled; and if at last some unlucky urchin blundered through inattention or ignorance, no greater punishment was needed than the black looks of his comrades, censuring him for depriving them of a song.

As the failures occurred less frequently, the singing became quite a feature of the school, all standing, with their hands clasped behind them, heads erect, and shoulders back, thus resting body as well as mind while they sang,

"I think when I read that sweet story of old,
  When Jesus was here among men,
How he called little children as lambs to his
  fold,
I should like to have been with him then."

Wednesday was a half-holiday, and the morning was devoted to various kinds of handicraft and singing.

Mrs. Morgan encouraged the boys to learn to knit, sew on buttons, darn their stockings and mittens, as well as make fish-lines, braid whip-lashes, and whittle toys.

The girls brought blocks of calico for bedquilts, straw for braiding hats, and knitting.

After the work was well under way, Mrs. Morgan would read or tell a story, historical events usually suggesting the theme.

One day Jamie electrified the school by reciting "Casabianca;" and from that time speaking pieces became the "reward of merit," Mrs. Morgan promising as a great favor to teach the best boy some verses "by heart," for the succeeding Wednesday; and they who recited,

"Poor and needy though I be,
God, my maker, cares for me;
Gives me clothing, shelter, food,
Gives me all I have that's good,"

never forgot the words.

"My school governs itself," said Mary Morgan, one evening nearly three months after its beginning. "The very boys I was afraid might give me trouble seem to try as hard to please me as I do to please them. I overheard that comical little Sammy Brown telling Jack Rodgers that by-words 'was jest a baby way of swearin', 'cause teacher said so.' And I notice, too, that they are all getting quite polite to each other as well as to me. Not a day passes without a gift of flowers—a hollyhock or nasturtion from their door-yards, or wild flowers with mosses and ferns: the tin cup I have for a vase is always filled. And they are getting on nicely with lessons, too. Jack Rodgers is learning multiplication and division already, and will soon get into fractions. But having so few books is a great bother. Some will learn their spelling-lesson in ten minutes, and be on the lookout for mischief, while others would keep the book an hour. So I have arranged to let them hear each other go over the lessons, in a whisper of course, the one waiting for the book playing teacher, which hurries the stupid ones considerably. I find they take a great deal of pride, of late, in seeing how quickly they can learn a lesson. If I can only keep on a few weeks longer, I can teach them writing; that is, if your husband ever finds time to make those desks, Bessie."

"'Deed, ma'am, William wud be mair than glad to do yer will, but the wark's over-lang for the days, an' the nichts na' fit for sic a job."

"Oh, I'm not particular *how* it is done, so I have a shelf put up around the room for the books just a little slant, so that the children can rest their slates on it as they write. We have so little paper in the store, it would be useless to begin using it; so their home-made slates and pencils must answer until there comes a freshet, and I can send to my brother in Philadelphia for what we need. I have made out a list to send him, but the weather will soon be too cold to use the room; so I expect nothing better this term. If you will stay with me, Bessie, maybe I can teach again."

"An' hae a braw new scholar i' th' schule, eh? I wonder what bonny name will ye'll enter i' th' buik 'mong the lads and lassies? John is na' sae bonny, but—"

"I feel very sure we shall call her Miriam. 'Twas my mother's name," said Mrs. Morgan, softly. "Do you know, Bessie, I do so love to read of the mother of our Lord. I wish there was more about her in the Bible. I don't want to pray to her, you know; but I love to think about her, and how she must feel for all women."

"What popish nonsense is that you're talking, Mary?" said her husband, rising suddenly from the doorstone, where the evening shades had concealed him. "A woman of your sense ought to know better than to talk such stuff as that. Why, you'll be having a crucifix hung up by your bed, next, and a string of beads to pray on, and all the rest of it. I'm astonished at you! Perhaps you better send for a priest to come here and form a church, you're so anxious—"

"Oh, John! John! don't talk so! Please don't! You frighten me when you speak so loud. It makes my heart flutter so! I did not know you were sitting there."

"Well, what if you didn't? What do you talk such popish nonsense for? I don't know why it is, but I can't speak to you lately but it sets your heart a-fluttering! You never used to be so silly. I think I have enough to make my heart flutter! There's Long John been peeling over forty cords of bark on my land; pretends he don't know where the line is, and intimates that *I* don't. I'll prosecute him, sure's he lives!"

"I thought he wanted tew settle," said Big Bill, who had just entered.

"Settle? Yes, he offers to pay for the bark; but what's that? Am I to have my property damaged that way —hemlock-trees cut down that I want standing—and then let him settle on his own terms? Wrong is wrong, and right is right! And here are store-bills coming due next month, and not a cent to meet them. Goods trusted out, and not a dollar in the country till after we get a freshet; and no signs of rain either!"

And the man strode out of the house and down to the saw-mill, the wheels of which had long stood idle for want of water.

"Ah me! puir winsome leddy!" said the kind-hearted Scotchwoman, kneeling by Mary Morgan's side, and chafing her cold, trembling hands, "I wad ye cud greit an' let out the heart-ache."

"Oh, Bessie, I'm silly to get frightened at nothing!" she answered, laughing hysterically. "He didn't mean it; he never used to talk so in our own dear home. But now—though I have been so much stronger since you came, you dear, kind woman—but I feel— Hark! is that wind?"

A low, shuddering moan crept through the trees, then a quick gust of wind swept through the house, extinguishing the light, slamming the doors, and awaking Jamie and Davy, whose screams added to the confusion.

A flash of lightning, a peal of thunder, a downpour of rain came almost in the same instant. The men came running from the barn and mill, drenched to the skin in the momentary exposure.

The storm had crept unseen over

the western hill-tops, and broke with fury in the narrow valley. A blaze of light—a horror of darkness—a crash of cloud artillery that shook the earth and filled every heart with terror; then a cry of bitter agony from Mary Morgan's white lips; and they carried her to her room, and laid her, fainting, on the bed.

All night the storm raged without: the horses pranced and neighed, trembling in their stalls; and the cattle ran to and fro in their pasture, seeking shelter from the storm. The brook sprung out of its sluggish sleep, and dashed and foamed over the rocks it shrunk from months before.

The trees moaned and shivered with the violence of the wind. The blue blaze cleft the darkness every instant; the thunder roared, and the mountains gave back their muttered defiance. The clouds spread their black mantle up the valley to the source of the stream, threatening destruction to all the property along the brook.

Yet inside the tiny cottage on the river-bank raged a far more fearful conflict. It was a conflict between life and death, while remorse, grief, sympathy, and anxiety were helpless, trembling witnesses!

No human aid could be obtained; only the God of nature could decide the struggle! and the night dragged wearily away, while with staring, senseless eyes Mary Morgan looked death in the face, but knew it not, and clung to life, unconscious of the grasp.

Slowly the clouds passed away, the thunder reverberating in the distant mountains. Slowly the pale light of dawn crept over the eastern hills.

More slowly death retreated, and the light of reason illuminated the pale face of the mother.

Her eyes sought the little bundle in Mrs. Rodgers's arms.

Bessie leaned over the pillow and whispered,

"Ye hae yer will. It *is* Miriam!"

A happy smile swept over the face, and then—

"Being faint with joy, the mother slept."

CHAPTER V.

"For us the wealth-laden world laboreth ever;
For us harvests ripen, winds blow, waters roll;
And he who gives back in his might of endeavor,
I'll cherish—a man ever dear to my soul."
GERALD MASSEY.

THE next morning the river was pronounced only two feet below a rafting freshet, and still rising. Being a "lightning fresh," that is, one caused by thunder-showers, its height and duration depended on the direction the last night's storm had taken; and it might "run out" as rapidly as it had risen; so no time was lost by those who had lumber to send to market.

Before sunrise the river's bank was thronged with men and teams; and the business of rafting began. Long John was engaged to raft the toggle-timber, and Sam Jenkins the logs; while Big Bill took charge of the sawed lumber.

Hemlock-scantling rafts differ only in size; while a piling or toggle timber raft has the appearance of a number of large poles huddled together with little regard to size; the constructor's skill being shown by collecting the largest number of sticks in the smallest space and shortest time, with the fewest possible fastenings.

The raftsman's skill culminates in the construction of a log raft. That their proficiency in so placing each log that its largest and smoothest side be uppermost, and all defects be hidden, is of art most artful, can be proven by the purchasers.

Mr. Morgan watched the men roll the logs down the steep bank into the river, leap lightly on them from the shore, and ride them to their places in the raft with such apparent ease that he was vexed to think he had yielded to the demands of the log-riders for the highest wages.

"That's more like play than work," he said to Jenkins, as he walked up the bank to select another log. "I think *I'll* take the place of one of your men."

Sam cut a wedge from the plug of tobacco in his hand, turned one eye upward to squint at the clouds hurrying across the sky, and in his peculiar drawling tones, ending each sentence with an "uh," quietly replied,

"Mebbe ye wouldn't like it 's well 's

ye think ye would. 'N cf you should send off one of these boys, I don' know whar ye'd fin' another 'twouldn't rather worruck 'an play 'ith logs in that there current: darned ef I do. I'm agoin' tew run daown a double-length naow, an' yeou kin ride daown 'ith me, an' see haow ye like it. Roll in that twenty-four-foot, boys!"

"None of your tricks now, Sam," said Mr. Morgan, who thought he detected mischief in the solemn lines of Sam's countenance.

"I was jest a thinkin' w'at yer wife 'u'd say ef— Hed'nt ye better giv' me yer watch to kerry fur ye? Spile it to git it wet, wou't it? But ef ye stan' stiddy, 'ith yer heels square on top th' log, an' yer toes turned aout, I guess I kin git yer daown t' th' raft. Ye'll hev to dew some purty lively dancin' fust, though: the roll off the bank sets the log a-spinnin' mighty rapid; an' then yew'll hev to handle yer feet middlin' lively goin' under the lash-poles, ur th' 'll trip ye intew th' river quicker 'an lightnin'. Thar she comes! Wait till I maount her, an' steddy 'er daown a little. Naow, then, jump!"

Mr. Morgan picked up a pike-pole, and, taking a flying leap, came down upon the log so heavily Sam was nearly thrown from his balance; but by the skilful use of his feet and pole he stopped the log rolling, and guided it to the raft. Morgan stood firmly, his eyes upon the men who were fastening a single-length log to the projecting sticks which held the raft together.

"Naow, jump the lash-poles!" yelled Sam, obeying his own command.

Mr. Morgan sprang over the first and second as the logs passed swiftly under them; but the third caught his foot, and he fell headlong into the river, barely escaping being drawn under the raft by the current. He crawled upon it, while the men shouted with laughter. Angered by their rudeness, but too wise to betray the feeling, he accepted the joke, saying,

"That skip-the-rope movement was too much for me, boys; but I can ride a log as well as any of you. I'll ride them down to the point here, and you can place them with your boat-hooks."

A sly wink from Sam betokened mischief.

"Wall, I want a twelve-footer nex'. Ye'd better try a smallish un fust, hadn't ye?"

"I'll get the log you need, whether it's large or small," Mr. Morgan answered, impatiently. "I could have been half-way down with it while you've been talking. You hang on to your words as though you liked the taste of them, and grunt as if every sentence hurt you."

"The glibbest talkers ain't allers the fastest workers, Mister Morgan; an' though I like fun, I hope my words ain't so bitter as to taste bad, nor so sharp as to hurt me nor nobody else," Sam replied, with more dignity than one would have supposed possible for the lank, freckle-faced young man to assume. "An' naow, sir, ye'd better take a fool's advice an' leave log-ridin' fur them as understan' it. Leastways, ye'd better dew yer practisin' in still water."

"When I want your advice, Mr. Jenkins, I will ask for it; and it might be well for you to remember who is the employer and who the employed in this business."

"All right, Mister Morgan; but somehow we mountain men hev free ways. We live free, work free, an' talk free, an' actilly b'lieve we *be* free. We hain't got to usin' gold weights to weigh men with here yit; an' ef ye live, an' work, an' talk 'ith us, yeu'll hev to take a joke 'ith us."

"Well, well: it will be no joke if this freshet runs out before this raft is done! Now let's make up for lost time; and I will get that twelve-foot log."

The oxen had already hauled the log to the roll-away; and as he arrived, it went thundering down the bank, and plunged into the water, dashing the spray high in air.

"Light on 'er 'fore she gits in the current!" shouted one of the men.

Morgan sprang; the log whirled rapidly beneath his feet — his feet danced more rapidly to keep on top of the log; faster, faster the log rolled as the current caught it; a slip — a plunge—and he disappeared beneath the water. He rose, swam to and mounted the log, only to be rolled under it on the gravelly bottom; rose again; caught his pike-pole, then sank, and was borne out into the swift current.

Sam leaped from the raft and caught him by the arm. Swimming to the shore, he drew the half-drowned man to the bank, and helped him to the house; while Jack Rodgers sprang upon another log, overtook the estray, and brought it to land.

All were as busy in doors as out.

Mrs. Rodgers's "men folks" having no lumber to run this freshet, she remained to assist Bessie in the unaccustomed labor of preparing provision for the rafts.

Even Jamie and Davy were furnished employment in looking over beans, beating eggs, and keeping a roaring fire under the kettles where whole hams and huge chunks of pork were boiling.

"Keeps 'em from pullin' the blankets off that blessed baby every minnit, ennyhow," said Mrs. Rodgers, "ef they dew hinder 'bout ez much ez they help. I guess they've kissed her han' more 'n fifty times a'ready. Wall, it's a marcy they 'er so much tuck up 'ith havin' a little sister! They hain't never thought o' goin' to the river an' gettin' drownded 's their mother's allers 'fraid they would when th' 'fresh' come. Wall, *I*'m allers a-crossin' a bridge 'fore I git to it; an' then like 's not find thar hain't no bridge thar, nor never wus."

And she thrust a big pan of beans and bacon into the stove-oven, while Bessie placed another of pumpkin bread beside the pile of doughnuts, which seemed to Bessie's unsophisticated eyes sufficient for a regiment of men.

The channel of the Delaware being narrow and rocky, with frequent rapids, it is necessary to find a landing every night, the men seeking lodging in taverns or farm-houses, wherever it can be obtained; often a score in a room, their beds on the floor — any place where they can lie stretched out —talking, laughing, singing, or sleeping, from dark till dawn.

Then rising, with shouts and jesting, they hastily swallow their breakfast of fried ham and eggs, buckwheat-cakes and coffee, and hurry to their rafts while the white mists of night still hang heavily over the river, spring to their oars, push out, and glide down the stream.

Dinner is a cold lunch, and a well-filled dinner-box a necessity.

Dry clothing and a cup of hot tea had restored Mr. Morgan's vitality, but not his equanimity; and the face that stooped to kiss his little daughter, though smiling, was not an amiable one.

"Are you sure you are not bruised, or have not taken cold?" inquired his wife. "How did you happen to fall in? I couldn't hear all that was said in the kitchen."

"Oh, 'twas nothing serious; don't worry about me. I'm not the worse for it, and shall raft scantling this afternoon."

"Oh, father! mayn't I help you? Who's bossing it—Long John?"

"No, Bill Morris. You help? Well, I guess you better wait a few years. But I'll tell you what you can do. I'm going to have Fred help raft, and you and Jamie can attend to the store. Only, mind you don't eat the candy."

"'Tend store? Oh, that's lots of fun! Can we sell things?"

"Yes; if you get the money for them. Don't let any one go behind the counter."

"Is Fred strong enough to raft?" inquired Mrs. Morgan, feebly.

"Yes; he's stronger than he looks. I don't suppose he'll be of much use, but 'twill do him good. He thinks too much about his white hands and rich relation. His uncle sent him up here to work some of the nonsense out of him; and I think rafting will do it."

"Mister Morgan," said Mrs. Rodgers, coming to the door, "ken that clark o' yourn fix them pervision boxes? Tea-boxes is the handiest ef ye've got enny empty; an' there's holes got to be bored in the sides, to put rope-handles in. Leastways, that's the best way to fix 'em."

Promising to see the boxes made ready, Mr. Morgan hastened to the river to join the forces of Big Bill; but Morris seemed disposed to find him employment elsewhere.

"Tell ye what 'tis, Mister Morgan," he said, "thar hain't no time t' lose ef we git off on this fresh; an' I jest wish you'd go an' hurry up them teams. We hain't got more 'n half th' fillin' fur the cribs down here yet. An' sen' down a bag o' wedges an' a bundle o' grubs, ef that thar shiftless Mose has got 'em made yit. Can't you take Fred an' go up on th' hill an' cut a couple o' dozen oak or hickory saplin's? Git 'em 'bout four foot long, an' two an' a half or three inches through. Kinder grub 'em up so's to leave th' bulge o' th' root fur the head o' th' grub. Guess that'll keep him busy fur a spell," he added, as Mr. Morgan walked briskly away. "He's a nice man, Mister Morgan is, but 'pinionated as a mule! He's boun' to see into th' hull business o' raftin'; an' he's so chuck-full o' ideas, he'd see some new way o' doin' everything; an' nothin' so conflusticates a lot o' men's to make 'em do a thing they understan' in a way they don't understan'. I'm powerful glad to get shet o' him till we git these 'ere cribs in. Hallo, Mose! like to got them grubs here 'n time fur nex' fresh, didn't ye? Guess Mister Morgan put a leetle spring into ye. What's he doin'? Hope he'll stir up them teams, an' git that thar stuff down here 'fore long."

"Wall, I seed him an' Fred down by th' lumber pi-iles; but I didn't see no wagon a-loadin'," Mose replied.

"Well, I hope they'll move faster 'n your tongue, when they dew git started. Fur th' land's sake, put down them grubs, an' help lift this crib off! Guess ye was born on a Saturday, Mose, an' purty late in th' afternoon tew! Yew allers work an' talk as ef thar wa'n't no more to dew this week."

Mose put down the grubs he had been holding upon his shoulder, and lazily picking up a handspike, he placed it under the corner of the crib, and putting his shoulder against the stick, inquired, "Reddy, be ye?" Then, with a giant's strength, gave a lift and a shove that threw the crib off the slide and his corner to the water's edge.

"Why didn't ye keep yer eend up?" he chuckled; "yer a purty big ma-an, Bill Morris, an' likely ye was born tolerably airly in th' mornin'; but yeou can't pull an even whippletree with me yit."

"Wall, Mose, you be the blamedest critter I ever see! Yer stronger than an ox when you're a mind to do anything. Now you jest take holt agin, an' git this 'ere crib onto th' slide and into th' water."

"Wall, I guess I've got to go down an' see to that toggle-timber naow. Mister Morgan he wants *me* to steer it, an' I w-o-n't trust nobody to hang an oar for *me*. 'Sides that, thar cleark said he was comin' daown to ra-aft: an' I wan' to be tha-er t' see th' fu-un."

"Fred goin' to raft toggle-timber? Wall, I swan! He'll git the starch tuck out o' him, I'll bet!" exclaimed Morris. "Jehoshaphat! look there! ef there hain't that York Yankee comin' down th' creek on a float o' lumber. Here we've ben a-haulin' it through th' mud on wagons, an' never once thought o' floatin' it! Blamed ef I hain't reddy to bag my head, an' sell it fur a pun'kin."

"That's a smart idea o' Mister Morgan's," said Long John, coming down the bank. "Guess we kin hev all th' teams a-haulin' logs now. But ef he brags any, you jest twit him o' ridin' logs."

"Come, all hands," shouted Mr. Morgan, pushing the float to the shore, "pull out this scantling before we go to dinner. There goes the horn!"

CHAPTER VI.

"The pure sweet fountains chant of heavenly hope:
The chorus of the rills is household love:
The rivers roll their song of social joy:
The ocean's organ voice is sounding forth
The hymn of Universal Brotherhood."
SARA J. HALE.

A SCORE of men entered the kitchen, after stamping the mud from their feet upon the door-stone, and using the tin wash-basin and crash-towel hanging outside the door.

With much scraping of chairs and shuffling of feet upon the bare floor, they seated themselves around the well-laden table.

A few heads were bowed while Mr. Morgan murmured words of thanks to the Giver of all Good; and then the work of emptying the dishes began, Bessie and Mrs. Rodgers refilling them as soon as their contents were exhausted. Indeed, a looker-on might have supposed the consumers and suppliers were each trying to overcome the other.

But in twenty minutes the suppliers conquered; and the consumers one by one left the scene of conflict, until only Mose remained to demolish the piles of potatoes, corned-beef, and pumpkin-pie still left upon the table. In five minutes more he, too, retreated, and the women were left to dispose of the *débris* of the meal.

The clerk accompanied the men in his usual city dress, they exchanging glances, and muttering their guesses that "them store-clothes won't look so slick long."

Reaching the river-bank, the group divided, each party going to its own place of labor. Fred joined the forces of Long John above the logs and below the scantling-rafts.

Running lightly across the loose sticks which lay between the shore and the raft, Long John left them whirling and plunging behind him.

Seeing the men were waiting for him to pass over, Fred followed. The small, slippery logs rolled and sunk beneath his feet; but to the evident surprise and disappointment of the spectators, he reached the raft with only one bootful of water.

"Wall, tha-at wa'n't bad fur a greenhorn!" exclaimed Mose, who had hastened to the bank, and stood with his hands in his pockets, and a grin of expectation upon his leathery face. "I've seed ol' han's do wus 'n tha-at!"

"Oh, that's nothing," said Fred,

lightly; "though I believe Long John set those poles spinning and plunging on purpose to give me a cold bath. I am sorry to disappoint you all, but I don't think I can afford to entertain you as Mr. Morgan did. If I can't keep my balance and footing with any of you, let me know it, please;" and the young man executed a brilliant rigadoon upon the log, whirling and bowing to an imaginary partner. "I have practised walking a slack-rope, riding a horse bare-back, and leaping and tumbling with circus-boys in New York rather too much to be taught anything in that line by you fellows," he said, with a toss of the head and a half-contemptuous smile.

"That's so, boys," said Long John. "You thought you'd have a leetle fun seein' a greenhorn ride an' raft toggle-timber; but you'll hev to go to school to him to learn to do it *circus fashion.*"

Fred, uncertain how to take the laugh which followed, determined to outdo them all, and proposed to ride one of the timbers about the size of a sloop's mast to its place in the raft.

But Long John, with an expressive glance at Fred's soft white hands, ordered him to try boring holes first.

"Take this long auger. 'Tain't nateral fur you to stoop; an' you kin use this an' keep yer chin level with yer ears."

"I was taught that man was created upright," retorted Fred, "and the place for his chest was under his chin; but you fellows shoulder your chests and go bent over like humpbacks."

"Well, well, we've fooled away too much time already," said Long John, impatiently. "Carry yer chest and chin where you please; an' ef you stan' upright, see 't you bore them holes down right."

Fred's voice rung out loudest in the laugh that applauded this witticism; but his contemptuous "you fellows" was not forgotten.

His gymnastic exercises had so strengthened the muscles of his arms, shoulders, and loins, that probably no man upon the raft could drive an auger with greater ease and rapidity than he. Intent upon again surprising them, he walked across the raft with the auger upon his shoulder; but he quickly learned that a toggle-timber raft was a series of traps for the unwary; for the second stick sank as he stepped upon it. He sprang to another, but his foot slipped, and he came down astride it, and up to his waist in water.

"That's circus fashion, I s'pose," said Long John; "much obleeged fur th' show: but ef you've got cooled off, I'd like to hev ye go to work."

With an exclamation more emphatic than polite, Fred succeeded in drawing himself out of the water, looking more heated than cooled.

"You call this timber rafted, do you? only the forward end of the sticks fastened! The slippery, squirming eels!" exclaimed Fred, as, after several slips and many falls, amidst a running fire of comments from the men, he scrambled across the raft.

"See Fred a-coonin' of it!" shouted Mose. "Look out, ur ye'll git yer che-est wet!"

"Good at tumblin', ain't he?" said

another; "practised 'ith circus boys, ye know."

"Got yer foot in, but lost yer balance, didn't ye?" said Long John. "If you had rafted the timber properly, I shouldn't have got my boots full of water," Fred answered, good-humoredly. "I'd like to see any man walk on these loose poles with a couple of gallons of water in his boots! There's room enough for a horse to fall between them in some places."

"Mebbe so: a hoss's cousin kin, we know."

"Pretty good, Uncle John; you're quite a poet! To walk your raft would take a go-at," retorted Fred, laughing. "Now I'll get even with the slippery fellows by boring them."

"Use yer auger then, and give yer tongue a rest," growled Long John, "or ye'll bore us 'stead the timber."

"Wall, John, yev got yer ma-atch in that youngster. I guess he's 'bout as tonguey cz yew be; an' he han'els that thaer auger 's tho' he's use' to it."

"Well, I guess he'll larn a leetle somethin' yit 'fore he's through raftin'," Long John answered, giving a final blow to a bow which held a log to its lash-pole.

"Likelier 'an no-ot," answered Mose, chuckling. "Neow I'm goin' up to help Big Bill a spell. S'pose he's growlin' fur more grubs 'fore this time."

While the men were making a boom to catch and hold the lumber from being floated down the brook, Morris was inducting Mr. Morgan into the mysteries of rafting scantling.

"Here goes fur the las' crib," he said. "Ketch holt o' this ere plank, will ye? Turn 'er up sideways, an' stick grubs thro' them auger-holes (guess it would be better to hev th' heads all on one side, wouldn't it?). Turn 'er down now, heads under; now this one. That's all right. Now another; keep it straight on the slide! There, now, the runners is ready for the side-pieces. Take any of 'em; they're jest alike. Now lift 'er; hold her stiddy till I git the grub an' auger-holes so's they'll match. Your eend right? Now slide 'er down! Now fur t'other two. All right! Now han' me that there axe, will ye? Ye see I jest cut into this grub an' split down a sliver of it tew th' plank; an' then drive the wedge into th' grub an' the auger-holes to onct; an' thar can't nothin' work this frame apart. Now fur th' fillin'. Any o' them there eighteen-foot 'll dew; but the las' plank must be jest wide enough t' fit tight an' wedge 'em all in. Nex' comes th' caps: they're put on th' grubs, jest like the runners, to hold th' fillin' firm. Thare, sir: we've got th' las' crib ready fur lanchin'! Guess we kin git off to-morrer forenoon, sure. Hallo, boys! come an' help git this crib in!"

"No, no, Bill. Just put rollers under it, and we can get it in alone. These bits of lash-poles are just th' thing."

"Rollers? Well, I swan! I don' know but we kin. Blamed! I don't see why I couldn't thought o' that m'self. Here I've ben liftin' nuff to bust a blood-vessel, an' got th' crib all yanked out o' shape too. All ready? Heave-o-*he!* Slides in stiddy 's a board, don't she? S'pose you an' me kin couple th' crib alone?"

"Well, I think Sanders and Jim can get the lumber down as fast as you will need it, and you can have the other boys on the raft. They seem to have plenty of time for fooling on that toggle-timber."

"Wa'n't that ruther rough on Fred? Raftin' those leetle logs ain't no fool of a job; an' Long John hain't no more feelin' fur a greenhorn than a pine knot."

"'Twill do him good, do him good! Take the conceit out of him. I only hope Long John 'll get the raft finished before night."

"Oh, he'll git it done. There ain't no better worker 'long this river. Wall, now we want one o' them planks 'long-side o' ye—t'other one, with a hole bored in one end and two in the middle. Now jest slip the endhole over the middle grub; an' th' middle holes fits into these 'ere grubs on this crib an' that jines the cribs an' holds 'em stiddy," Big Bill ejaculated, between the blows of his axe, which drove the plank firmly to its place.

"I see," responded Mr. Morgan. "This end overlapping, strengthens the raft—one each side, and one in the middle. Now I suppose the bottom is done."

"Yes, sir. Come, boys, more lively there! we've got to git one course on by moonlight, ef we don't afore. There 'll be a boomin' fresh by mornin', judgin' by th' clouds, an' we've got to pull out 'fore noon. Sanders, haul out more o' that twelve-foot stuff. Got to begin with that, Mister Morgan, so 's not to break jints 'tween th' cribs. Each course must lap over the ends o' the one under, you know. 'Twould be a purty shaky concern to git over Cochecton falls an' Lackawack dam ef th' timber wus all th' same length. Take as many steersmen as there was cribs 'fore she'd run under Trenton bridge. Hello, Mose! thought we's so nigh through you'd venture down here, did ye? I jest wish ye hed to buckle right down to work like the rest of us once—blamed if I don't!"

"Wall," drawled Mose, "I ca-ant see no use in workin' hard 's ye kin the hull time; and I'm jest ez well off as any on ye. I've got 'nuff t' eat, an' 'nuff t' we-aur, an' thar hain't no smarter woman 'n I've got 'n all creashun."

"That's so; ef she wa'n't ye wouldn't allus hev plenty tew eat; but—"

Shouts of laughter from the toggletimber raft again attracted their attention, and Mose sauntered away to learn the cause of their fun.

Fred was again the victim. The auger turning in his ungloved hands made them smart furiously; and he looked about for some new employment.

Fastening the logs in place by wedging the wooden bows into the auger-holes looked simple and easy; and the moment one of the men went ashore for more plugs, Fred dropped the auger and took up the axe.

"Hold on; I ain't swopping jobs!" the man called out.

"Oh, I want to learn the whole business. I know all about boring holes. Give me a plug, like a good fellow; and show me how to get these loops of wood apart. You fasten them together to keep them bent, don't you? They spring out nearly straight, now they're apart. Well, you mountain men have heaps of ingenuity, or Yankee-nuity, rather. The middle of the bow cut thin to let it bend, and the ends shaped like wedges; then the ends of each loop caught in the loop of the other to hold them in shape. I say, you just change works with me for a few minutes, won't you? And then I'm going to ride logs."

The man good-naturedly picked up the auger, while Fred, after driving the bow in its place, put a plug in the hole beside it, and raised the axe for one vigorous blow which should drive it firmly in.

The axe came down—the plug flew up—and poor Fred staggered backward with one hand over his nose, and the blood trickling between his fingers, the rebounding plug having struck him full in the face.

"Wall, neow, that's rough!" exclaimed the man with the auger. "The tarnel ol' plug must a knowed you's a greenhorn. You quit yer laughin', boys! I'll bet you've bin hit on th' nose yerselves, an' hain't forgot the feelin' nuther."

"Much obliged, Brown; but I ain't hurt, only got the nose-bleed," said Fred, dipping his handkerchief in the river and pressing it to his face. "Pour a little water on the back of my neck with your hand, will you? There, now I'm all right."

"I vum! ef you ain't 'bout the pluckest chap fur yer size I ever see'd. Accidents will happen—can't allers hit a thing squar' on th' head —but ther' ain't nothing like accidents fur provin' ye'r good timber."

"That's so!" assented the other men, as they resumed their work.

Some long sticks lying on the upper banking ground were wanted; and Fred, although his hands were badly blistered and his nose stinging with pain, immediately volunteered to bring them down.

"Better try one o' these in the eddy fust," said Brown.

Fred hesitated.

"Yes, we hain't got no time to chase arter runaway logs, nor drag th' river fur drownded boys," added Long John.

"Don't fret your gizzard about *me*, Uncle John," Fred answered. "You won't be called upon to mourn the untimely loss of life or lumber on my account;" and, pike-pole in hand, he carefully but quickly picked his way across the raft and loose logs to the shore.

The required sticks were rolled in. Jack Rodgers sprang lightly upon the foremost, and steered it down the stream, while the log glided through the water like a huge snake. Fred leaped upon the next one, using his pike-pole as a balance-stick, standing upon the rolling log with perfect ease and grace, singing,

"What the city boys don't know, don't know,
The Delaware boys can't show, can't show;
For they work all day and dance all night,
And are ready for a row, a fire, or a fight.
And all the girls are crazy to catch a city beau,
That's so, boys; that's so, that's so."

"Steer yer log toward shore," called a man from the bank.

"Let him alone," said another; "do him good to git a duckin'."

"It's gittin' a strong pint to Jarsey. I want to see him git her aroun'."

The log was gliding toward the opposite shore with no apparent inclination of joining its companions in the eddy.

Fred tried to change its direction by placing his pole on the lower side of the log; but the current was swift and strong; the pole caught against a stone; the log struck the pole, and, like a flash, Fred was thrown headlong into the river.

The shouts of the men mingled with the roar of the water in his ears as he rose to the surface. He saw the log on his left hand, and beside him the pike-pole bobbing along, the iron point sinking to the bottom. He grasped the pole and swam to the log. Remembering Mr. Morgan's experience, he decided not to mount it; but plunging his pike-pole deep into the end, he swam to the raft, towing the log behind him, and puffing like a steam-tug.

The men laughed and cheered; and even Long John was forced to admire the pluck which redeemed the promise of saving lumber as well as life.

"Wall, Fred," he said, pulling him upon the raft, "you're a purty good steamboat, ef you ain't much of a log-rider. But we've hed enough of your circus performances. Every man an' boy has hed to quit work an' watch your shines; and I hain't agoin' to hev any more foolin'."

"Sa-ay, Fred," called Mose from the bank, "guess ye've got to stop raftin' neow. Mister Morgan says there's some wimmen t' th' store th' boys ca-an't wait on."

Fred seated himself upon a pile of plugs, and deliberately pulled off his boots and emptied the water from them; then slowly drew them on.

"I'd really like to try another stick," he said, looking up the river; "but business before pleasure—even the pleasure of hearing Uncle John growl. So here goes for a trade between butter and buttons, or cheese and calico."

The morning sun saw the glittering hill-tops rising like islands in a sea of mist. A white frost had gilded the hemlocks, silvered the rocks, jewelled the moss, while the valleys were filled with white billowy fog, which rose, cloudlike, upward, then drifted into fragments, and floated away. Soon the sunbeams, gliding earthward, lighted up a busy scene.

One raft was pulling out from shore; some boards were being added to the cargo of another; while Big Bill, everywhere present in person or voice, was giving final directions in regard to the scantling raft which he was to steer.

"We've got three courses clean thro'," he was saying to Mr. Morgan, "an' that's enuff fur th' ends; but we can take four more layers in the middle (each course runs ten foot back o' t'other, ye see); an' them cherry an' bird's-eye maple boards kin go ef you say so, though the river won't git no higher this fresh. Hello, Sanders! got them tie-pieces bored yet? All right! Now, Mister Morgan, ye kin help put blades in these 'ere oar-stems. I'm mighty particular 'bout the oars on the raft I steer. A poor oar makes a poor hand! Wall, I guess this 'll strike th' water th' hull length; though I'd ruther hev a maple blade, an' a leetle thinner at th' fur end; this is purty springy, though. Sanders, jest bore another cross-piece fur a head-block, will ye, while I git these oar-pins ready? You see, Mister Morgan, it's a particular nice job to git the oar-pin in plumb; so I ruther tend t' that myself. Now, let's run out the oar an' git its balance. It ought to hang so 's ye could raise th' blade out o' the water by pressin' down on the tip end o' the oar-stem with yer finger. Kin ye do it? All right. Now hold 'er stiddy while I mark 'er fur borin'. You see I bore one auger-hole clean thro', and *two* holes part way, an' so make a taperin' mortice ending in a auger-hole: that lets the oar play up an' down 'thout wabblin'. Now les' ship 'er! Hangs a leetle too low; ought to come to my waist. Brown, toss over that butt of a lash-pole! That 'll do fur an oar-block. All right now! While you're finishin' th' loadin', boys, I'll git th' dinner-box. See 't yer ready when I be."

"Wall, don't stay to kiss yer woman more 'n onct, fur th' water's fallin'."

"I meant to took my wife 'long, Sanders, but Mis' Morgan can't spare her now. I swan! I hope she won't cry," he muttered as he went up the path to the door.

He found Bessie awaiting him with a smile and a kiss; but no tears ventured farther than the brown lashes of her blue eyes.

"If you see me mither, or ony o' me kin, tell 'em I'm happy a' th' day."

The dinner-box was ready, some clothing tied in a colored handkerchief on top of it; and Mr. Morgan, after a hasty "good-bye" to his wife and children, helped to carry it to the raft. The rope was untied from the tree and thrown on board. The men sprung to their oars, while those upon the shore pushed and pried. Jamie and Davy shouted; Fred waved his hat; Bessie stood in the door-way and let the tears flow unchecked, until the autumn-tinted hill, the sunlit river, and gently gliding raft mingled in a rainbow-tinted mist.

Two weeks passed, and the raftsmen were all home again, with gifts which more than atoned for their absence. Besides the messages from the old home, and the new bonnet for Bessie, Morris brought a package of books for Mrs. Morgan, which gladdened the hearts of the whole household.

A week later Mr. Morgan returned in better humor with himself and the world than since the purchase of his Delaware estate, having disposed of his lumber at good prices.

CHAPTER VII.

"Folks say a wizard to a Northern king
At Christmas-time such wondrous things did show,
That through one window men beheld the spring,
And through another saw the summer's glow;
And through the third, the fruited vines arow;
While still unheard, but in its wonted way,
Piped the drear wind of that December day."

WILLIAM MORRIS.

WINTER came: the snow lay three feet deep upon the ground. Paths from the barn and store and the well-beaten roads alone broke the white wilderness stretching from the cottage to the wooded hills. River and brook were hidden, roofs and trees loaded, and still

"All the air was dizzy and dim
With the fall of glittering, fluttering snow."

"What is snow, mother?" inquired Davy.

They were sitting by the window; Mary Morgan with her babe in her arms, and her boys beside her, wearied by a snow frolic with Big Bill.

"The snow, my son?" his mother said, dreamily. "I think it is the christening robe of the New Year."

"I remember when Davy was christened, mother," said Jamie. "'Twas in Grandpa Walton's church, and Uncle Dave was sponsor. Who's New Year's sponsor, mother?"

"*Hope*, I guess. She makes the promises, and keeps them as well as sponsors generally do."

"And who is father and mother to New Year?"

"Time is the father, and I think Earth must be its mother."

"Where be they? I don't see 'em," exclaimed Davy, climbing upon a chair, and flattening his nose against the window-pane. "Where's New Year?"

"With God; he'll send it to us soon."

"Mother Nature's hair is getting white," continued Jamie. "See the hemlocks on the hill. The baby year is going to have a soft bed; the wind is fixing the blankets so 's to be all ready. See!" and Jamie pointed to a whirling mass of snow hovering over and then settling down upon the meadows.

"And now they're shaking up the pillows. Oh, look! see how the feathers fly," and he laughed merrily as the large snow-flakes fluttered against the window.

"Yes, I see," said his mother; "and the clouds are weaving beautiful fleecy garments for the New Year to wear; and Frost is making sparkling jewels and dazzling toys for it to play with."

"Well, *I* can't see anything but a snow-storm," said Davy, impatiently; "an' there ain't no bed, nor baby, nor nothin'."

"Oh, you prosy little mortal! there isn't a particle of poetry in you. You are as like your name-author as a little pea is like a big one! I hoped we would get a letter from your uncle David this week. I want one for my Christmas present."

"And to-morrow is Christmas, isn't it?"

"Yes, Jamie."

"Will St. Nicholas find us here in the woods, do you s'pose?"

"I think so; though he cannot bring any nice toys so far; so a little must satisfy my boys."

"How's he going to get his sleigh through the drifts, I'd like to know? Jim said the snow was over the logs so the oxen couldn't haul 'em out. An' I don't believe reindeers is bigger 'n oxen; be they, mother?"

"*Are* they, Davy. I never saw St. Nicholas's reindeers; but if he can't come with his sleigh through the drifts, he can on foot. Hark! didn't some one knock?"

"Oh, it's him, Davy! it's St. Nick, I'll jest bet anything!" cried Jamie, pressing his face close to the window to catch a glimpse of the man knocking at the outer door of the adjoining room. "He's all dressed in fur, an' he's awful big! Run and see!"

And he laughed merrily as Bessie opened the door, and the stranger entered the kitchen, while Davy rushed frantically out to welcome St. Nicholas.

A large, portly man, in a wolf-skin overcoat and fur hat, was stamping the snow from his feet, as Davy walked up to him and, looking earnestly into his face, said, "Be you St. Nicklas?"

"Me, St. Nicholas! Well, no, sonny, I guess not; but"—seeing the disappointed look stealing over the little face—"you see the ol' fellow couldn't get here, 'count o' the drifts, an' so *I* come."

"Oh, goody, goody! Hollo! Jamie, he's come. 'Tain't *him*, but he says he sent him. Oh, mother, ain't you jest as glad as you can be? I'll bet he's got a letter or suthin' for you too, cause that's what you want; an' you're awful good, ain't you, mother? An' suthin' for Bessie, too!"

"Davy, Davy, don't go wild, my son."

And Mrs. Morgan came from the inner room to greet the visitor.

"How-de-do, how-de-do, Mrs. Morgan? An' how's your family? All well, I trust. You do not recognize me, eh? I'm called Noyes—Squire Noyes. Most everybody knows me hereabouts. But I never had the opportunity of visiting your domicile before—that is, since your occupation and transformation of it—until this inclement evening. Exceedingly inclement, truly! The snow is nigh unto five foot deep, and my beast of burden stands shivering without. Is your man about? Ah! how-de-do, how-de-do, Mr. Morgan? I trust I see you well!"

"Very well, sir; very well," responded that gentleman, shaking hands cordially with the stranger. "Take off your coat and sit down to supper with us. The men have put your horse in the stable, and you can't get any farther to-night."

An hour later they sat around the blazing wood fire, Squire Noyes the centre of the group, with a boy on either knee.

"Do you live with old St. Nick?" Davy was inquiring.

"Well, no, sonny; I don't know as I do live nigh neighbor to him. What made you think I was him?"

"Why, you look jest 'zactly like him; don't he, Jamie?

" 'He was all dressed in fur; an' his eyes how they twinkled!
An' his droll little mouth was drawn up like a bow;
While the beard on his chin was as white as the snow;
An' he shook when he laughed like a bowlful of jelly!' "

he added, triumphantly, as one by one these points of resemblance recurred to his mind, while the squire was obliged to put both the boys off his lap as he united in the roar of laughter which followed Davy's apt description.

"Well, well, well!" he exclaimed, wiping his face with a red bandanna, "I'm glad I look so much like a saint; maybe I'm his brother. Anyhow you just hang up your stockings as you did to your grandpa's. Ef the ol' fellow kin get here, he'll come. An' you get your ma to hang up hern, just for the fun of it; and Mis' Morris too. Ol' Kriss Kringle (that's what they called him when I was a boy), he likes grown-up folks too."

"An' little sister's stocking, too," said Davy.

"Certainly; though I apprehend her wants are all supplied."

"Do you know what he's going to bring us? Bill bet he'd bring us hand sleds."

"Quite possibly he may. I flatter myself that I have an idea. You see 'twan't more 'n a fortnight ago, I see the clouds one evening as red as them coals of fire; an' I have been assured that when the sky looks like that ol' St. Nick is baking his cake for Christmas. An' likelier 'n not he'd be making 'lasses candy at the same time. But now, I tell you, he'll never come while we sit here and have such a blazing hot fire. We've all got to go to bed, an' the fire must go out, an' everybody go to sleep, and then I apprehend he'll put in an appearance. But should any individual try to get a squint at him, he'll get nothing but a gad, or a snowball in *his* stocking. Now you go an' get your ma's, and the baby's, an' Mis' Morris's, an' I'll hang 'em up with your'n right here 'front of the fireplace."

Mrs. Morgan was putting little Miriam into her cradle, and Bessie making preparations for the morning meal. Davy's movements were unnoticed; and the stocking basket was brought to the fireside.

Hammer and nails were found by Jamie; and in a moment the men were laughing, and the women astonished at the sight of a long white stocking flanked by a gray one, a tiny red sock, and two blue ones, all suspended from the mantle.

The gray dawn was drifting through the windows, when two little figures crept quietly from their trundle-bed and stole into the kitchen.

Morris had been there before them; and a fire crackled in the cook-stove at one end of the room, and roared and sparkled in the fireplace at the other, lighting up the row of stockings and the words MERRY CHRISTMAS in evergreen letters on the white wall above them. Over the doors were rustic arches of mingled hemlock and laurel, and each white curtain was festooned with evergreens and scarlet berries.

But the boys saw only the five stockings, stuffed to the toes with St. Nicholas's gifts, and beside the fireplace two tiny red sleighs.

For a second they stood in mute astonishment; then, with shouts of delight, they seized the ropes of their designated sleighs, and commenced drawing them across the floor.

"But the stockings!" shouted Davy. "I want mine right away, quick!"

Morris, entering, placed the treasures in their upraised hands. Their loudly expressed joy soon aroused the household. A big red apple; a doughnut, resembling either a man, a monkey, or a bear in shape; a primer; a fish-line, and a pair of little red mittens were in each stocking.

A doll, with cloth head, adorned with ravelled yarn for hair, a thin skin of cambric over the pink muslin cheeks and lips, and inked eyebrows arching over the bead eyes, leaned out of Baby's stocking as though meditating a leap to the hearth.

The long gray-and-white hose hung undisturbed until Mrs. Morgan and Bessie, more surprised than the boys at St. Nicholas's remembrance, sat down by the fireside to examine their contents. Gingham for aprons was first pulled out; then gloves, apples, and a handful of nuts; but something flat and thin remained in the foot of each stocking.

"My certie!" cried Bessie, "but auld St. Nick is na coif! 'Tis a letter I have, an' frae me ain mither, I ken weel. What hae ye, missis?"

"A letter too, from my brother. I never knew St. Nicholas to be a mail-carrier;" and Mrs. Morgan looked smilingly at Mr. Noyes. "But he could not have brought me a more acceptable gift."

"Weel, weel, we hae muckle daffin'! The letters maun bide till bra'kfas's weel awa';" and Bessie slipped the treasure into her bosom, and hastened to put the griddle over the fire, turn the slices of frying ham, drain the boiling water from the potatoes, and set the coffee-pot upon the hearth, before setting the table for the morning meal.

Meanwhile Mrs. Morgan was hastily scanning the pages of St. Nicholas's best gift, assisting the children in dressing, and admiring their Christmas presents.

"Now, mother," said Davy, skipping across the floor with his sled at his heels, "I kin take you ridin' downhill. You set behind an' jest hang on, an' I'll steer! Is that a real sure 'nuff letter from Uncle Dave? What does it say? Noffin' 't all 'bout me? Oh, goody, goody! breakfus' is reddy, an' I'm hungrier 'n a bear! Well, I'm *mos'* hungrier, mother."

The morning meal was over; the men gone to their labors at mill and barn; the boys started up the hillside to find a clear place for coasting, when the treasured letters were again opened, and each sentence carefully and thoughtfully read.

"My brother has a plan that I hope you will like as well as I do, Bessie. He wants us to come down the river on a raft next spring. Here is what he says: 'With a cabin built on the raft for a shelter from the winds and possible rains, plenty of straw and blankets, you could keep yourself and baby comfortable, even if the weather should be chilly. The scenery must be grand through the mountains of the Upper Delaware; and below the Water Gap it is indeed lovely. Just fancy the country clothed in spring's fair verdure; the mossy rocks; the mist-like pink of budding foliage; the thick masses of evergreen, changing as you glide along to the blossoming orchards and verdant fields. Wreaths of radishes, bouquets of asparagus, garlands of garlic, shall greet you! Banquets of spring chickens and green pease will await you. Cabbages and catfish shall lie at your feet. The city shall be in readiness to receive you, with door-steps newly cleaned. Let nothing but ill-health or unfavorable weather prevent your coming.'"

"Eh, mem, the thocht o' gain' to the auld hame makes me hert loop i' me briest! Ah, I'll bide weel content ef we can gang awa' i' the spring. Hoots, but I darna lippen too 't! Not that I'm at a' mecserable, mem, but the wark's some wersh like, an' we're baith fashin' fur a change. Yer brother's o'erfond o' daffin'; he's sae merry-hearted. Wad ye like a bit o' my letter noo? Ye see, mem, I tellt her o' th' fine blackberries on th' brambles, an' the big gran' wuds, wheer there's na eend o' bonny blossoms a' sae fair an' fragrant; an' noo she tells me o' the fruits on the fairm at hame: 'We hae gathered thirty bushels o' pears, as big as yer twa *neeves*'—that's two fists, mem—'out'n the arichard yer daddy bought sin' ye been awa'. Ye never saw sic big anes in a' yer life; an' peaches grow jist like apple-trees in th' Auld Country. Naebody has th' brick wa's to fas'en th' trees tae here. We hae muckle o' grapes; but ye were made acquaint wi' them, an' dinna like them sae weel, I ken, as th' gossarts up at th' Ha' i' th' auld hame.'"

"What are gossarts, Bessie?"

"Gooseberries ye ca' them; but they're nane sae sweet as th' anes the auld gardner wad be givin' me frae the squire's garden i' Scotland. Ah, hoo I wad like to sind an air o' corn to auld Sandy! I canna mak' him unnerstan' hoo th' grain grows on a cob, a' set i' rows, jist like pearly teeth, frae ane eend to t'ither; nor hoo it's wrapped round aboot wi' th' bonny thrieds like soft spun silk, an' th' braw green leaves ane above anither. He jist minds him o' aits an' siclike grains, an' winna b'leve corn grows higher 'an his heid wi' a stalk like his airm. He'll ne'er unnerstan' 'less he comes awa' t' see."

"Mistress Morgan and Bessie, do come out and ride downhill with us! It's perfectly glorious out-of-doors, and coasting is the jolliest kind of fun. Do come, won't you? We have the boys' sleds and a deerskin, and the crust will bear a horse's weight."

Fred's voice reached them before his face, flushed with exercise and radiant with mirth, appeared in the door-way.

"Do bundle up the baby and let me take her. You want to come, don't you, Mira?"

The little girl smiled, and cooed assent.

"Why, Fred! you dear crazy boy! to think of taking an old woman and her baby out riding downhill. We will look out of the window and see you. But Bessie is young; she can go."

"'Course she can," said Morris, also entering; "I ain't goin' to draw lumber on a Christmas-day. I'm going to take you to a frolic over the river to-night, Bessie, ef ye'll go; an' I may as well put in the hull day. So you jest get on your fixin's, an' we'll have a ride fust. Bundle up your ears, for Jack Frost is waitin' to give 'em a nip. We'll cum down that hill like a streak o' greased lightenin'."

"My certie, Willy," exclaimed his wife, "wad ye mak' yersel a gay young spark agen by crackin' me pow agen a rock? Ye better 'ware th' wuddie ere ye do sic a thing as that," Bessie answered, her laughing eyes contradicting her pretended alarm. "Never ye fear my breakin' yer head; ef I'm ever hung on the *wuddie*, 'twill be fur crackin' the pow o' some fellow that's winked at you."

"Wad ye let me stay wi' th' wean, mem, an' let ye come oot?" said Bessie, looking at her husband for approval for her sacrifice of the sport; "or wad ye hae yer ride efterhin?— Aiblins yer frightit at th' wee sled-dy?"

"I am a little afraid of tumbling off, and very much afraid of spinning downward through the air. But you will like it, so go on."

Placing the baby in the cradle, Mrs. Morgan wrapped a shawl about her, and followed the coasting party out into the sunshine. From the uppermost trees on the furthermost hills to the door-stone at her feet spread the glittering snow, broken only by icicled rocks and frosted trees; a dazzling scene, from which the eye turned to watch the figures climbing the nearest hillside: Jamie and Davy in advance, Bessie's tartan plaid and Fred's gay scarf contrasting brightly with the blackness of rocks, and evergreens, and the whiteness of the snow.

Up, up the steep path they climbed (made straight and smooth for rolling logs) until they reached a rock a quarter of a mile above the road. Then they paused, Fred seating himself upon Davy's sleigh, the owner crouching between his knees. A moment's pause—

"All ready? Hold on tight, Davy!"

And downward they flew, past

rocks, trees, bushes, stumps—faster, faster—the air rushed against them, bearing away breath, sight, feeling, and leaving a bewildering whirl! A stop, and Davy saw the barn-yard gate and the cattle and chickens around him.

"Get up, Davy, and see Big Bill come down. That deerskin will be no easy thing to steer. Now they're off. Whew, how they fly! They'll hit that stump—no, they don't! They've run into that bush; I knew they would. On they come! Bessie has lost her hood. Hear her laugh! Here they are! My gracious, Bill, that's what I call fast flying! How do you like it, Bessie?"

"My certie!" she exclaimed, catching her breath. "O-oh it's fine! Les' try it agen, Willy; an' go na farther than th' oonmainnerly bramble that sto' me snood."

"All right, I'm ready for another; an' I'll try an' keep clear o' the bush. I'll bet that *buckskin* never went so fast afore, not when the hounds wus after it. Davy, your ma is waitin' thar by the door fur you to tell her how ye like ridin' downhill."

"Fred, you better bring Jamie down nex' time. I guess he's kindy 'fraid to venture all alone."

True: Jamie was seated on his sled, with heels braced firmly in the snow, dreading the laughter of those who had dared the danger, yet dreading the danger more.

"Oh, pshaw! what's he afraid of? We came down safely. Come on, Jamie!" yelled Fred.

"Stay there, Jamie!" shouted Bill. "I'll come an' fetch ye! He don't know nothin' 'bout steerin' a sled. Likelier 'n not he'd upset an' skin his nose, ef nothin' wus."

Again they climbed the steep hillside, until they reached the clump of briers and laurels, where Bessie's hood yet swung in the wind.

"I'll bring Jamie down, Bill," said Fred. "You needn't go any farther."

"All right: we'll wait till you go by. I hain't no notion o' bein' run into by your sled; and this plaguy skin is ez likely to swing round and slide sideways ez to go ahead."

As they stepped from the "runway" upon a moss-covered rock, a white rabbit bounded away, a flock of snow-birds fluttered to the tree-tops, twittering a moment, then settling down again upon the spot of bare earth the overhanging rock had sheltered from the snow. The crimson plumes of the sumac, the brown foliage of the oak, and the scarlet and yellow berries of the bitter-sweet gleamed among the dark-hued hemlocks and deep-green laurels, while the golden sunlight filtering through the forest gilded and illumined the scene. Far below them lay the valley, clad in glittering white.

Before the store, horses and sleighs were standing, their owners coming out now and then to stow away their purchases in the straw under the seat of the rude home-made vehicles. At the mill a group of red-shirted men were rolling logs and piling scantling; while the ring of the file upon the steel, as the sawyer sharpened his saw, sounded clear as a silver bell. The river was a narrow field of snow, hedged by steep banks, and broken only by holes some fishermen were cutting through the ice.

"There's the square a-settin' tip-ups; don't you see him down in the eddy? He'll hev fish enough fur dinner, I'll bet."

"'Deed noo," exclaimed Bessie, "we mus' mak' haste awa', or the partridges weel be ill dune for deener. Haud awa' wid ye, Mister Fred, an' ne'er stan' starin' theer like an unco gawk! Faith, though, I could bide i' these bonny green wuds a' th' day. See the winsome birdie, Willy! ane wi' a scarlet coif an' t'ither wi' bonny blue kilt an' brown breeks. Coom awa,' lads, or ye'll get na deener this day!"

"Here we go!" shouted Jamie; and instantly they darted past and flew down the hill. The deerskin was adjusted on the glittering snow, Morris holding the bushes, while Bessie seated herself behind him, her skirts tucked closely about her, and her arms clasping her husband's waist.

"All ready now? Whew!"

A long gasp; a mad rush of bushes and trees up the hillside; a grating of the steersman's heels in the icy crust; a swift whirl as the smooth skin swung to the right; a backward slide; and they stopped beside the garden wall.

"How do you like coasting, Bessie?" Mrs. Morgan asked, as she was removing her wrappings.

"Hoots, mem, it's jist gran'! Theer's nair birr to 't an' slidin' (though it's mony a clyte I've had in slidin'), but it takes ane's brith awa'. Dinna speer me 'bout it; jist hae a try at it yer ain sel."

But the sun's rays soon softened the snow, and riding on the crust was abandoned.

The Christmas dinner was prepared. Roasted partridges and pigeon-pie were flanked by pyramids of mashed potatoes and hulled corn, yellow turnips, and crimson beets. A blackberry pudding and pumpkin-pie, with cranberry jelly and golden cheese, furnished the dessert.

"Mother," called Davy, pausing with a wedge of his favorite "bren'-butter" at his lips—"mother, this is Jesus' birthday, ain't it?"

"Yes, my son."

"I s'pose he's *real* glad we're havin' such a nice time down here. Ef he wus here now—and wa'n't grow'd up, you know—I'd let him ride on my new sled jes' as long 's he'd a min' to."

The mother-heart understood the self-abnegation of the boyish impulse, and her face smiled approval before the father's voice uttered its harsh rebuke.

"David, never let me hear you speak of the Omnipotent King of Heaven in that manner again. Do you know he is able to destroy you this instant for such irreverent thoughts? It is plain enough where you get such ideas; but I call them downright blasphemy."

"I know, John"—and Mary Morgan's face flushed, and her voice faltered—"I know you and I do not feel quite the same on this subject; but it seems to me Jesus was a boy, and a man, just to give us a pattern to live by; and if he had been born ten years ago instead of eighteen hundred, and here instead of Bethlehem, he would have shared Davy's sled with pleasure."

"Well, well, I don't see where you have any authority in the Holy Scriptures for such irreverent ideas; and for my part, I want my boys to be brought up to regard the name of their Redeemer as something too sacred to be talked of with levity; and I don't want to hear any more of it! —Let me help you to some more partridge, squire; and take another cup of coffee."

The clatter of knives and forks went on, but the frown on her husband's brow and the mist gathering in Davy's eyes clouded the sunshine in Mary Morgan's heart, and the old pained, perplexed look came to her face.

"Can you go and play with little sister, Davy? I hear her waking: your pudding shall be saved for you."

The little fellow choked down the sobs, and ran hurriedly into the next room, where his voice was soon heard mimicking the baby's crows of delight, and singing one of Bessie's favorite cradle songs:

"Creep awa', my bairnie, ye're ower young to learn
To tot up an' down yet, my bonny wee bairn;
Better creepin' cannie than fa'in' wi' a bang,
Duntin a your wee brow—creep afore ye gang.

"Ye'll creep, an' ye'll hotch, an' ye'll nod to yer mither,
Watchin' ilka step o' your wee donsy brither;
Rest ye on the floor till your wee limbs grow strang,
An' ye'll be a braw cheil yet—creep afore ye gang.

"The wee birdie fa's when it tries ower soon to flee,
Folks are sure to tumble when they climb ower hie;
They wha canna walk right are sure to come to wrang:
Sae creep awa', my bairnie—creep afore ye gang."

CHAPTER VIII.

"Three-storied larnin's pop'lar now: I guess
We thriv' es wal on jest two stories less;
For it strikes me ther's such a thing as sinnin'
By overloadin' children's underpinnin'.
Wal; here it wus I learned my A B C,
An' it's a kind o' favorite spot to me."
HOSEA BIGLOW.

BABE MIRIAM increased in size and beauty daily. Shy, sensitive, she clung to her mother and Bessie with unvarying affection, received the caresses of her brothers with evident delight, and the admiration of the workmen with timid pleasure; yet the child shrunk from every attention of her father with apparent terror.

In vain did Mrs. Morgan strive to overcome without directly referring to this strange repugnance, grieving secretly with bitter self-reproach at her own unconquered weakness of months before, which now threatened to mar their daughter's inheritance of happiness. For the father, quick to perceive the babe's shrinking from his slightest touch, resented the aversion, and grew apparently indifferent to her, not unfrequently complaining that the baby occupied more time and attention than necessary, and was annoyed by its mother's and brother's loving words and tender caresses.

Nothing delighted Bessie more than to take the little girl in her arms and sing to her the ballads of Bonny Scotland.

A weird, sweet melody would make the little lips quiver and brown eyes fill with tears; if quickly changed, the face was as suddenly irradiated with smiles; if continued, the tears would leap out over the dimpled cheeks, and the little form be convulsed with grief. Nothing but a gentle lullaby would then quiet the sensitive child, who never cried loudly, but passionately as a woman.

To the mother the babe was more than pet, plaything, and employment. Day by day she grew to be the confidante of all her cares. A feeling of reverence mingled with her love, as the dark steadfast eyes looked earnestly into her own, as if with subtle instinct they gazed into her inmost soul, recognizing each aspiration, comprehending every limitation, with calm trust foreseeing, and with loving loyalty defying all.

Hours of silent, blissful communion were these, when the infant head rested upon the mother-heart, and fancies came thronging to her mind demanding utterance.

After such an hour she wrote these lines:

TO THE BABY.

Your eyes have opened on a world
Of gladness and of sorrow;
But naught you fear,
O baby dear!
The shadows of to-morrow.

Your mother's face, the moving forms,
Your little clumsy fingers,
All make surprise:
In your bright eyes
A thought half wakened lingers.

Or are they only germs of thought
Your mind is just receiving?
Your face reveals—
And yet conceals—
A wonder and a grieving.

I half believe, my little girl,
'Tis not the things around you
That make your eyes
So wondrous wise,
But mem'ries that surround you.

Say, are they mem'ries, little one,
That fill your eyes with wonder?
Some that are glad,
And some so sad?
Eyes smile with tear-drops under.

I wish your lips could form the thoughts
Your eyes are half expressing.
Have you a Past?
Boundless and vast,
Of peace, and joy, and blessing?

Are visions of a life that's gone
O'er your senses stealing?
And do you grieve
For what you leave?
What will dispel the feeling?

Maybe you know the spirit tongue!
Are voices now addressing
Some words of cheer
I cannot hear?
I'm weary of my guessing.

I only know, my precious child,
This life is just beginning,
With loss and gain,
With peace and pain,
With pardon for the sinning.

Weakness to conquer, doubts to crush,
While daily strength attaining;
With light we're led,
With manna fed
Till heavenly stature gaining.

And if we consecrate each day
As holiest of the seven,
Christ's will is done,
His kingdom come;
And earth is fair as heaven!

Then do not falter, O my own!
Or grieve at coming sorrow.
Your Yesterday
Is in To-day,
And all joy in To-morrow.

The wintry days grew shorter and colder. March came and passed away, but brought no sign of spring. A sudden storm raised the river, and at midnight a roaring and crashing was heard, and a voice shouted,

"The ice 's goin' out!"

The men hurried to the river-bank and mill. The lanterns went flashing and glimmering in the darkness; voices rung out above the noise of pelting rain and howling wind; then, one by one, the men came back to the house, announcing the danger past, the lumber safe. When morning came the storm was over and the ice gone.

Preparations for rafting began, although the snow lay thick upon the ground, and the weather freezing cold. Each sunlit day was followed by one of storm, and the hope of a pleasant journey on a raft grew daily fainter.

. "Ah me!" Bessie cried, as the second week in April brought a snowfall that again whitened the hills, "will the gloomy winter ne'er gang awa'? I mind me faither's tellin' the bairns

"'Hoo Mairch borrowed from Aprill
Three days: an' they were ill.
The fairst day was snaw an' sleet,
The second day was wind an' weet;
The third day there cam' a sair freeze,
An' froze a' the bonny baird's 'nabs t' th' trees.'

An' I'm thinking Mairch has paid 'em back wi' a score mair o' the same sort."

"Giving more than compound interest, you think," replied Mrs. Morgan, glad to divert Bessie's thoughts from a contemplation of the dreary scene outside. "When was that bargain made?"

"Ah, 'tis lang sin' syne. 'Twas a fierce battle 'tween th' Scots an' the Romans; and their gods would hae it ended ere the year was dune; 'twas when the new year cam' i' Mairch, ye ken. Weel, they foucht on, an' whiles th' las' day was near dune, an' the Romans were winnin'; then the Scots cried out for more time, an' the gods lat them hae three mair days—borrowed from the nex' year, ye ken — but tak' a' th' fairness out o' ilka ane o' them so 's to be mair creedit to 'em suld they win."

"And did they win?"

"Oh ay, mem! 'Twas a great victory, spite o' weet an' cauld; an' th' three days hae jes' keepit th' ill weather e'er sin'. Mayhap the morrow may be fair."

And she looked out upon the gray sky faintly tinged with the sunset's yellow hues.

But the morrow brought a cold east wind. The river was low enough for the rafts to start; and one by one they were completed, pulled out into the channel, and carried away by the rapid current.

"Hoots, mem!" exclaimed Bessie, dashing the tears of disappointment from her eyes, "we ha' na time to be douce an' dourie wi' th' gardenin' an' house-cleanin'. Willy was awa' 'fore milkin', an' th' co's a' lowin' fur him noo;" and, taking the milk-pail, she hurried to the barn.

Before a fortnight had passed, the men had returned, the lumber reaching market with few accidents.

The proceeds were largely invested in dry-goods and groceries for the store; and the teams were sent to meet them at the terminus of the canal. The gardens and fields were ploughed and planted; the berries had not begun to ripen. Between these busy seasons the children grew clamorous for school.

Books, slates, pencils, and paper had been procured; and one bright May morning little Miriam's cradle was brought into the room, where new seats and desks had been constructed, and the child's school life began.

To the great delight of the urchins, she smiled her approval at all the exercises, and expressed her interest by clapping her dimpled hands and crowing as only a baby can. Bolstered by pillows in her cradle, or lying on a blanket on the floor, she amused herself by watching the children, or shaking a string of spools and the wooden rattle manufactured for her by Morris.

A special reward of merit for the younger scholars was a seat beside the baby, playing "Bopeep" until little Miriam laughed outright.

"Altogether a model baby for a school-room," said Mrs. Morgan to Mrs. Rodgers, when a fortnight of the term was ended. "Jamie brings her to Bessie if she frets; but she oftener falls asleep over her play, and after a long nap wakens with a smiling '*a goo*.' Her example is worth something in keeping restless bodies quiet. But I see I must invent some stimulus to study; get up some competition for a prize, I think. Mrs. Rodgers, can you tell me how I shall make the scholars get their lessons?"

Mrs. Rodgers was trotting little maid Miriam to "Banbury Cross" to buy the baby a plum; but the "white horse" suddenly stopped as she replied,

"Make 'em git their lessons? Why, I don't know of nothin' better 'n a switch, 'nless it's a *gad*. Land's sake alive! I don't see how you've got along 'thout givin' some on 'em a lickin' 'fore this. time. You know how I laughed at you las' year when ye sed ye wa'n't goin' to hev no whippin' in your school; an' I declar' for it, I was jest 'mazed to see how ye managed them thar young uns! An' I sed to my ol' man, says I, Mis' Morgan's allers preachin' 'bout rulin' by love 'stead o' fear, an' I'm beat ef I don't believe thar's suthin' in it! An' I s'pose it does do better fur to coax 'an drive sometimes, and with *some* young ones. Now, thar's my Jack; land's sake alive! the whippin's that thar boy's stood an' never whimpered, and never give up nuther! My man throws it in my face yit that I never broke that boy's will. Well, I hope the Lord 'll git arter him, an' give him no rest day nor night till he gives up an' gits religion. Seems like he's kindy alterd sence he's ben agoin' to school to you. Not that my Jack is worse nor other boys; he's a sight better 'n many a one 'at don't live a hundred miles from this house! But, then, Jack is set on worldly pleasure; an' I'm powerful 'fraid—" And the mother sighed.

"But you's askin' 'bout some way o' makin' the young uns git their lessons. Now, I never went to school only a little spell; but I mind how the master use' t' take every one of us that didn't know our lessons perfec', an' stan' us all upon the floor, an' tie us all together in a ring with a big cord 'round our wrists, an' then he'd bring out his gads—used to keep a dozen on 'em seasonin' agin the rafters—an' he'd draw his whip long his han', kindy feelin' of it, an' a-glarin' at us (land's sakes! how our hearts 'ud pitty-pat!), an' then he'd raise it up an' give it a whirl (tell you, we'd jump an' yell), an' down 'twould come on somebody's bare feet an' ankles. Why, that feller jest enjoyed it! He actilly used up more 'n forty whips on us young uns; an' he didn't teach but three months neither. Tell ye! we ginnerly hed our spellin' when we know'd what was a-comin' ef we didn't! Though thar was some that got so scared ef he jest looked at 'em, they didn't know nothin', an' *they* was allers gittin' licked. So I s'pose it takes differ'nt ways fur differ'nt kinds; an' I guess you're 'nough sight wiser 'n I be 'bout such work, anyhow."

"Well, I want these boys and girls to do right because it *is right*, and because it is more safe and more pleasant. I think that is the way God teaches us. He shows us what is wrong, and if we will do it, the wrong itself hurts us; but if we do right, the right itself makes us happy. And I think if the good people would always be the most pleasant people, young folks would try to imitate them; and if the right way was made pleasantest, the children would all try and go that way; so what I want is something to coax them along in the right way. Bessie, can't you think of something? I cannot afford gifts, you know, nor get medals."

"Weel, I dinna ken what wad gie the bairns here maist gude; they're sae muckle sculduddery! But I mind a custom in the parish schule where the maister hed a sou'reign, an' a crown, an' a shillin', wi' holes i' them, an' a ribbon put through; an' th' lads an' the lassies wha stood heid i' their ilka class wore ane o' them hame th' nicht; an' verra proud were we when we won the honor, tho' we parted wi' the prize i' the mornin'."

"Did they ever lose them?"

"That ne'er happened but aince. A big lad wore the sou'reign hame, an' did na' fess it back the morn— 'twas los', he said. Weel, the maister took a strip o' white paper, stiff like, ye ken, an' he put on it in sic big letters, 'This lad hae los' our sou'reign' —an' pinned it on his back. Then he put a bit o' leather wi' a cord 'bout his neck, stead o' the prize (for he wan it agen); an' 'fore nicht he bro't the sou'reign to th' maister's han'; an' it was ne'er los' agen."

"I wonder how that would do here? A dollar for the first class with a blue ribbon, a half-dollar for the second with green, and a quarter-dollar with red ribbon for the A B C class. Then the one who left off head the most times should have the piece of money to keep. Why, Bessie, I think that is a capital plan! I will speak to Mr. Morgan about it this very evening."

"An' wha' for s'uld ye spake o' the maitter at a'? Ye hae the siller, I ken."

"Yes, my brother sent me a number of pocket-pieces with the gifts to the children. Yet I feel as though I ought to ask my husband's opinion about it."

The family were gathered about the hearth-stone that evening—for though the days were sunny, the nights were cool—and a bright fire leaped and sparkled in the fireplace.

Jamie and Davy were popping corn in the hot ashes; Babe Miriam gleefully watched the sport, enthroned in her mother's arms. Two men were engrossed in a game of checkers, with chips and buttons for men. Bessie and her husband sat together in the cushioned settle in the chimney-corner, while Mr. Morgan, with account-books before him on the table, leaned his head upon his hands, absorbed in thought.

Dreams and aspirations of youth, hopes and plans of manhood, mingled their contrasting forms and varied hues in a kaleidoscopic vision. Past and present grew confused. Where were the desires of earlier years; the anticipations of usefulness, the self-abnegation, the fervor? Was this backwoods life a result, or a contradiction? Was money-getting a means, or an end?

"I have some new scholars to-day," said his wife.

"Hm-m," he responded, without raising his head.

"Two English children, by the name of White: quite good scholars, I think. Do you know anything about the family?"

"Just come. Live near the gristmill."

"Oh, they are new settlers. John, I want to ask your advice about a plan for coaxing the children up the hill of knowledge;" and Mary Morgan turned toward the table with an expectant smile.

Her husband gathered up his books.

"You must manage your school without any of my help. I've got enough on my hands without being bothered by that. Only, I want to tell you, once for all, I won't have the young ones hanging around the store! They are a perfect torment, with wanting a slate-pencil, or a stick of licorice, or a bottle of ink, or a few peppermints, a dozen times a day! and bringing pails and baskets for things their mammies sent for. Then when your school is out, in comes the whole drove; and bags, and buckets, and half-gallons, and quarter-pounds, and names, and young ones, are all mixed up for half an hour. Fred don't know one young one from another, and is continually getting things charged to the wrong persons."

"I'm sorry," said Mrs. Morgan, "that my school should annoy any one; but I cannot help the children doing errands for their parents."

"Well, you can keep them from running into the store play-spells and noonings; and they can keep their baskets and bundles until school is out. As for the rest, you can whip them, or do anything you like. I don't care; and I don't want to hear anything about it."

And John Morgan, unheeding the surprised looks of his children, or the disappointment in his wife's face, picked up his books and went to the store.

"What ails papa, mother?" said Davy, coming to her side with his tin cup filled with parched corn.

"I don't know, dear; I suppose his business bothers him. But it is bedtime now for young folks."

"'Tis, hey?" exclaimed Sam Jenkins, sweeping the checkers into a box just as his opponent was crowning a king. "That means me; an' I hain't goin' to set here an' be beat agin at no sech baby game as checkers is; hanged if I be!" And amidst the laughter of his companions, he climbed the steep stairs leading to the men's room, followed by his victor.

Big Bill took a candle, and, lighting it by a brand from the fireplace, went to his room; and Bessie, after finishing preparations for breakfast, covered the fire, and followed him.

But Mary Morgan sat for hours with her sleeping babe in her arms,

MIRIAM'S HERITAGE. 57

the smouldering
 held the secret
es and chilling

 of merit" were
ed to the school
The eagerness
il studied show-
o be the first to

s pierced by the
laid beside the
at recorded the
and recitations

in her happiest
ghing quietly as
per, or twisted a
d her taper fin-

arded to a blue-
d the one-sylla-
, and knew the
y, and township
lent.
sed triumphant-
of spelling, but
formidable ques-
esident of the
o is governor of
bright half-dol-
nded by its gay
of a curly-head-
d scarcely wait
o his jacket be-
ard to show the

the class took
d followed him,
they were "jest
correct answer
vrong one.
le," Mrs. Morgan

said, holding up the remaining coin, "I wonder who will wear this silver medal first? But, remember, if you miss to-night, you may win to-morrow; so keep trying. First class in spelling!"

All the largest boys and girls left their seats, and ranged themselves before the teacher's desk in a long row, carefully toeing the mark.

"Henry, this is your class," said Mrs. Morgan, turning to a pale-faced, white-haired boy near the door; "you can go to the foot to-day that you may win a place at the head to-morrow."

The boy's face flushed crimson, making the whiteness of his hair and eyebrows more apparent as he rose and walked awkwardly to his place at the foot of the line of giggling urchins, who stared at his blue cloth "roundabout," adorned with rows of brass buttons from the bottom of the waist to the top of the shoulders. The tightly fitting black pantaloons contrasted strangely with their loosely hanging cotton trousers; and the leathern gaiters stumbled along as though feeling out of place among the bare feet of the other boys.

"Number," commanded the teacher.

"First," said Jamie, who stood at the head; "Second," "Third," "Fifth."

"You stand *fourth*, Polly Brown."

"No, ma'am; I stood *fifth* yesterday, and I hain't got above nobody," said the girl, twisting the corner of her checked apron and glancing shyly down the class.

"How is this?" inquired the teacher; "who stood above Polly?"

"Wal, I guess I wus up thar yisterday; but I'd sooner stay here, ef it's th' same tew you," answered Jack Rodgers, who, being a man in height, felt out of place among the smaller children.

"I prefer your keeping your place, Jack; it saves time and trouble, and I don't think Polly minds your being above her. Now number again!"

"*Theme*," pronounced the teacher.

"*Truth.*"

The words were spelled as rapidly as pronounced.

"*Eighth.*"

It was Jamie's turn; but his eyes were fixed upon a spider weaving a web across the window-pane.

"Next."

Jamie started, and blushed as he realized he had lost his position.

"I'm sorry, my son; but you must stop that habit of day-dreaming. Dan, it is your turn."

"E-a-g-h-t-h," said the boy, confidently.

"Next."

"E-y-g-h-t-h," faltered Beckie Sanders.

"Next."

"E-i-g-h-t, *eight*," said Jack.

"That's not the word. Next—*eighth*."

"E-a-y— Oh, I don't know," exclaimed Polly, the tears starting to her eyes at losing a chance to go up head.

"The word is very easy; only think how it looks on the page. I do not see how any of you can misspell it. Try it, Sammy."

"A-i-g-h-th," said Sammy, triumphantly.

"Next."

"A-y-gh-t-h," said the next boy.

The interest grew intense; the head and foot of the class unconsciously kept stepping forward to see the spellers, until the straight line became a curve.

The new scholar was quivering with excitement. His fingers were clasped and unclasped in impatient agony lest some one above him should spell it correctly. His face twitched, his eyes dilated, his breath came quick and hard.

"Next," said the teacher; and his turn had come.

A triumphant smile swept over the crimsoned face; he drew himself up, and in a shrill *crescendo* voice began,

"He-hi-g-haitch-t-haich!"

The last letter was a scream, and he started instantly for the head of the class.

A burst of laughter convulsed the whole school.

Mrs. Morgan closed the book, and gave the command to "number," trying in vain to control her face sufficiently to restore order.

Little Miriam began to cry with fright; and it was for her sake the noisy boys tried to suppress their laughter.

"Henry White has won the medal for the day," announced the teacher; "and though he misuses the letter *H*, no doubt he sees as great blunders in our speaking. So let us all help each other to *speak* right, and *act* right—no one getting angry at a joke, and no one carrying a joke too far. The class is dismissed. Put your desks in order, then go out quietly. Good-night."

CHAPTER IX.

"A mistiness broods in the air—the swell
Of east winds slowly wearing autumn's pall,
With dirge-like sadness, wanders up the dell;
And red leaves from the maple slowly fall
With scarce a sound: what strange mysterious rest
Hath Nature bound the Lotus to her breast?"

MOLLIE MOORE.

"IF this 'ere spell o' weather holds ut, you may as well git your traps ady fur Jarsey, little woman," Mor- s said, as he stamped the mud from is feet at the kitchen door.

"Hey, Willy," Bessie exclaimed, ausing with a ladleful of golden but- er over an earthen jar, "be ye daffin', oo?"

"Not a bit of it, little wife; I'm in ead airnest. The river's riz six inch- s sense las' night, an' ef it keeps on aisin' there'll be a fresh, sure."

Mrs. Morgan came from the other oom with Miriam in her arms.

"Are you very certain we can go?" he asked, her face lighting up with leasure dimmed with fear.

"Wall, no, marm; I hain't certain ' nothin'. But there's a raft all eady, 'ceptin' the loadin', an' there's fresh' lackin' 'bout ten inches. The louds are puttin' in thar best licks ow, an' I'm goin' to the mill to look rter some cherry boards we're goin' o take fur loadin'. So ef you tew wimmen really want to go 'long, why you'd better be gittin' reddy; an' ef yer don't want ter, an' won't nohow, why, ye might be gittin' up a dinner-box fur us poor fellers what hev to go anyhow," and, laughing, he walked away.

"Eh, mem, 'tis maist unco gude to be true. But I'll gang on with the airnin', an' we hae enough breid. S'all I mak' ginger-cake? An' wad ye like some corn-beef, or wull the ham be sufficient?"

"If we can go, we had better take a box of provisions for ourselves besides the men's. I will make some sandwiches. My trunk has been packed nearly all summer—except a few things for the children; and baby's cloak and hood are not quite done. It does seem too good to be true. Oh, how I hope nothing will prevent our going! Mother Rodgers said she would come any time and keep house. A rainy day never look- ed so cheery before."

The preparations went on rapidly; and when Mr. Morgan returned, wet and weary, from a two days' collecting tour, he saw faces so expectant of bliss they were almost tearful. He had met with better success than he had anticipated in collecting store debts, and, with more than enough money to pay for running the lumber, he was very willing to give his family a pleasure so long deferred.

Another day was spent in preparation. The boys were wild with delight. Jamie constructed a ship, with paper sails, to float beside the raft.

Davy prepared fish-lines and hooks and a box of bait. And little Miriam, appearing to understand that packing up was the order of the day, collected her dolls and their clothing, her rattle-box and primer, and stowed them all under the pillow in her cradle.

"How she will miss her rock-a-bye!" Mrs. Morgan said, as the curly head lay down for a noonday nap, singing a sleepy song without words, while her mother gently touched the cradle as she sewed.

"Never went to sleep 'thout rockin', did she?" said Mrs. Rodgers. "Wall, neow, Jack, can't you holler out a log an' make a cradle fur her, like you wus rocked in?"

"Don't b'lieve I've got time, mammy," Jack answered. "But tell you what kin be done; I kin git an empty box an' nail it on a piece o' slab, an' I guess likely she'll rock-a-bye herself in that. Won't ye, sweetheart?"

The child opened her sleepy eyes, smiled dreamily, and reached up her tiny hands; but sleep conquered.

The hands dropped, the eyes closed, and the smile faded into a dream.

Jack stooped and touched her forehead with his lips.

"Don't ye let nothin' happen to her, Mis' Morgan. Seems if I'd never want to set eyes on you agin if ye didn't bring her back all right."

"Why, Jack," exclaimed the mother, startled by his look and tone, "what could happen? Isn't it safe— the raft I mean? And you have built a cabin and made a place for fire; why, I expect we will have a splendid time."

"Course we will. I didn't mean nothin'," and he laughed uneasily. "I was thinkin' if she should git sick in Philadelphy;" and his lips quivered as he turned away.

The night was half spent before all was ready for their journey; but the new day was only dawning when Morris roused the household with his hearty "Hurrah, everybody! Time to be up an' at it!"

Jamie and Davy tumbled out of their trundle-bed, and were half dressed in their new suits before the kitchen fire was lighted, getting buttons and button-holes mixed, garments inside out and hind side before, in a way impossible to any creature but a hurrying boy.

"I'm jest a-gittin' gladder and gladder every minute!" Davy declared, dancing around on one foot, while lacing the shoe on the other. "Mother, when a feller feels as if he could fly, why can't he?"

"Because his body isn't as light as his heart, I suppose."

"Well, I'd rather sail on the river

than fly in the air, anyway. If I was a bird, I'd be a duck."

"Well, you're a goose, and that's clear enough. Come, hurry up, Dave; breakfast is ready—come on," said his brother.

Passengers and baggage were upon the raft, as the first rays of sunlight leaped over the hill-tops and tinged the river with a ruddy glow. The white cottage gleamed through its mantle of green and scarlet foliage, and at its back the forest waved red and yellow banners amidst its ranks of evergreen, while the whole earth seemed dressed for a holiday.

"All aboard now! An' ef ye can't git a board, git a slab!" shouted Big Bill. "Man yer oars! Now, then, intie her. *Jarsey!*"

Slowly the space of water widened between them and the shore. Slowly at first, but more rapidly as they glided away, the cottage and the river-bank seemed receding. Fred waved his hat; the men shouted, "Good luck to ye!" And Mrs. Rodgers, with a gay handkerchief about her head, and a smile on her earnest face, looked the presiding genius of the scene.

"Fred looks lonely. Poor fellow, I wish he could come too."

"Well, I think there's enough :ome," her husband answered, gruffly. 'I guess somebody's got to stay to see to things."

"I suppose that means *me*, Mister Morgan," Bill said, good-humoredly; 'an' I'll allow there wa'n't no special use of both of us a-comin', seen 's the raft 's sold an' the loadin' bargained 'ur. But, ye see, it's fashionable to take a trip after yer married, an' this is Bessie's and my weddin'-tower. Ain't it, little woman?" to the rosy-cheeked wife, who, with her blue hood pushed back, and golden hair waving about her face, was gazing at sky, hill, and valley, as if a new world had opened before her.

"Toots, Willy," she said, blushing and dimpling with delight, "'tis a better journey than the newly wed can know; an' this is a fairer day than the spring-time can bring. See how sweet and content the valleys lie 'twixt the hills."

"That's so, little wife; harvest-time is better 'n plantin'. An' when you an' I go up to th' house, an' see th' ol' folks standin' in th' door a-waitin' for us— *Pennsylvania!* Lively, boys!" And Morris brushed the back of his hand across his eyes.

The men sprung to their oars; lifting the tips of the stem at arm's-length, and, dipping the blade deep in the water, they put their strength to the oar, which bent almost to the point of breaking as they went tip-toeing across the raft; then, quickly lowering their hands, lifting the oar-blade out of the water, ran back again, repeating the movement until commanded to "Holt!"

"Pretty close shave, Bill," Jack Rodgers remarked, quietly cutting a piece from a plug of tobacco he held in his hand.

"A miss 's as good as a mile, they say; but hanged if I b'lieve it."

"That depends a good deal on the miss, an' suthin' on the mile. We know you're kindy 'fraid o' Miss Susan; but guess it's a good travelled mile between ye, ain't it? Honest, now, it did look as if that miss was goin' to be a hit. I let the raft sag over a purpose; wanted to stir you up an' git yer gait, so 's I could see what sort o' han's I hed to depend on."

"Well, what do you think of us?"

"Oh, you'll do; you jest fairly lifted 'er. See ef ye'll do as well for'ard at Butler's, Foul Rift, an' Wells's. The las' time I come through here, I'd jest as live scrape agin that rock as not—didn't want to *stave*, ye know, but enjoyed comin' purty nigh to it; but now"—glancing at the cabin where the women and children were sitting—"well, now it's different; an' I won't take no more chances this trip. Davy, where's yer fish-line? Bring yer bait-box, an' I'll show you how to hook a sucker. Jamie wants to ketch an eel, don't ye? or would ye ruther take my oar fur a spell, while I go an' lay down on the straw? That las' pull kinder winded me. Here, Davy, you set down here, an' let your line drop 'tween th' rafts. There's room to haul up a bigger fish 'n you'll ketch. See what a lot of pin-fish! Tie yer line to this grub, an' git Bessie to give ye a piece o' bread to crumb up an' drop in here. More fish 'll come thar than you an' Jamie can both of you count."

Leaving the boys so well employed, Morris seated himself beside his wife. Jack was lying on the straw with little Miriam in his arms, crowing and cooing at a branch of red leaves he fluttered beyond her reach. Mrs. Morgan glanced a little uneasily at the deserted oars, as the other men sauntered to the provision-box, and, abstracting a pie, cut it into quarters, and began leisurely to devour it.

"I did not suppose you could let the raft go at all without guiding it," she said to Jack.

"Oh, it's got the right pint, an' this is still water. Bill knows this river from the Forks to Trenton as well as you know the path through your door-yard. He can tell by lookin' at the hills on either side where we be, 'n then he knows 'bout how fast we're runnin', and could calculate to half a second when there's pullin' to be done if he wus blindfolded. He'll set thar 's unconcerned as an owl for 'bout three minutes, an' then you'll see him jump an' yell 'Jarsey.' Want to go to your bye-o, sweetheart? Well, yer bed's soft as straw an' blankets ken make it; an' here's yer own little pillow. Now, then, rock-a-bye, Beauty."

The water rippled and twinkled, splashing musically against the raft, the winds rustled the gay foliage as they glided close to the shore, and the white clouds and brilliant-hued hills were reflected in the clear waters till they seemed floating in mid-air, with the sky above and beneath them. Even Morris seemed impressed by the solemn grandeur of the scene, and, rising quietly, said, "Come, boys." Jack gave the cradle a final rock; the men brushed the crumbs from their bearded lips, and each sauntered to his oar.

"Jarsey!"

The water, which had been smooth as a mirror, began to swell and roll; now it dashed foaming upon a rock, now rushed fiercely across the raft.

l creaked; the nuts laid upon a towel beside them;
, and main. while the men went by turns to their
outed Bill. own box, sliced bread and ham with
the other side their pocket-knives, rinsing down huge
:d hard, though mouthfuls by draughts of river water.
he water grew   Jamie sat on a pile of boards with
t; and a long his elbow on his knee, and his head
) spread before resting on his hand, with a biscuit
or a wave from half-way to his lips; but his thoughts
were engrossed in the beautiful scene
, bad place?" before him.
Jack returned "Mother," he exclaimed, at length,
"do see that creek come tumbling
rus nothin' but down the mountain; the water turns
ill that rough, to mist before it reaches the river!"
till ye git to   "Your dinner will be *missed* if you
low fresh like don't eat it," said Davy, snatching the
)arin' an' pitch- biscuit from his hand.
don't you be   "My son, don't be so rude! Davy
steersman, an' is almost as fond of punning as you
s raft through are, Morris."
man's aboard."   "Yes; I guess it's kinder ketchin'.
y, "when's din- I got it of Long John, an' Davy he's
I am as hun- ketched it from me; 'n fact, I sorter
felt 's ef I 's indebted to the family,
?" Bessie asked. ye know, an' orter train him up to
of 'em *stealin'* 'muse ye, somehow. An' as I hain't
to have a con- no drum nor whistle fur him, I set
asty minnows! him to making puns, an' now he kin
·s just smelled make 'bout 's bad a one as I kin; can't
ed one eye up ye, Davy?"
But I caught   "Pretty near; but Fred will beat
all of us. Ain't it funny we're all so
punny?" And the boy ran away to
·, and a big ap- assist Jamie in launching the ship.
ht away, won't   Like a panorama the varying scenes
glided by. The rugged mountains
n'. Come awa' disappeared, and autumn-painted hills,
iic dinner ye'll surrounding verdant valleys, fruitful
orchards, or pleasant homes were seen
re distributed; on either hand. Then the river nar-
the bottles of rowed, and the waters grew black as
pie and dough- they reflected the hemlock-trees and

fern-crowned rocks overhanging the way. Again it widened, and villages with church-spires and tavern signs appeared. The men hallooed to raftsmen on shore; some children waved their hats to Jamie and Davy. Then a turn in the river hid all sight of human habitation. Bessie leaned upon her husband's oar in earnest talk. The other men, with slow steps to and fro, kept the raft in the current. The boys were sailing their ship upon the unruffled water behind the raft, while Mr. Morgan, shading his eyes with one hand, was closely examining some figures in his account-book. Babe Miriam slept on in the shade of the cabin.

For a long time Mrs. Morgan mused; then, taking paper and pencil from her bag, she wrote:

Autumn, wistful-faced and dreamy-eyed,
Is wandering down the mountain side;
Throwing back the veil of mist
From the brow by sunbeams kissed,
And gathering close about her form
Her robe of colors rich and warm,
While murmuring a sweet refrain,
As she gathers golden grain,
Ripened fruit, and brilliant flowers,
From verdant fields and woodland bowers.
She saunters through the valleys fair
Where misty splendor fills the air;
And wanders o'er the rocky height
Veiling the hills with purple light.
She pauses now: is it to hear
The voices of the bounteous year?
The falling nuts, the rustling corn,
The bird songs welcoming the morn,
The cricket's chirr-chirr, the blue-jay's call,
The river's murmur through it all?
Ah, tear-drops gather in her eyes
As, with a sudden, sad surprise,
She sees her flowers are faded, dead!
And dry leaves rustle 'neath her tread.

A breeze rustled the paper in her hand, and a shadow fell upon the river.

One of the men, glancing at the cabin, said, "Hope that thar shanty 'll shed water. Goin' to hev it over and under too purty soon."

"Guess we'd better land 'fore we reach Lackawac, hedn't we?" drawled another, as Mr. Morgan hastily put up his papers and looked at the white mist drifting across the hills.

"No," he answered, shortly; "we'll make this trip in four days."

The water grew darker, and the trees rustled ominously, as the women and children huddled together on the straw of the tiny cabin, and the mist hovered over them, and settled down in a chilly, drizzling rain.

"Bessie, comin' to Cochecton Falls now!" called Bill.

The boys and Bessie sprung to their feet, and ran out to see the water dash over the half-hidden rocks.

"Looks like sheep jumping over a wall, don't it?" Davy's shrill treble rung out, above the tumult of the waters and the loud voices of the men.

"Oh, mother," gasped Jamie, "do look! It's like monsters leaping up and dashing the water to foam."

Mrs. Morgan stepped to the door of the cabin with her babe in her arms; heard the confused roar and rush of waters around them; saw the foam-capped billows rise and fall; felt the timbers heave and shake under her; and, calling her boys to her side, sunk upon her knees in prayer as the raft glided safely into smooth water.

"Some purty tough pullin' there," Jack said, as he sauntered to the provision-box for a "chunk o' cake."

"Neow yeou jest keep inside here till we git to Lackawac. Ain't nothin'

to-day, 'less it's the
ldy. Guess we kin
⟨p⟩rtable shake-down
here's so few rafts

⟨sa⟩y!" made him drop
⟨t⟩o his oar.
⟨h⟩ad hailed at Calli-
⟨se⟩en them, and was

⟨t⟩o Big Eddy?" their
⟨ai⟩l.
Lackawaxen," Mr.
⟨in⟩ reply.
⟨Ⅰd⟩n't risk making
dark with wimmen

⟨u⟩nder the blanket,
⟨k⟩in, stood by his fa-
⟨ther⟩ had descended be-
⟨tween⟩ the hills that now
⟨⟩ to a narrow stream.
Davy cried, "we
⟨can't⟩, nohow. See! the
⟨ligh⟩t across the river
⟨⟩"
⟨add⟩ed. There was no
⟨o⟩n either side; but
⟨⟩, and before reach-
⟨ing⟩ that barred the
⟨⟩hill seemed to draw
⟨⟩arrow entrance to
⟨w⟩ith rare good luck
⟨fa⟩vorable current and
⟨in⟩ the eddy without
⟨th⟩e surging counter-
⟨s⟩ide, which frequent-
⟨de⟩lay for hours, some-
⟨⟩ floating object that
⟨⟩s. The entire vol-
⟨ing⟩ through a chan-
⟨hu⟩ndred feet in width
⟨⟩ wide eddy creates

great whirlpools which are dangerous to rafts in high freshets, and tosses logs and trees as a cat plays with a mouse.

The current below being rapid, Lackawaxen was soon reached. The Lackawaxen River joins the Delaware at this point, and the Delaware and Lackawaxen Canal crosses it here. A dam creates a pond through which the water flows slowly; but the momentum given the raft by the rapids above makes it difficult to stop at the landing. Dusky shadows were fast obscuring the shore; while the sound of the waters pouring over the dam was to Mrs. Morgan's terrified fancy like a roaring lion in the way.

"Better let Jack handle that rope, Mister Morgan," said Morris.

"No, I will attend to that myself," he answered, shortly.

"Well, Mister Morgan, you kin handle that thirty-foot rope an' snub on the rafts when we come to 'em, ef you want to; but you let Jack handle the long rope an' snub 'er up on the snubbin' posts that are set 'long th' shore."

"Well, well; you talk as if you owned this lumber, and I was one of your hands."

"I calculate I'm capting of this craft, Mister Morgan, an' whatever's done while the raft is movin' 'll be done 'cordin' to my orders; 'n ef ye don't like 'em, ye kin go an' set down. Wish to gracious you would! fur a greenhorn's allers in th' way when a difficult landin' 's to be made; an' this ain't no fool of a job before us."

Mr. Morgan turned away in evident ill-humor, while Jack carefully coiled the rope, one end of which was fastened to the raft, and prepared to jump on shore as soon as the raft was sufficiently near.

"*Now*, Jack!" Bill shouted.

Jack leaped to the shore, rope in hand, and threw it in a double coil around a large post; letting it render fast enough to avoid breaking the rope or its fastenings, thus gradually slackening the speed of the raft. Post after post was reached, used, and passed; but the current still bore them on rapidly. The mist aided the fast-coming night in obscuring the outline of the bank, and it was necessary to keep the forward end out from shore to avoid sticking or striking other rafts, which might cause it to swing out into the stream and go sideways over the dam; which would be fatal to the raft, if not to its passengers. Mr. Morgan could remain inactive no longer, and seizing the thirty-foot rope, sprang upon a log raft just reached, saying,

"I see I've got to stop this raft, if it stops this side of destruction!" And he tied one end of the rope around a lash-pole. The raft moved on; a sound of snapping followed, then a sharp crack, then — whiz! — a groan, and a splash.

The rope had broken, and the end, striking Mr. Morgan in the breast, knocked him breathless backward upon the logs. He regained his breath and feet, as Jack brought the raft to a standstill, and led the way to the tavern, apparently deaf to the jokes of the men. The light of a candle beamed like a ray of hope across their weary pathway as, encumbered with luggage, they stumbled along, rain above and mud beneath them. The men around the fire made room for the wet and cold women and children; and the supper of fried ham and eggs was soon served and eaten.

"Guess likely we kin give yer wimmen folks a room by themselves," said the landlord, "though we're purty middlin' full." And a half hour later, they were tucked between blankets of colored wool, and sleeping as soundly as though sheets of finest quality and purest white enfolded them. Not one hour by Bessie's mental time-piece, but eight hours by the clock in the hall had been spent in slumber, when a loud rap on the door and booted feet in the next room aroused all but Miriam from their sweet, restful forgetfulness. The little girl was gently wrapped in blankets, cloak, and shawl; and while the men hastily swallowed their allowance of pancakes and coffee, Bessie refilled their pot with tea, procured a supply of boiled eggs and a bottle of milk, and, aided by the boys, carried their extemporized breakfast to the raft. The air was cold and damp, the foliage dripping and torn. The river, black as ink, flowed sullenly along beneath a dull gray sky. Jack sprung on board with his arms filled with dry straw and some pine-knots.

"Goin' to be a tedious day, I'm 'fraid; but we'll hev it 's comfortable as we kin, anyhow."

Mrs. Morgan sat upon a pile of boards, with her sleeping babe in her arms, as the raft left the shore; while the boys nestled in the straw at her feet, watching Bessie prepare the morning meal. Unconsciously they were nearing the dam.

"Eh, mem!" screamed Bessie, "they've sunk!"

The front part of the raft had dropped down and disappeared. The boy's faces were fixed for a shriek of terror, but the cry had not reached their lips when they, too, glided over the glassy slope; the hinder part of the raft dropped down, and all were safely over the dreaded dam.

"I had not time to get frightened," Mrs. Morgan replied to Jack's inquiry. "We were over before I knew we were there."

"But Bessie thought Jack had gone to feed fishes. How she yelled!" said Morris, teasingly.

Bessie picked up the knife she had dropped, and resumed her work of cutting bread and beef, singing merrily,

"Although me faither was na laird
('Tis daffin to be vaunty),
He keepit a gude kail-yaird,
A ha hoose an' a pantry;
A gude blue bonnet on his heid,
An' orlay 'bout his craigie,
An' aye until the day he deid
He rode on gude shanks naigie."

The rain now began falling heavily. The fire Jack had kindled smoked drearily and went out. The wind penetrated every crevice of the rude cabin, and the children grew restless and fretful. In vain Bessie sung her funniest songs, and Mrs. Morgan told her most charming stories. The boys grumbled at the storm, and Miriam wailed for her "bye-o" until they each fell asleep. The fire, rekindled, tempted the women from the dark cabin to warm their chilled feet; but the blaze which sprung up at Jack's coaxing breath proved a deceptive one; there seemed no heat in it; and the smoke turned to whichever side of the fire they stood. With smarting eyes and aching feet they returned to the straw couch, hoping they, too, might return to dream-land. The long morning passed away. The rain dropped slowly and unwillingly, then ceased, and a ray of pale sunlight fell on babe Miriam's face as she opened her eyes in smiling acceptance of its promise that the storm had gone. Trying to catch the sunbeams in her dimpled hand, she awakened the boys by her merry laughter. Their tiny ship and tangled fish-lines were called for, and their enjoyment seemed restored.

"Oh, what walls of rock! Do come out and see, mother," Jamie called. "They hang way over the river. Have they got a name, Bill?"

"Yes; they call these Carr's Rock. Don't look 's if they'd ever git a railroad runnin'. 'long-side o' that mountain, does it? Yet that's right where they're goin' to put the road, they say. I'll bet they'll run off some time. My gracious! wouldn't it make a smash-up, comin' right slam down on these rocks, an' into the river? You boys better stay purty near your mother and Bessie now, so 's to take keer o' 'em, ye know, fur we've got rough water ahead."

"What places are they, Bill?"

"Well, Davy, it's purty rough most the way from Pond Eddy to Port Jarvis; there's Stairway, an' Butler's, an' Sawmill Rift."

"Is there any danger, Morris?"

"No, Mis' Morgan; not with good han's an' good light. Sometimes the fog rises jest enough to coax the raft out o' Pond Eddy an' then shets right down on 'em so 's they can't see neither shore. Then's the time there's trouble at Sawmill Rift."

"They are going to put a bridge across the river at Sawmill Rift," said Mr. Morgan.

"Well, they may as well stretch a boom across an' stop every raft then, an' better too; fur ef they put a pile o' stun' in th' river there, it may kill men 's well 's stave lumber."

With pieces of their fish-lines and bits of boards the boys had been imitating the horses on the canal, dropping the "ropes" as they passed and repassed each other on the imaginary tow-path, enjoying the sport far more than their mother, who started nervously as they ventured near the edge of the raft to push off their boats.

"Davy, are you not tired of being a canal horse?" she called, as the boy for a second time stood in the way of the steersman's oar. "Come here, and I will tell you a new game I have just thought of. Here are two pennies; one for you, and one for Jamie. Now, there are a great many things upon them you never noticed. I can see thirty-five letters, some berries and leaves and stars, two borders, an eye, a neck, locks, a date, an ear, and several other things. Now, if you will find all of these, you may have the pennies; and the one who finds the most shall have half a dime."

"Can't I play that too?"

"Yes, Jack, if you will find the name of a fruit, a grand church, a scholar, the end of a river, and an animal."

"Well, I do say! Do you mean to tell me all them things is on a penny?"

"No; not the things, but the names. You see these figures, 1839; well, that's a *date*, and a date is a fruit."

"Oh, ho! I see now. But an animal, an' a scholar, an' a— I swan, the *mouth's* the end o' th' river, ain't it? I'll bet I'll hev 'em all in a jiffy;" and Jack returned to his oar with a cent in his hand.

"I've found the animal," he said, as after a pull to Jersey he sauntered back again. "It don't grow round here, though, an' 's a sort o' rabbit, ain't it? Now, s'posin' I sh'u'd find more things 'an you boys an' yer mother all on ye c'u'd, then I win all yer pennies, wouldn't I, Davy?"

"Yes, sir; but I bet a dollar you can't do it," the boy replied.

"Mother"—Jamie lowered his voice to a whisper—"wouldn't that be gambling?"

"Davy," she said, "what is gambling?"

"Why, taking what you hain't given anything for."

"Precisely. Now, Jack, I have found the top of the hill, a cover, and a fastening to a door."

"Wall, now, I never see the beat! She's bound I sh'll earn all I git out o' this speculation, ain't she, Davy? But I say now, Davy, what's bettin'— hey? 'Tain't airnin' nor givin', is it? S'posin' I took ye up an' won yer dollar?"

"Yes, boys, that's a question to be

thought of. And, Jack, what is *speculating?*"

"Wall, I guess I got 'nough thinkin' before me to las' to tide-water."

And he walked back to his oar; but Davy had pocketed his penny and Jamie his half-dime, and neither the temple, brow, pupil, nor locks had been discovered.

"Good gracious!" she heard him exclaim, in reply to something Morris was saying, "he don't mean to take *her* to ol' man Post's, does he?"

"I don't know 's any worse fur his wife 'n mine," growled Bill.

"I wa'n't thinkin' o' nobody's *wife*," Jack answered, in a lower tone.

"But blamed ef I kin see why we can't run on t' th' nex' landin'."

"Jes' his cussed contrariness, that's all."

Mr. Morgan stepped briskly forward, saying,

"We'll tie up at Mulliner's."

When the raft was landed, Jack stepped to Mrs. Morgan's side:

"We're goin' to the dirtiest place 'long this river," he said, "an' you better wrap the baby in a big shawl an' hol' on to 'er till mornin'. I've hear'n o' men bein' snaked out o' bed an' clear 'cross the road by— But then, I won't lie; the place is bad enough an' tell the truth."

CHAPTER X.

"All things journey: sun and moon,
Morning, noon and afternoon,
Night and all her stars."

THE SPANISH GYPSY.

THE mist was rising like wreaths of smoke from the river, and settled in a bank of white fog over the weather-beaten building where they were to find supper and lodgings. The screams of crying children, and the scolding tones of a woman's voice were heard before they reached the door. Mr. Morgan rapped, and the noises suddenly ceased; the door opened, and Mrs. Morgan saw a tall, gaunt female with a young babe in her arms, and two dirty children holding fast to her skirts, while others peeped shyly at the strangers from the dark background of the room.

"We can't keep ye, nohow," she said, her hand on the latch. "We hed a lot o' raftsmen here las' night, and they nigh upon tore the house down, and eat us clean out. Ain't got no accommodations for raftsmen, an' don't want none."

"But we've got some women and children here, and it's too late to go farther. You won't have any trouble with my men; they are all quiet fellows; and if you can't give us supper, we'll furnish our own and pay you too."

She hesitated a moment, and then, stepping back, told them to come in and not leave the door open no longer; despatched two of the tow-headed boys for wood; told the unwelcome guests to "take cheers an' make themselves to hum;" put the baby in the largest girl's arms; sat the two little ones on a bench with a force that made them wink, and began to put the room in order with such a clatter and despatch that Mrs. Morgan sighed for the quiet of the cold cabin they had left.

"Hello, Bill! Hello, Jack!" the woman responded to their "How de do, Mis' Post?" as they brought the provision-boxes and blankets into the room.

"Heerd ye ben gittin' ye a woman, Bill," she said, standing the splint broom in the corner, and placing her hands on her hips, as she stared at Mrs. Morgan and Bessie, whose face flushed scarlet with indignation. "Be either o' these women yourn?"

He laughed as he answered, "Pshaw! who's been talking such stuff 'bout me? That lady with the blue hood on is Mis' Morris, goin' to her ol' home in Jarsey; an' the other with the baby is Mis' Morgan: her husband owns the best lot o' land an' timber of anybody in our country; an' ef you use us purty well to-night, you'll git a good many shilliu's out o' us fellows."

"Yes, a pinched lot o' shillin's, an' git my þlankets tore up, my pillars bust open, an' some o' my best crockery broke to smash! I tol' Abe las' night that the fut of a raftsman shouldn't never step over that thar door-sill, an' here's my house all clattered full o' ye agin."

"Land's sake, Mis' Post, ye don't call this house full *now*, do ye? Why, I've seen more 'n fifty men layin' spread out on this floor to onct."

Mrs. Morgan glanced around in astonishment. The fireplace and a door each side of it filled one end of the room; a curtained recess, with a pantry on one side, and a cupboard on the other, filled the side and described the size of the room, while two small uncurtained windows gave sufficient light to show the bare, mud-tracked floor, pine table, two long benches, and a few wooden-bottomed chairs ranged against the wall. Some bright tins hung over the cupboard reflecting the fire-light's glow, and strings of dried apples and pumpkin festooned the ceiling.

"Wall, las' fresh we had a hundred an' four to supper. Some on 'em slept in the barn, an' some on 'em stayed here in the house. I wun't say they slept, fur they didn't, nor nobody in their hearin'. Sech goin's on nobody never seed 'fore nor sence. I bet they hed some licker 'long with 'em. I don't believe fellers could a' carried on as they did 'thout the devil helped 'em. Jake, you go down cullar and git a panful o' taters; an' don't be gone all night, nuther. Sall, gim me that young un, an' you go 'long an' hol' th' candle, an' git a chunk o' pork."

"Where's Abe?" Morris asked, after the fried pork and boiled potatoes were placed upon the table.

"I dunno; heerd a raft had stuck at Fiddler's Elbow this forenoon, an' guess likely he went up to git a job; he hain't got nothin' to dew to hum," and she laughed sarcastically as she poured the tea in the cracked and grimy cups, and placed one at each plate, before the benches were drawn up to the table.

The outside wrappings of the women and children had been removed, and rolled up in a blanket by the thoughtful Jack, who also warmed a cup of milk for Miriam, using the contents of the provision-box instead of the table. Miriam laughed gleefully to see her own china mug and spoon, and while she ate, Jack was again busy at the fire. A plate of hot buttered toast and eggs roasted in the shell were placed on a chair by Mrs. Morgan, who excused herself from the table to feed baby, and with a tin cup of tea she made a comfortable meal. Her husband looked annoyed, and their hostess muttered something about her "vittles not bein' good 'nough for quality folks;" but the meal was soon ended, and preparations for bed-making began. The benches and tables were placed against the wall, ticks stuffed with straw were brought from the chamber above, as the roof leaked too badly to make sleeping there agreeable, and spread upon the floor, with heavy blankets for covering.

Morris and Jack held a brief consultation, and as Mrs. Post disappeared in the stairway, they seized the cleanest-looking tick and ran out-of-doors, returning before she appeared with the bed newly filled with fragrant hay. They swept a place clean for it, and, stretching a blanket from one chair-back to another, made a low partition between this bed and the others, leaving it open next the fire.

"Now, Bessie," said Morris, "you an' Mis' Morgan can have a middlin' decent bed; an' ef you'll use your shawls for blankets, you'll have a tolerable comfortable night. Jack, you an' me kin bunk on this side th' fireplace. Jamie, you an' Davy roll yourselves up in this big cloak an' lay 'long-side o' me. Now, then, the rest o' ye kin go whar yer a mind to."

Was there a bit of malice in the plan that placed Mr. Morgan against the wall?

The trundle-bed was pulled out, and the little Posts were tucked away; the talking ceased; the fire burned low. From the men's beds came prolonged snores ending in a gurgling sound, strangely like suppressed laughter, as Mr. Morgan tossed restlessly, throwing the blankets from him; then, after a vigorous shake, spreading them over him again. The boys cried out now and then, but never wakened; and inside the curtained bed slumber reigned undisturbed. Before the gray dawn streamed into the room Mr. Morgan's voice aroused them.

"Come, come, boys!" he said, carefully brushing his clothes, "let's pull out from here; we'll run to Shoemaker's to breakfast."

"I don't know 'bout that, Mister Morgan. 'Tain't likely we could land there now, an' we'd be losin' time too. As we hed such a good sleep, I guess we'd better ask Mis' Post to give us something to eat. Les' have some eggs boiled in the shell an' some fried ham. I don't want any pancakes; do you, boys? We'll save Mis' Post the bother o' bakin' them, an' take bread out o' the dinner-box. She'll hev suthin' cooked while we're gettin' these things down to the raft, and some dry straw into the cabin. Guess 'twon't rain no more. Mis' Morris, you might make some tea in that big pot o' yourn to take out t' th' raft."

The beds were thrown in a heap in a corner; the table drawn out; the breakfast swallowed; and they were off again. The stars glimmered faintly through the clouds that, radiant with welcome, were hurrying to meet the god of day. The moon had paled, and was fading away; the sky glowed, the river sparkled, the foliage glittered above and around them.

"Oh, mother!" exclaimed Jamie, his face reflecting the rapt look of her own, "this is a new day!"

"Yes, my son, fresh from God's hand."

The loud voices of the men jarred the sweet stillness of the morn; and the baby's eyes opened wide with wonder on the unfamiliar scene.

"'A sea of glass mingled with

ire;' 'A pure river of water clear .s crystal,'" murmured Mrs. Morgan. "What a glorious, beautiful world it s! and, oh, what disgusting creatures n it!"

"Toots, mem! I'm thinkin' we escaped weel. Deed noo, ef we were orn an' bred in a' that filth an' deestiution, wad we be like her, think ye?" rith a backward gesture toward the iouse still visible.

"Born in and of it—why, I suppose we would, Bessie—and yet I don't :now. It seems as if I would grow ut of it, and above it. I do not think he real *me* would settle down in uch squalor, into whatever body or ircumstances I was placed; could ou?"

"I dinna ken, mem; but I hae mair o be thankfu' for than I e'er kent fore." And, wrapping Miriam in a hawl, she walked up and down the aft, studying a new problem. The lay, so fresh and fair at its beginning, ;rew wearisome, and the boys begged to be set ashore, confident they ould outrun the raft gliding so moiotonously along. Their ship was a vreck, their fish-lines broken, the sunhine hot, the wind chilling, the glare n the water distressing, and the cabn too damp to sit in with comfort. The hills and trees, the villages and arms, had lost their charms to the oys, accustomed to so large a playground and an endless variety of musements. But babe Miriam was erfectly content in her rustic cradle, a handful of straw and a piece of ravlled rope for playthings. Bessie sat n a pile of lumber, knitting, and fan:ying the blissful meeting with the loved ones at home. And Mrs. Morgan, with a bit of paper resting on her Bible, pencilled thoughts which had long waited this leisure for expression.

"Coming to th' Gap purty soon; it's jest below this rift," Jack announced, and the boys looked eagerly ahead to see the mountains yawn at their approach, while Mrs. Morgan and Bessie, anticipating a rapid current rushing through a narrow gorge, were glad to pass before the sunlight was gone. The mountains were flooded with glory, the river reflecting every curve, rock, tree, and every tint of foliage, as in a mirror.

"There's the Gap!"

No yawning chasm, no boiling caldron, was there; only a perpendicular wall of rock on either side reaching up into the cloudless sky, and the river winding gently between, clear and calm as a lake. Every eye was lifted in silent wonder at the power which had cleft this mighty mountain in twain.

"Nothin' but ice could have tore things up so," Morris announced. "An' then that stun-heap on the Pennsylvan'a shore—acres and acres o' round stun, all rounded and pounded up— 'twas ice done that. Them stun got froze in a-comin' along down—some started from Beaverkill, an' some farther up—an' they was turned over an' over, an' rounded off, an' ground down, an' got smooth as pebbles; an' they piled up an' piled up agin this yer mountain, an' the water biled an' surged till suthin' giv' way, an' then —through they come! an' the water swashed 'em up on that thar shore, an' thar they be yit. Golly! I'd like to been where I could a' seen it done. Now, ain't that a purty picter, after all them mountains an' rocks?"

Like the lifting of a curtain, the scene had changed. A wide valley stretched out on either side; with orchards and fields, farm-houses and barns, as far as the eye could reach.

"Mother"—Jamie's hand nestled in her own—"mother, it looks like another world! just as if we had left the rough workday world behind us, and that"—pointing to the sunlit valley before them—"that was Sunday."

A tall, well-dressed man stood upon the shore, and as the raft grated upon the pebbly beach he sprung on board and clasped Mrs. Morgan in his arms.

"Oh, David! Oh, my brother!" And the glad tears sprung to her eyes. "How did you get here? How did you know I was coming?"

"I have expected you at every rise of the river since you went into exile, little sister. Glad to see you, John. This is Mistress Morris, I am sure," shaking hands with each. "Well, boys, have you forgotten Uncle Dave? I've grown gray since you saw me, haven't I?" taking them in his arms—"and you have grown heavy. Backwoods life agrees with you, evidently. And here's my only niece; bless her little heart! not a bit afraid of her uncle. Why, Mary, she's a perfect beauty! How did I get here? I came up on a Durham boat. I was tired of the city, and the supercargo of this boat being sick, I concluded to take a trading voyage, meet you, maybe, and have a good time. I've been here before, hunting and fishing; grand country, isn't it? but very rough."

"Rough? Oh, David, come up to our place! What would he call *that*, John?"

"A better country for hunting and fishing than this. But come; let's get ashore. We've stopped here for a load of slate, and will stay till morning."

"Ah, I'm glad of that, for so do I; and, Mary, I want you to change conveyances and finish the journey on a Durham boat. I saw you before you reached the foot of the rift, and was about to board your craft and capture you, when I saw your raft preparing to land. There is a comfortable inn here," he said, as they ascended the hill, "and there are several places worth seeing. Is your home near here, Mistress Morris?"

"Ah, sir, I wad it were! I'm weel wearied o' the raft; but my hame is anither day's journey ayon."

"If Mr. Morgan is willing I should go on the boat with my brother; you will go too, won't you, Bessie?"

"Ah, mem, I'm unco sweir to leave Willy an' gang to the auld hoose alane."

The rest of the day was spent in examining the Cold Air Cave and the Echo; enjoying the magnificent scenery from Mount Minsi; watching the men load the raft with slate from the quarries, and inspecting the Durham boat, which was taking in a cargo of butter, cheese, honey, grain, and vegetables for the Philadelphia market. It was a queer-looking craft, some sixty feet long, with oars at least a third that length, a plank walk for the row-ers on deck, and a rude cabin below. A ballast of slate, and barrels of cider and flour, were already in the hold; and upon the deck were heaps of pumpkins and cabbages, with a confused mass of Yankee notions and dry-goods for which a group of farmers were bargaining. The dread of going through tide-water on a raft, and the pleasure of having her brother's company, decided Mrs. Morgan to take the boat for the rest of the journey, and Mr. Walton accompanied Morris to the raft to consult her husband.

"They're loadin' them rafts too fur for'ard," Bill said, as they walked down the stony road. He found Mr. Morgan directing the men to put a tier of slate still nearer the ends of the raft. "Mister Morgan," he called, "you're a-loadin' them rafts too heavy and too fur for'ard!"

"I've contracted to take that pile of slate, and it's got to go on these rafts. The middle is under water now, and the rest of the slate must go on the ends."

"I suppose you know the river is fallin', an' Foul Rift and Wells's is ahead."

"Well, well, if you're afraid to steer them when loaded, I can find a man who is not; and I shall use my own judgment about the loading. These rafts are not moving *now*, Bill."

"All right, sir; you hev more at stake than I hev. I guess I'll git off at Upper Black's. Bessie wants me to go home with her; so 'f you kin find a steersman to suit ye, you'd better git one."

In the early morning the rafts pulled out. The Durham boat started an hour later, but, aided by pushing poles, it overtook and passed them at the head of Foul Rift. The "goodbyes" were waved and shouted to the mother and her three children as they ran quickly by the raft; but the roaring water just ahead attracted all eyes to the coming danger. The oarsmen each took an immense bite from the plug of tobacco they shared between them, grasped their poles tightly, braced their feet firmly, and were ready.

"Those rocks are called Harrowteeth, and that reef of rock 'The Wing,' Mr. Walton shouted; "many rafts dive as they go over that; and the other is 'The Foamer.'" The water boiled over it in a roaring wave, and went seething and foaming below. "Those black rocks on the left cause many a wreck."

"Oh, the raft!" screamed the boys; "they'll go all to pieces!" and Jamie hid his face in his hands.

"Oh, don't be frightened, they will get through all right; two steersmen and a captain aboard," Mr. Walton laughed, assuringly; but his eyes were also fixed on the raft, which came rushing through the water at racehorse speed, dashing the spray over the slate on which Morris and his wife were standing. He had resigned his oar to the new steersman, yet would have sprung to his assistance but for Bessie's frightened face and pleading eyes. The raft ran a few inches to the right, and the forward end grazed a rock, throwing the other end dangerously near the rocks on the Pennsylvania shore.

"Jersey!" screamed the steersman; and the men, with the strength excitement alone can give, pulled the raft away from the threatened danger.

"Holt! holt!" cried the steersman, "t'other way! Pennsylvan'a!"

Too late. The raft went over the reef with "a pint to Jersey," dove, one end struck the bottom, and the two rafts parted company with a crash, a shower of broken slate, and a babel of yells.

Morris and Bessie, the steersman, and one man were left on the raft that kept the channel, and reached the smooth waters below. But Mr. Morgan, Jack, and the other men were left in a dangerous situation; their stoven raft darted toward the Black Rocks that looked like huge teeth in the frothing mouth of a devouring monster.

"Les' swing 'er!" yelled Jack. "Cross pull! 'Hind han's, Jarsey! Pennsylvan'a, Tom!"

The raft swung around. Before it reached the rock, Jack unshipped and drew in his oar in time to save it, and ran back to the middle of the raft as it mounted high upon the rocks, then swung off with a large loss of slate and considerable lumber. With hard pulling they succeeded in getting their shattered raft through to the smooth waters below the rift, where Morris had already tied the other.

"Oh, please do stop and take Bessie on!" said Mrs. Morgan. "I know she is nearly wild with fright."

"What say you, Jones? Do you think we can take two more passengers for a day?" Mr. Walton inquired.

"I reckon so," said the pilot.

"They've got to raft over now. I tol' Jake he'd never get that double raft over the Wing, with such a load, 'thout divin'. Big Bill might a' done it, for he'd got the hang o' the raft, an' knows his men. A pull too much is as bad as no pull, in that crooked channel. Hold her stiddy, boys, till we find out what Bill's going to do. No use landing fur nothing."

But Bessie had decided to remain at a farm-house near, while Morris assisted in picking up the lumber, which would take the remainder of the day. He conveyed this decision to them by his gestures and stentorian voice; and the *Durham* again started down the stream.

"Who is that manly-looking boy who saved the raft?" inquired Mr. Walton, as he walked up and down the deck with Miriam in his arms.

"That is Jack," the boys answered. "He's just the best fellow ever lived, 'cept Bill."

"Your up-river men are not a bad kind, if these are specimens; but raftsmen in the city are as rough and wild as untamed bears, and more noisy."

"I cannot imagine Morris or Jack acting like rowdies," Mrs. Morgan answered. "Jack only needs education to make a noble, useful man. He is devoted to the children, which perhaps makes me partial to him. Where's Jack, Mira?"

The little girl turned and looked on every side. "Wha' Zack?" she said. It was her first intelligible utterance, and was received with delight by her mother, and shouts of applause from the boys. Pleased with her success, the child tried to imitate other words; and before her eyes closed for the noonday nap, she called her brothers by name, and made several amusing attempts to say, "Unty Dave."

The long-separated brother and sister found much to talk about in the long, fair day, while the children amused themselves about the boat. No common rift attracted their attention after Foul Rift. The *City of Easton*—the new steamboat—brought them from their cabin as it went puffing by. Queer Water, with its whirling, boiling waves, and Haycocks, where the water leaps over huge bowlders, were scarcely noticed. Durham, where the boat was built, received but a sleepy glance; and after a promise that they should be called in time to see the boat go through Wells's, they crept into the narrow berths, where their sister was already sleeping.

Skilfully guided through the rapids, and urged through the slack waters, the boat glided smoothly and swiftly by the low, level shores, where twinkling lights revealed the unseen dwellings. The bark of a dog borne across the waters, and the faint, sweet sound of a violin ebbing and flowing on the breeze, seemed floating to their ears from a far-distant world. Above them came the stars one by one, only paler and colder than the earth-stars that flickered and glimmered from the homes on either side.

"Are they not both promises of rest and peace?" thought Mary Morgan; "only the lower lights will go out by-and-by, while the lights above will last forever! This seems so like a dream, brother," she said, "as though we had left the shore of Time, and were floating away into Eternity. All the past seems as near as yesterday."

He drew her to him with caressing arm; but no words were spoken until through the white mist, like a sudden glory, shone the radiant moon. Each tiny ripple in the water caught its gleam; dim outlines of hills were revealed, and quaint shadows of mast and fluttering sail lay on the deck. The distant roar of water, and sharp, emphatic orders of the pilot aroused Mrs. Morgan from a dreamy reverie, and brought the boys from their berths below to her side.

"Is that Wells's?"

"Yes," said the pilot, "and you boys must keep out of the way. I reckon there'll be trouble with that raft ahead, Mr. Walton. They're at least twenty foot too far Jersey, and there ain't a inch to go on with that sized raft. Some fool of an up-river steersman trying to run through Wells's by moonlight, and with a fleet full sixty foot wide!"

"I thought they always hired regular Wells's steersmen to take them over the falls."

"They used to; but lately some of 'em have steered light rafts through. And I s'pose this steersman thinks he can see as well to-night as in the daytime; but moonlight is deceiving. Ah! he sees his mistake, and is trying to pull over; don't believe he can pass the entering rock, though. *There she goes!* just as I expected! Now she's swinging right across the channel! Blame the up-river fool! Boys, we've got to squeeze through Jarsey of the entering rock. Keep your ears open an' yer eyes peeled. *Jarsey! holt!* Jim, look out for those loose logs — they'll punch a hole in us if they strike! Mr. Walton, take that pole, will you, and help me, so I can send another man for'ard? Be ready at the word to lift 'er round. Jarsey — stiddy — holt, for'ard! This way, Bill! quick — straighten 'er up! Holt! There, now we're all right; but 'twixt logs and rocks it looked squally for a minute."

"Well, I thought we's a goner!" said Davy. "We did go against a rock, Uncle Dave, didn't we?"

"No; but a big rock ran right up the river and gave our boat a punch in the side: I saw it. Now the show is over, we had better turn in. The fog is rising, and we may have to anchor till daylight. So good-night."

The morning mist was rising, and the spires of New Jersey's capital were seen by the boys' eager eyes, as they tumbled up the steep stairway to the deck.

"Oh, mother!" Jamie called, as she too followed Mr. Walton and Miriam from the cabin into the fresh air of the cool gray morning, "you said you would show us where Washington crossed the Delaware."

"What do you know about Washington?" his uncle asked, laughingly. "Did you vote for him, last election, out your way?"

"No, sir-ee, we didn't!" exclaimed Davy, "'cause he's dead: and we know lots about him. Once his pa gave him a hatchet, an' he went to cuttin' down trees; and his pa got mad about it, an' said he'd just like to catch the boy what done it; an' 'cause George couldn't tell a lie, he had to own up. Now, what's the reason he couldn't tell a lie if he wanted to, Uncle Dave? An' what did his pa give him a hatchet for, if he didn't want him to cut down trees? That's jest what I'd like to know!"

"I give it up;" and Mr. Walton threw up his hands and rolled his eyes in mock despair. "You mustn't ask me any such conundrums, boy; they're too much for me. I don't know why that first apple-tree ever grew that has caused us all so much toil and trouble. But I rather think the reason why George Washington couldn't tell a lie was because it seemed like a mean thing to do, and he'd rather take a thrashing than be a liar. Hadn't you?"

"Course; if my pa'd say jus' as his did, 'Come to my arms, my son!' an' hug an' kiss him, an' maybe let him ride his horse to water; but—"

"David," called Mrs. Morgan, who was on the opposite side of the boat with Jamie, pointing out objects of interest they were passing, "what was Philadelphia called by the Dutch?"

"Coalquanock; it was only a hamlet then. Now, don't ask me what it means, for I don't know; but I learned a funny thing the other day about the place where my wife is stopping — Penn Yan. It is one of the pleasantest little villages I ever saw, nestled in a valley and near a lake. Well, it got its name from being settled by two families, one from our own State, and one from New England. They took the first syllables from their old locations and joined them. Now where were they from, Jamie? There's a puzzle for you."

"But, David, isn't your wife at home?"

"No, she is not, Mary, and has not been since June. She has a lot of fashionable folks around her who make our house a place to dance and feast in all winter; and then whisk its mistress away in the early summer to *recuperate* by dancing and feasting in some other place. She spent several weeks at Cape May; then went to Niagara, and is now at Penn Yan. However, I have a good house-keeper, and a carriage with as pretty and gentle a span of ponies as can be found this side of Kentucky; and we are going to have a thoroughly good time together. Besides the State-house, where the Declaration of Independence was signed; the Mint, where our money is made; the market, where the catfish and cauliflower I promised you are exhibited, and the Arcade, or Peale's Museum, there is a very fine panorama on exhibition. Boys, don't you want to go to Jerusalem? Very well, I will take you where the whole city is spread out before you, as though you stood on a hill and looked down at the people in the streets.—Caught the ebb-tide all right, haven't we, Jones? Now we will soon reach the city."

CHAPTER XI.

"And she would talk so weirdly wild,
And grow upon your wonderings
As though her stature rose on wings,
And you forgot she was a child."

GERALD MASSEY.

THREE years glided by, and again autumn had come. Few changes had been made in the settlement on the river-bank; but near the mill Morris had built a home for his wife and baby boy, and a mile away a school-house was nearly completed.

Little Miriam — a healthy, happy child, the idol of her mother, the playmate of her brothers, and the pet of the whole neighborhood — sat upon the cottage steps one balmy morning, singing. Her bright flossy curls were floating in the wind, and her faithful guardian, Bruce, a large gray mastiff, stood by her side. Jamie had been sent by his father to collect a store debt from a farmer ten miles away, and Davy was assisting Fred in the store; for this was Saturday, and the folks from all the country around had come to trade the produce of dairy and farm for groceries and clothes. Within the cottage the sound of beating eggs and the odor of pumpkin-pies proved that the mother's hands and thoughts were fully employed. Maid Miriam grew restless.

"Ets do some'rs an' do somefin!"

Bruce wagged his tail approvingly. She glanced at the mill, but that was forbidden ground; at the house above it, but Robin always slept at this hour, and Bessie would not let him be wakened. Then she looked toward the woods—the very thing— "Ets have a pitnit! I det some cats;" and the merry little girl ran into the house, seized a basket which Bruce had been taught to carry, put a handful of cookies and her tin cup in it. "Dess doin' itta ways," she informed her mother, and was gone like a flash.

Mrs. Morgan hastened to skim the pan of milk she was holding, and then went to the kitchen door. Neither child nor dog was in sight.

"She is gone to see Davy, dear little trudge," she said.

The bread was ready for baking, the cream waited to be churned, the kitchen floor must be scrubbed, and dinner prepared; one duty following another, until noon came, bringing the men from their work, and Davy from the store.

"Where's your sister?" Mrs. Morgan inquired.

"*I* don't know; haven't seen her since breakfast: probably she's at Morris's. She never goes far, and Bruce is with her; so she's safe enough from snakes and cattle. I'll look her up after dinner."

A load of impatient customers called Davy from the table before his dinner was eaten, and kept him busy for an hour. Supposing he had found and left the child with Bessie, Mrs. Morgan finished her Saturday's work; then, putting on her bonnet, she crossed the brook and tapped at Mrs. Morris's open door. To her surprise, little Miriam had not been there that day; neither was she at the mill, riding on the "carriage" that carried the log to and from the flashing saw; nor at the store curled up under the counter, looking at the blue and yellow covered primers. She must have gone in the woods; and the mother, anxious but not frightened, hurried up the mountain side.

Meantime, the tiny maiden was trudging over the stony road, her white sun-bonnet shading her laughing eyes, one dimpled hand holding the flowers she had gathered, and the other grasping Bruce's shaggy mane.

"We's havin' fun, we is," she remarked, confidentially, to the dog. "Nuffin' hurts *us*, 'cause we's *dood*. See! da's a pitty snake," and she let go of the dog to pick it up.

Bruce dropped the basket, gave a sudden spring, caught the snake, and with a dexterous jerk threw it outside the pathway. The child laughed merrily, pronounced the motionless reptile "Fas' asleep;" and as Bruce picked up the basket, the two walked on—one conscious of duty performed, and elate with victory; the other as unconscious of innocence as of guilt; feeling only the joy of vitality within and around her.

The light of every sunrise and every sunset was condensed in the foliage of the forest. Here and there a lusty hemlock stood as though exclaiming, "No time-server I. We evergreens absorb and transmute the sunlight of every season into unfading verdure."

Little Miriam stood breathless on the hillside, and looked around her. At her right, a little brook leaped from the summit of a pile of mossy rocks, and bubbled and foamed over the rocks below. At her left, emerald ferns and golden-rod mingled; while from trees above, the gold and crimson of a summer's radiance fluttered to her feet. Birds warbled as in spring-time; insects danced merrily in the sunlit air; squirrels frisked and chattered over the nut-strewn ground.

"Oh! oh!" the child exclaimed, in rapture. "B'uce, see! Oh, pitty! pitty!"

But Bruce had no eyes nor ears for the beauty which thrilled the child's soul with ecstasy. A rabbit flashed across the road; the basket was dropped, and the dog gone, crushing the ferns and daisies, trampling the brilliant leaves, pulling down the velvet moss which grew on the wayside rocks.

"B'uce, B'uce, tum bat he'e," called his mistress, "tum wight he'e!"

"Here I am," said a voice behind her. "By Jove, you're a little beauty! isn't she, major?"

"I should say so! What's your name, little one?"

The child stepped back and viewed the strangers curiously, but made no reply.

"Where did you come from?"

"I tum f'om my home," she said, with dignity.

The men laughed.

"And who do you belong to?"

"I b'yong to mysef."

"Indeed; whose land is this?"

"Mine," she said. "B'uce, you tum he'e!"

The dog sprung from the rocks above to the road, and, with a threatening growl at the strangers, stood beside the child.

"So this is the Bruce you called," said the boy who had first spoken. "Bruce is my name. Won't you tell me yours?"

The little girl looked at him with the grave, critical air children sometimes assume; then, her expression changing into mirthful mischief, she said,

"I is Bairdy Fissledown."

"Birdy Thistledown! Well, upon my word you are well named. Are you a fairy?"

"'Es, sa."

"I thought so; and Bruce is a human you have bewitched into a dog?"

"'Es, sa."

Her eyes were sparkling with delight, her whole form quivering with excitement.

"Say, major, let's sit down and rest a while. Perhaps this birdy will give us some music of fairy-land."

"Take care she don't bewitch Bruce number two. If she were a few years older, I wouldn't risk it. The settlement cannot be more than a mile away, and I'm going on."

"All right. I'll be at the store in half an hour," the boy answered.

"Come, Birdy Thistledown, let me lift you on this rock; and I'll lie down here in the moss and look at you. Now, will you sing?"

"I dess I 'peak a piece, faist," she said; and standing upon the rock, her bonnet pushed back, the blushes glowing and fading in her dimpled cheeks, the hands demurely clasped, she began,

"Ma'e ad a ittle yam;
Its f'eece wad w'ite as shnow,
An' eva'wha' 'at Ma'e went
De yam was su'e to do.
It fahaid hn' to 'cool one day—"

very slowly the words were pronounced, as though stepping carefully over uneven ground, then safely past, her speech flew over the remaining lines—

"W'ich wad adainst de yule,
It made de chillin yaff an' p'ay
To see a yam at cool;"

and the little elocutionist sat down. Her audience clapped his hands and shouted with laughter.

"'Top!" she exclaimed, authoritatively. "You stare 'e bairds."

"Oh, pardon me! I forgot I was applauding a bird. So that is the language of fairy-land. It reminds me of the verses, 'Mary had a little lamb,' that I've heard little mortals say; only it was sweeter and shorter."

"I've dot a yam," the child said, looking dreamily at the opposite hillside; "an' it talts."

"Oh, yes, of course; you have bewitched it."

"Es; it tan sing."

"Certainly. Where do you keep it?"

Her eyes wandered from the hill to the brook, then up to the misty sky.

"In 'e c'ouds."

"Oh, my stars!" exclaimed the boy; "what a witch you are!"

"Ain't a wits! I'se Mir'on; an' I wants my dinna. B'uce, det dat bastet." The dog obeyed.

"Ah, that reminds me, I have a lunch to get rid of. I suppose yours is fairy food. Now, if I should eat it, would I be a fairy like you?"

The little girl surveyed his long length of limb stretched out upon the mossy bank below, then said, decidedly,

"No, sa."

"Oh, I wouldn't? Well, I'm sorry. But perhaps this dog will turn mortal if he eats this beastly ham. Here, Bruce," and he tossed the stale sandwich to him, but the dog, taught to refuse food from strangers, turned away and mounted the rock by the little girl. "Most remarkable pair! Nectar and ambrosia for both of them."

Very quietly they sat; the dog taking the tiny morsels of cake from the child's hands.

"Now I want a d'ink," she said, taking the tin cup from the emptied basket, and springing lightly from the rock.

"Fairy Thistledown, let me get the water."

But he was too late. Knowing he sprung to catch her, that he was close behind her, she leaped from the shore to a loose stone, stumbled, and was on the brink of the fall, when his hand caught her.

"Oh, Birdy! Birdy!" he cried, "you might have been dashed to pieces!"

She threw her arms around his neck, trembling from head to foot. Bruce barked a fierce disapproval of the entire scene; and as the young stranger was carrying the little girl back to the wayside rock Mrs. Morgan came rapidly up the road, and stood before him.

"What does this mean? My child! my darling! are you hurt?" she exclaimed, taking the child from his arms.

"I'se bad aden," she sobbed. "I wun an' I fa' down. He dood boy; he tetch Bairdy."

A few words explained all.

"She is the most fascinating little creature I ever saw," the young man said. "Such a vivid fancy. She told me she had a lamb that could talk and sing."

Already little Miriam, with a child's happy faculty of forgetting danger or pain, was gathering Michaelmas daisies and golden-rod for a fresh bouquet; and the mother's eyes followed her anxiously.

"Her imagination is too vivid. I try to repress it and teach her to say 'I pretend,' when she begins her long stories. She really seems unable to distinguish between the real and imaginary. In her plays she carries on conversations and enacts scenes which seem actual facts to her, referring to them afterward as something truly occurring. And yet she is very truthful: a deception, however slight, gives her keenest pain, and she is often absurdly exact in her statements."

"Well, she is a genius; no mistake about that. Pardon me; but was she born among these hills?"

"Yes; her name is Miriam Morgan. You are going to our settlement, you said?"

"Yes, madam. I am on Major Morrill's engineer corps; we were recommended to apply to Mr. Morgan for a comfortable boarding-place while at work on this division of the railroad."

"Ah, then you are one of the gentlemen we are expecting; and you can go home with me now. Come, Miriam."

"Tarry me, mover!"

"Please let me carry her. I have a baby sister at home, and—"

"'Es, 'ou tan tarry me;" and the tiny despot raised her hands as he knelt to take her in his arms.

Going down the steep, narrow road, Mrs. Morgan scanned him closely. Tall for his years, which might be eighteen (she afterward learned they were two less); plainly but neatly dressed; close-cut curly hair, almost golden in hue; bright blue eyes in which a smile seemed ever lurking, and cheeks flushed by exposure till the forehead seemed ivory white in contrast; a quiet dignity and refinement of manner, ready speech, and brisk walk—all these impressed Mrs. Morgan favorably as the best companion possible for her boys; for the railroad was coming nearer, and every town and settlement, tavern and farmhouse, was besieged by workmen and their officers seeking board.

"We can accommodate two," Mr. Morgan said, the week before; and now they had come.

"You have a sister; have you brothers?"

"No, ma'am. There are only my mother, little Dora, and myself. Father died before she was born. We live with my mother's brother in Virginia. He has educated me for a civil engineer; this is my beginning."

"A life of adventure and exposure; full of hardships and temptations to be conquered," Mrs. Morgan said, musingly, as though she saw this youth's future mapped out before her.

"And who is your companion?"

"Major Morrill. I never saw him until my uncle introduced us a fortnight ago. They were college chums; he is a kind-hearted, jovial fellow, not strictly temperate, but very gentlemanly. I hope you will like the major," watching the pale face and drooping eyelids. "We will make as little trouble as possible."

She raised her eyes to his.

"There is only one way you can make me trouble, for work is not trouble. My boys are obedient, respectful, *honorable*. Help me to keep them so. Will you?"

They were standing on the brow of the hill overlooking the little hamlet. Very pretty and peaceful it looked, hedged in by the variegated hills, the sunlit brook gliding through the emerald meadows, and the calm blue river reflecting the cloudless sky.

"I see Damie!" cried Miriam, catching sight of her elder brother riding up to the store door. "An' da's Davy too! 'Et me wun!" And the little maiden sprung from the boy's arms, and skipped down the path.

He turned to Mrs. Morgan with outstretched hands.

"I don't know what I can do or say, ma'am, to keep your boys from evil, but they shall never be hurt by any word or act of mine; and if I can help them, I will."

"Thank you," the mother said, taking both his hands in hers: for a moment they looked in each other's eyes. "Now let us go home. Do you see that little, low house all overrun with vines?"

"Yes, 'm: I was sure that was yours. It looks like a pleasant place to rest in, and a happy home to remember."

"God grant it may be to us all! How shall I introduce you?" she asked, as they entered the gate.

"I have almost as many names as a prince royal; but you may call me Theodore Montgomery."

Happy days followed at the woodbine cottage; for though the young engineer faithfully carried chain and added columns of figures for his chief, he yet found leisure hours for romping with little Miriam, and idle days for hunting and fishing or gathering nuts, with Jamie and Davy, and sometimes Fred or Jack, for company. From these excursions the little girl was excluded after she carried the basket of trout to the water, "Des to div' 'em a d'ink," and let them one by one slip from her dimpled hands and swim down the brook. And so loud were her lamentations over a brace of rabbits brought home by an elated marksman that all game was kept from her sight until prepared for the table, where it was only *meat* to her anxious inquiries and eager appetite.

Her intense love of the beautiful, and equally intense abhorrence of everything uncouth or unclean, had a silent influence over the workmen, to whom she ran with delight, or shrunk from with disgust, as their manner or dress pleased or offended her fastidious taste. Quick to learn, and of retentive memory, the child learned poems and songs, verses of Scripture, and Mother Goose's Melodies with equal delight.

Morris, being an enthusiastic Whig, taught her the songs of his party; while Major Morrill, being a violent Democrat, taught her a Locofoco song. With a voice clear as a bell and sweeter than a violin, she sung or recited equally well, the indistinctness of her baby utterance giving an additional piquancy to the language. The perversity of her sex was often shown in her selections, regardless of requests or coaxing; and the major was often provoked, and the rest amused, when he asked for "Henry Clay is getting Gray," to hear the merry voice sing out,

"'Ha! ha! ha! such a nominee
As Dames Tay Polt of Tennessee.'"

And Mrs. Morgan was once mortified at hearing her, instead of the verses "Poor and needy though I be"—requested by a dignified colporter—with a most roguish look and absurd gesture, recite,

"'Da' was a man tum to ou' town,
He was so wond'ous wise,
He dumped into a *was*pberry bus'
An' *sc'watched* out bof his eyes!
An' wen he saw his eyes were out,
He wun wiv might an' main,
An' dumped into a *doose*berry bus'
An' *sc'watched* 'em in aden!'"

Her imitative powers were wonderful, and many a comedy and tragedy was enacted by herself and her dolls. But a loud laugh or loud applause offended her.

"Mover, Feo' waffs!" she would sometimes cry, with tears of real distress brimming her eyes, when the poor boy was nearly bursting his sides in efforts to restrain the shouts that her quaint or comical expression had caused.

"She would make her fortune on the stage," he said one evening, when she had been entertaining them for hours.

"I hope the future has a better fortune for her than that," her mother answered, quickly.

"Do *you* think actors bad? I thought you had no prejudices: you seem so wise, so generous."

There was a bitterness and sadness in his tone that puzzled Mrs. Morgan, and caused Major Morrill to look at him with a half-smile.

"I fear I have prejudices, Theodore, like other folks, which were educated in and have never been reasoned out. I am not acquainted with any actors or actresses, and never was inside a theatre, and personally know nothing against them; and yet it would be a great grief to have any one I loved or respected adopt *acting* as a life-work."

The youth's face flushed slightly; but a question of Fred's about coon-hunting in Virginia turned the conversation.

"Are you as decided in your views of amusements and temperance as your husband, Mrs. Morgan?" Major Morrill inquired, as the boys began eagerly talking at the opposite side of the room.

"I don't know that we ever compared opinions, but no doubt they are similar."

"Pardon me for asking a question which I see you think a rude one; but Mr. Morgan is so exceedingly strict! told me he would not allow his boys to play *checkers!* never tasted a drop of liquor in his life! Now, pardon me —I don't wish you to think me rude —but really I never heard anything like it; and was curious to know if you thought as he did. You see, I was raised differently, and—"

"All *games of chance* seem to me foolish, if not sinful. There are, of course, games of skill and tests of memory which are amusing, and may be beneficial if not so absorbing as to cease to amuse. But on temperance I can imagine but one opinion among sensible people. A human being unable to control appetite is lower than a beast! But I do not believe there *is* such a being. When the appetite and passions are strong, the *will* is correspondently strong, and can control if the person desires it."

"Why, madam, do you mean to say you believe a man who was raised on liquor, ate the sugar out of the punch-bowl, and tasted liquor at the still when a mere baby, could toss off a glass of brandy without winking before he could say the multiplication-table — do you suppose a man raised like that could help being a drunkard?"

"I *do*. I heard a man say it was as easy to quit drinking as to open his hand. Suppose the liquor was even that near his lips — he opened his hand, and — glass and liquor were on the ground. But, seriously, it would be a hard struggle, and a long one, to conquer a habit that had grown with his years; and a man might need a mild stimulant, like coffee, and his nerves might be very irritable. But then the exultation of victory, the knowledge that he is lord of himself, the calm of the conqueror! For he that ruleth his own spirit is mightier than he that taketh a city."

The major started to his feet, and walked up and down the room; then paused before her.

"Had I met you before, madam — had anybody said that to me twenty years ago — But I'm afraid it's too late now! Your boys will be trained right, and Theo shall never be what I am. Good-night, ma'am, good-night!" And he went out into the darkness.

Jamie had lighted the dry pine twigs in the fireplace, less for warmth than illumination; and as the flames leaped up, the shadows were driven into corners and behind the furniture, and the room glistened and glowed like an enchanted palace.

"Mother, let us sing our evening hymn before we say good-night. Come, boys. You start it, mother."

And the voices, timid and faltering at first, but clear and fervent at the third line, joined in a familiar tune:

" For friends and for friendship, for health and for home,
We thank thee Our Father, wherever we roam.
We thank thee for hunger, which gives food a zest;
We thank thee for labor and bless thee for rest.

" The lakes and the rivers have blessings in store,
The field and the forest will each day yield more.
Give strength, we beseech thee, give wisdom and power,
To aid in each duty and gladden each hour.

" We thank thee for pleasures, for freedom from sin,
For love that makes us with the whole world akin;
We bless thee for guiding us safely this day;
We trust thee to-night, and we trust thee alway."

CHAPTER XII.

"And broad-winged Commerce, swift to carry o'er
Earth's countless blessings to her farthest shore,
Stops not, though forests marshal all their force,
And mountains rise to stay her onward course."

J. G. SAXE.

The New York and Erie Railroad was nearing its completion. The ties were piled by the road-bed; the rails were brought on wagons from towns twenty and forty miles away; and in a few weeks the scream of the iron horse would resound among these hills. In every town and hamlet, in every tavern and cabin, the railroad was the constant theme of conversation.

Many and varied were the opinions expressed: the game would be driven from the forests; the cattle frightened from the fields; the children run over by the cars. The impossibility of the trains rounding the abrupt curves; the certainty of the engines running straight forward into the river; the inevitable collisions between trains going both east and west on the single track; the absurdity, if not wickedness, of attempting to travel twenty miles in an hour, as the civil engineers boldly prophesied their doing—these subjects were gravely discussed with serious apprehensions.

"It's jest a-flyin' into the face o' Providence," Mrs. Rogers declared.

"How under the sun an' airth them railroaders dare to cut right thro' that thare ol' buryin'-ground is what beats me! Why, I should think they'd be afeard to go out nights lest spooks sh'u'd chase 'em."

"Wall, I hain't 'feared o' Uncle Jake nor Betsy Jones's baby; wa'n't nothin' but a han'ful o' dust in neither coffin; an' Mister Morgan made 'em take 'em up an' bury 'em decent," Sam Jenkins said, thoughtfully. "But how this 'ere body o' mine kin all go to nothin', and then how it kin all come together agin an' be raised up, that's what I can't understand nohow! An' some o' them thare bones 'll have a time gittin' sorted, I'll bet. They throwed the whole on 'em into a dry-goods box fust, till Mister Morgan had Bill Morris make some little coffins to hold 'em. But I'll bet they chucked a lot on 'em into the river, an' ploughed 'em under the road-bed when nobody was a-watchin' 'em."

"Wall, you don't never ketch me a-ridin' on that railroad! Makes me kindy quivery to think o' kears goin' right over them poor dead bodies. Oh-dear-me-suz!"

"Good gracious, Mis' Rogers, le's talk o' suthin' else! I've got to walk home on that thare railroad track to-night. What riles me most o' anything is them hootin', puffin', snortin' ol' ingines scarin' the deer forty mile off; an' they're gittin' skurse now."

"An' the sooner they're all gone, an' you hunters spend your time in clearin' up land, the better," Long John answered, testily. "S'pose the railroad 'll profit them 'at built it, an' 'twill be handier gittin' back from down the river; but we hain't no further use for't, fur as I see; an' likely 'twill bring a lot o' city chaps up here to show our boys how to fool away their time 'ith new deviltry."

Major Morrill and Theodore returned to woodbine cottage for a parting call. Mr. Morgan, Morris, Major Morrill, and the boys sat about the fire, eagerly talking; but Theo left the group and drew a chair to the table where Mrs. Morgan was seated. In low, earnest tones, he told her of his plans and hopes; while she, with words of loving counsel, deepened the good resolves made at the hour of meeting.

"I tell you, major, the railroad company will have the best of the bargain yet," Mr. Morgan was saying. "It is, as you say, a regular gouge game on the part of the commonwealth to extort ten thousand dollars a year for the privilege of running across two corners of the State; but mark my words, sir, in less than twenty years that will be the company's gain and Pennsylvania's loss!"

"I don't see that, sir."

"Nor I," added Morris.

"Well, you see this exonerates them from all State and local taxation; school-tax, road-tax, poor-tax, and so on. Now they will be shrewd enough to put their machine-shops on this land, which will save them a large and constantly increasing sum of money."

"That might do if there was a valley big enough to hold shops, side-tracks, and turn-tables; but there isn't."

"Well, sir, if the company cannot find a place, they'll *make* one! And forcing them to put the road farther back on the mountain to prevent the rocks falling in the river—"

"Yes, and altered the grade of over fifty miles!" growled the major.

"Even that is their gain. I have been on the Delaware long enough to see the ice pile up and the water overflow their first survey."

"Perhaps you think it will be for their advantage that the canal company forced us to come this way instead of going up the Lackawaxen, as first intended."

"I do. The Honesdale folks think their ditch is a wonderful thing now; but they will be begging for a branch road soon. This way is not much steeper grade, you say; and if you had gone up the Lackawack, we would never have had the pleasure of knowing you."

"That is true; and the comfort I have enjoyed in your house, the pleasure of knowing your family, ought to reconcile me to the company's loss, being my gain. But it's time we were off. Come, Theo."

They were urged to remain overnight, but insisted a sleigh-ride of a dozen miles behind a fast horse on a moonlight night was too great a pleasure to miss. "Particularly when we anticipate being south of the snow-line soon."

"I suppose Mira is asleep?" Theo said, as he folded his neck-shawl.

"She is easily awakened," her mother said, "and will be disappointed if she does not see you. Come in this room."

Major Morrill laughed. "That boy is perfectly bewitched about your baby; shouldn't wonder if he came after her some day. Here, Davy, just button my overshoes for me. You may live to be fat and fifty yourself, and hate to stoop as badly as I do."

Jamie was warming his overcoat, and Mr. Morgan and Morris talking of the morrow's work, as Theodore knelt by Miriam's trundle-bed. "Mira, little darling," he whispered, putting his hand under her head and turning her face toward him, "Theo is going away; won't you wake up and speak to him?" The dark eyes opened sleepily.

"Don't do 'way!" she murmured, laying one dimpled hand on his cheek and nestling the other in his own.

"I *must*, Mira. Will you kiss me good-bye?"

She clasped her arms around his neck and pressed her rosy lips to his. "Tum back aden, teo," she whispered; then turned her head away and was asleep.

He arose, and the mother took his hand. "My dear boy," she said, "it seems as though a son were leaving me. Keep yourself pure, Theodore, and come back again." She kissed him twice.

"God helping me, I will! The book you gave me is carried here"—he put his hand to his breast—"and will be often read. Will you accept this from me?" He put a small leathern case in her hand.

"Is it your miniature? Thank you, my boy. Now good-bye, and God keep you."

In a moment the partings were over. Months passed, and the "Little Orange" went puffing and shrieking by, to the wonder and delight of the people gathered on the river-bank. But their astonishment increased when the "Monster" paused opposite the saw-mill, and a man, swinging himself off the locomotive, hallooed to them to bring over some slabs.

"She's out o' kindlin', I gue-ess," Mose remarked. "Here, Jack, you might take over some o' them thare pine-knots I got to go a eelin' wi-uth. Jest split up a few sla-ubs an' put in my canoe, an' I'll pole over."

But a half-dozen men had attacked the slab pile beside the mill, and a float was half-way across the river before the canoe was untied. Axes soon cut the slabs to proper length, and the empty tender was supplied with fuel.

"Now, boys," said the engineer, "one good turn deserves another, they say. Just form a line to the river an' fill 'er up with water."

"Yer horse wants a drink, eh?" said Jack, taking a bucket.

"Yes, won't move 'thout 'er reg'lar

dram, an' there ain't a tank on this division yet. Pass 'em up lively, boys." Soon the puffing and wheezing began again; clouds of steam hovered around and above the crowd of curious countrymen who pressed nearer and nearer to the "snortin' critter," until with a shriek that sent them backward with sudden fright the engine moved away.

Soon the railroad was opened to Binghamton, and two trains bearing the officers of the road, members of the press, and leading citizens passed by; but a blinding snow-storm obscured the sight and obstructed the trains, while the intense cold and fierce winds prevented the people witnessing the novel sight.

A grand inauguration of the completion of the road to Lake Erie was anticipated. Rumors of the President of the United States and his Cabinet, Daniel Webster, and other men who stood almost as high in the nation's esteem, taking part in the celebration, created great enthusiasm, and a determination in each town to outdo all others of its size in display. Mr. Morgan became as zealous as any, and determined that his industries should be represented. A platform was erected beside the railroad track. Piles of lumber and bark were put upon it, and between them were spaces for groups of hunters with game, and tanners scraping hides and dressing leather. Silk for a banner was procured, and Mrs. Morgan and Bessie spent many hours in embroidering a wreath of ferns and flowers on one side of it, and on the other the name, in glittering tinsel, JOHN MORGAN.

At last the day came. From every house and hut for miles around men, women, and children gathered. Long before the hour appointed for the triumphal car, the track was lined and the platform crowded by the expectant people. With much difficulty and some angry words, a place was found for the tableaux: a prostrate buck with spreading antlers, a hunter with raccoon cap and leathern moccasons beside it; another hunter dressed in homespun, with a brace of rabbits at his back, and rifle poised at unseen game. On the other side of the pile of bark the tanners were at work. Walking rapidly to and fro, Mr. Morgan kept the boys from climbing the lumber piles, or standing between his exhibit and the track. How long the minutes seemed!

At last a puff of smoke over the hill—a shrill whistle—a low rumble, and the train was near. Again Mr. Morgan assured himself that all was ready: Jack held the banner a few inches higher.

Now! One deafening yell arose. Rifles and hides were dropped; the banner was thrown down, and the crowd rushed forward to clasp the President's hand. Davy sprung upon the car, grasped every hand within reach, jumped off as the train moved on, and joined in the parting Hurra-a-ah!

Their inauguration was over. A perfect Babel of chatter from every excited man, woman, and child about what they did and whom they saw covered Mr. Morgan's confusion and anger as he turned away and walked homeward, leaving Morris and Jack to remove the exhibit prepared with so much trouble and expense, only to be a failure, and the subject of rude jokes for years to come.

"A set of uncontrollable barbarians!" he muttered. "I've a mind to sell out, and go where there is some civilization."

Then, as he paused at the river-side and looked up the valley, he added, "But it is a fine estate and a magnificent heritage for my children."

A new outlet for lumber, leather, and farm produce was now open, and wealth in abundance, power unbounded, lay within reach. Thoughts of the responsibilities, the dangers involved in such possessions, struggled feebly and were put aside. The contented farmer, the enthusiastic disciple, were fused into the eager money-getter. Strange that while the "shalt not" of Divine authority is feared, the "cannot" of human nature is uncomprehended, and few understand the impossibility of serving both God and Mammon.

Before many months had passed, trains were running with some regularity; but an accident to one, however slight, detained them all, each having the right of way only when arriving at the stations when due, the right being transferred to another as soon as a detention occurred. No telegraph line being erected, a flagman would frequently run before the train to warn the engineer of danger, or drive the cattle from the track, the same curiosity that infected their owners seeming to draw them before an approaching engine. A ride on the cars was the ambition of every individual; the passenger-coaches with upholstered seats, gilded mouldings, and shuttered windows were the wonder of them all, and a journey from one station to another a treat only the enterprising young men could afford to offer, and only the most venturesome girls dare accept. Jamie and Davy had made frequent excursions on the flat cars drawn by horses before the first locomotive arrived, and since then had rung the bell and pulled the whistle of the "Little Orange." But a ride in a passenger-car, with a conductor to take one's money for a ride—that was a novelty yet to experience. A daily mail from the East and the West, besides the usual semi-weekly mail from across the country, kept the assistant postmaster busy for several hours each day; and he took the mail-bag Davy brought from the station with a weary look.

"A letter from Uncle Dave to mother, and a note to me. Listen, Davy: '*James Morgan, yourself and brother are urgently invited to attend an oyster supper at our house to-morrow evening.*' Signed, Robert and Maria Hotchkiss."

"Good! *James Morgan, Esquire, presents the grateful thanks of himself and brother*, et cætera, and so forth. But the ladies, Jamie, where are they? We might take Jane Rodgers and Lucy Jones; but Jane is *so* awkward, and Lucy would try not to appear verdant and so be ridiculously prim; and neither one could be induced to swallow an oyster. But they are the best of the lot."

"Suppose we take mother and Miriam? Nothing would suit me so well, and Mrs. Hotchkiss and Miss Jeannette would be delighted. Besides, Sam Jenkins wants Lucy to go with him for a ride in the cars. He has been trying to get a chance to ask her, but she dodges him: you see, she does not want to refuse, nor dare to go."

"There are enough girls who would be glad of a chance."

"Yes; but the chase has its charms; and Sam knows nothing worth having comes without seeking. You take the invitation to the house, Davy, and see what mother says about it."

But Miriam, who was seated on the door-step, sewing bits of calico together to form blocks for a quilt, answered his query by saying,

"Mother's gone to see Bessie, an' I'm going to s'prise her by doing this piece-work all my lone self."

Davy walked to Morris's door. Robin had been a bad boy that morning, and Mrs. Morgan found Bessie preparing a switch for a severe castigation.

"I told the bairn ne'er to climb oot th' winda'," she said, in reply to Mrs. Morgan's inquiries, "an' the laddie hae dune the vera thing he waur forbid an' pit his fut thro' th' glass o' th' hot-bed an' broke a' th' wee plants doon; an' he s'all smart weel for 't," giving the birch rod a vigorous twirl, while Robin, a sturdy urchin of seven summers, began to sob piteously.

"For what will you punish him, Bessie—the disobedience or the accident?"

"Eh, mem? I dinna unnerstan'."

"Are you going to whip him because he did not mind you, or because he broke the hot-bed?"

"Baith, mem; he knew I bade him not do 't, an' he lat himsel' doon on the glass as though 'twere solid earth!"

"And if his feet had come down on solid earth, would you whip him just the same?"

"Why, 'twad dune na hairm!"

"But he would have disobeyed you."

"Weel, mem, ye're right; maybe 'tis for the accident I was maist angered. But what wad ye hae me do?"

"I would teach him he must obey because my commands were right."

"An' if he winna?"

"I would show him disobedience brought punishment. If he was not sorry enough at grieving me, and the mischief done, I would punish him in some other way. But when Robin looks at the glass that cost his father a whole day's work, and the tomato-plants that will never lift their heads again; never bear any pretty lady-apples for his mamma—" The melancholy tone and reproachful face were too much for Robin's endurance, and, with a loud wail of anguish, he ran to Bessie and threw himself at her feet.

"I'll ne'er do 't agen, mammy! I'll mind ivery word ye tell me, 'deed I will! Ye may whip me an ye're a mind to, mammy; I'm sae awfu' bad boy." And the tears poured over the sunburnt face.

"Na, na, I'll not whip thee, laddie," the mother said, taking the child in her arms; "but ye must ken something bad wull happen to ye whene'er ye winna mind yer mither, for

God sees ye, if I dinna, an' he'll punis' ye."

The boy looked out with scared eyes at the far-away clouds that might conceal the All-seeing.

"But, Robin, our Father in Heaven keeps watch of us to keep harm away. He only puts a hurt into bad things so we will not choose them, just as your mamma puts lumps of salt in the sugar-bowl to keep her boy from eating too much sweet. See that butterfly, Robin. God made that, and all the birds and flowers. Isn't he good?"

The boy saw his father approaching, and ran to meet him, apparently heedless of the theological lesson he had received. But as Morris turned to the mill, which was forbidden ground to children, he paused and picked a daisy, looking from it to the sky.

"Robin is a good boy, Bessie. You need have no trouble with him."

Mrs. Morgan drew her work from her pocket, and leaned back comfortably in the cushioned chair.

"Eh, mem, 'tis a sair task for me! He's sae wi' fu' an' res'less, an' speers at me wi' questions till I'm near daft wi' him! An' gin he gangs wrang at th' lang-last, I'll hae to beir nabody kens hoo muckle o' th' wyte o' 't." And the young mother sighed. "I canna unnerstan' why the worl' 's sae fu' o' things 'at canna be touched. It's a' *Thou shalt not* on ither side. What fur s'uld there be ony temptations at a', mem? Why needs there be ony but gude things?"

Mrs. Morgan looked with surprise at the flushed, perplexed face.

"I never knew you puzzled your mind with such questions, Bessie. But I suppose God wants us to be something better than machines that must go one way, and cannot go any other. Suppose you had been so afraid Robin would get hurt by creeping that you kept him constantly in your arms: he would never have learned to walk; or if you kept him shut away from all danger, he would grow up an idiot. We must learn to obey first; then, as we grow wiser, to choose. Do you understand?"

"Oh, ay; I ken a' that. But th' responsibility o' a boy is just awfu'!"

"I do not feel it so. They are God's children more than mine. We are the parents of their bodies. He is Creator of their spirits. I do not know what he means them to be or to do; but I know he wants pure, self-controlled minds in strong, active bodies; and I— Here comes Davy; I am wanted at home." And she folded her work and put on her bonnet.

As they walked homeward, Davy put the invitation in her hand, and told his and Jamie's wish.

"Thank you both for the compliment, my boys," she said, with a face radiant with love and pride. "I am a happy mother to be the *one* lady in my sons' thoughts; but I must decline for myself as well as Miriam. I am too old and she too young, for such pleasures, now. Precious little wonder-woman! Ah, my children, how I do long for cultured minds and refined associates for you! But the Father knows best, and we have each other. Don't keep Jamie waiting, dear. And, Davy, if you give pleasure, it shall be given to you: remember that."

CHAPTER XIII.

"She is not sad, yet in her gaze appears
Something that makes the gazer think of tears."
MRS. EMBURY.

"Oh, mother, if I only *could* go to school!"

"Yes, daughter, yes."

The first voice was full of the quick impatience of youth—hope struggling with circumstance; and the other toned by experience and the hope deferred that maketh the heart sick. They were sitting together on the porch of the same vine-wreathed cottage—Mrs. Morgan and Miriam—a basket of unshelled pease between them, and brightly scoured tins in their laps, into which the emerald balls were dropping rapidly from their supple fingers. The fragrance of roses mingled with the odor of new-mown hay floated about them unheeded; the robin's warble and bobolink's trill brought no delight. Silent and thoughtful they sat, the mother and daughter, with the glad sunshine flooding the earth, and darkness in their hearts.

"Do you suppose he would sell any hay?"

The young girl's eyes wandered up the valley, across the acres of potatoes and corn, to the fields where men were raking, tossing, and forming into oval heaps the dried grass cut the day before.

"No, child; there won't be any to spare. We had to begin to feed it out in October last year, and the cattle have no good pasture till June. If they could have got that bark off last freshet, then—"

"Yes, *then* he would have bought that team of Jackson; I heard him say so. That's all he cares for; more teams, more lumber, more saw-mills, more tanneries, and everlasting lawsuits."

"Miriam!"

"Well, mother, isn't it so? Aren't we just slaving our lives away to get more lands and more money—and what good will it do us? Here's Jamie, just longing to study medicine; and Davy, wanting to be a machinist; and you losing your health and prettiness—for you *are pretty*, you dear, blessed little mother!—and I, growing up a great, big, ignorant girl, with oh, *such* a craving for books and society!" A big sob and a burst of tears choked her, and, jumping up quickly, she ran into the kitchen with her pan of pease, creating a great clatter with the kettles and stove; but when she returned to the vine-covered porch her face was tear-stained, but smiling; and she said, merrily, "Now, little mother, you're day-dreaming! I've caught you at it! And the pease are not all shelled, and the table's not set, and the lettuce's not picked, and pretty soon the tannery bell will ring, and all those hungry haymakers will be here to dinner. You needn't 'go to the ant,' though; you just keep near me. There's the milk to skim, cream to churn, butter to work over, cookies to make, currants to pick, and shirts to iron this very afternoon; and then by-and-by in the twilight, when supper is over, we'll sit out here on the porch, and I will tell you a story about an unsatisfied but not ungrateful girl, and what she intends to do with herself."

The mother's face brightened; the pease rattled in the pan, keeping up a merry accompaniment to the girl's eager talk of the work, Bessie's baby, Jane Rodgers's marriage, and Fred's anticipated visit with his bride after an absence of eight years.

"He will find us in the same little cottage under the hill. We were going to have a new house the next year after he left, and it has been the *next* year ever since. Oh, well, he will enjoy it more than a new, strange one. Even Bruce, dear old fellow! is here to welcome him. But he isn't the frisky puppy he was when Fred taught him to carry bundles from the store, bring in wood, and shut the door. See him, down there in the grass, raise his head and look at me. I believe he always knows when any one is talking of him. Yesterday he was lying by the stove door, and Davy said, 'Bruce is a homely dog,' and the old fellow dropped his ears, and looked at him so reproachfully from under his shaggy brows! Then Davy, without altering his tone one bit, said, 'But he's a good dog,' and Bruce wagged his tail, got up, and licked Davy's hand. I'm sure he used to understand every word I said to him, long years ago, when we wandered in the woods and I told him fairy stories. I am so sorry to see him grow old. If he could only go to heaven!"

"Oh, daughter!"

"Well, now, mother, Bruce has always been just as good as he could be. He never has neglected a duty—"

"Except when he left the basket of eggs in the road."

"And that was to drive a strange dog out of the yard. It was a question between two duties, and I know that he was sorry he did not choose right. He is strictly honest; he never took a thing that was not given him or he did not earn."

"Except dry sticks from Bessie's wood-shed."

"Oh, now, mother, that was real cunning, when our wood was all green and wet! He is a great deal better than some humans I know, and I'd a deal rather see him in—"

"There, child; you had better go get the pie and put it on the table, and sweep up the pods."

The fire was replenished and the table spread for dinner. Then the mother passed into the bedroom, closed the door, and, kneeling before a low chair, buried her face in her hands. Every day she entered *into her closet*, and as often received patience, strength, and peace. The old chair had become an altar and a shrine. Sacrifices had there been offered, burdens there laid down: while holy memories of a mother's counsel, a father's good-night kiss, and a brother's caresses centred about this rocking-chair. Rising from her knees, she sat upon its faded cushions, and, resting her elbows on its arms, bowed her head upon her hands. Thoughts flitted back to her girlhood days; those ardent hopes, eager, ambitious, vague longings; then the early marriage, the disappointments, the privations, the repressions.

"My daughter's life shall be different," she said.

A quick step on the porch, an impatient voice at the kitchen door, aroused her.

"Come, come, come! Here's all the men waiting for their dinner, and not a soul to get it. Miryum!"

"Yes, sir," she answered, coming up the steps with a pan of freshly washed lettuce in her hand.

"Come now, I ain't agoing to have any such work as this! I told you to have dinner at twelve o'clock, and here it is a quarter after, and it ain't half ready."

"The tannery bell hasn't rung."

"You haven't anything to do with the tannery bell; you might as well make your calculations by the cows coming home! But I want my dinner at twelve o'clock, and I ain't agoing to have a dozen men kept waiting."

"There, that's enough." Mrs. Morgan took the dish from Miriam's trembling fingers, and whispered, "Go to the store and call Jamie to dinner."

"Miriam is working beyond her strength every day, John," she said, as the girl went out again into the dazzling sunlight.

"Yes; very hard she works. She don't earn the salt in her porridge!" and the father went out on the back porch, where the men were splashing the water from the tin wash-basins on the long bench, and rubbing their hands and faces on the coarse towels hung above it.

"Guess 'twill rain 'fore mornin', Mister Morgan," said Sam Jenkins, arranging his bushy locks before the little mirror.

"Well, I want that hay all in before sundown, whether it rains or not," looking off to the west, where a pale mist hovered over the hills.

"Did Long John's cattle hurt your corn much?" asked a thin, wiry man, after a moment's silence.

"Done over forty dollars' worth of damage, and he shall pay me the full amount or I'll prosecute him. The fault was *not* in my fences, but in his breachy cow."

"I heard he wanted to settle it."

"Yes, on his own terms. I guess he'll find the law will settle it. But come; dinner is ready."

A formal and lengthy grace was said, but no further words except those necessary in passing the food, until one by one, their appetites being satisfied, the men rose from the table and left the house. Jamie lingered after the rest had gone. The five years had made the shy, sensitive boy a thoughtful, earnest, generous man. The same straight black hair, clear-cut features, dark-gray eyes, and curved lips unshaded by beard; the same gentle movements and sympathetic tones, which were the magic that unlocked all hearts, and a quiet, self-assured manner that the responsibilities of business had given. For Jamie was cashier and book-keeper in the firm of Morgan & Sons, keeping the accounts of the men employed in the three saw-mills and tannery, with a score of wood-choppers and bark-peelers, the teamsters and farm-hands, regulating their pass-books, and settling their disputes. Every spring and fall several weeks were spent in New York purchasing goods for the store. With all these labors, Jamie still found time to establish a circulating library and reading-room in the tannery boarding-house, and a debating society and temperance union, which held their meetings on alternate Wednesday evenings. If the duties of chairman, secretary, reporter, critic, librarian, and treasurer were ever onerous or annoying, added to his other labors, no one ever heard a complaint, and there was always leisure to attend to any family want, give counsel on any subject, or visit any sick person when called on, night or day. He used the forceps or lancet with a dentist's and surgeon's skill, and settled many a knotty point of law for country squires and attorneys.

Davy—reckless, fun-loving Davy—had become restless under the many cares, unwillingly assumed and carelessly executed. "These hills shall never hedge in my life," he had said, when as a school-boy he longed for a wider outlook and more congenial work. But daily duties and love for his mother kept him still hedged in and bound down to labor he detested.

"Up in the morning at six o'clock, getting yesterday's dirt out of sight, ready to smile on the first customer, inquire about the lame horse or sick baby, weighing out groceries, measuring dress goods, cutting off samples, dealing out hardware, tasting butter, wrapping up patent medicines, recommending pills, counting eggs, copying accounts in greasy pass-books, explaining charges, giving prices, hearing complaints, contradicting statements—all these employments have filled up this day, which is but a sample of every day"—Davy wrote to his uncle David. But the labors were shared by Jack, often performed by him alone, while Davy, careless of his father's reproof, spent days in sauntering through the forest, with rifle or fishing-rod in his idle hands. There were also debts to be collected; and in this part of their business Davy's easy, assured manner, mirthful jokes, and frequent laugh succeeded best of all. Days and sometimes weeks were spent in long tours on horseback or in a wagon, travelling among their customers, and returning with money, judgment notes, mortgages, or produce to settle their accounts. Often the machinery of the mills or tannery would need repairing, and then Davy had employment that pleased him. Self-taught, and with tools of his own making, not a wheelwright in the county could do a better job. His father often pointed out his work with pride and words of commendation, which he was careful his boys should not hear, believing praise was injurious to immature minds. When urged to give his children a more thorough education, and wider opportunities for culture, he declared they knew quite enough to transact the business assigned them; and when the varied talents of each were alluded to, he insisted they found ample time and space for their development.

"I came into this wilderness to make an opening for my family. Here is work enough for all the talents they may have," he would say. "Restless? Boys are always restless, and girls are always discontented! But they'll outgrow it. I intend they shall live here, and after I am gone my fortune shall be theirs."

Jamie pushed his chair from the table, saying, 'Mother, I've sent for a hired girl to help you through haying; and if you like her, she will stay all summer."

"Does your father know it?"

"I will tell him. It is my own affair, and I will see to her wages. She will be here to-morrow. And, mother, Davy is going on one of his long collecting tours with the little wagon. What do you say to letting Mira go with him? She needs a change, and they could go gypsying through the country, stopping at farm-houses at night. They will be within a day's ride of home when farthest away; but he may not be able to see all our debtors within a week. It is not the change she ought to have, but it is better than none."

"If she wants to go, she can; but I have another plan, Jamie, that I want your opinion of."

"James"—the voice of his father never seemed more harsh and exasperating — "what do you mean by keeping those men waiting while you idle away your time in the house? Here's Jones and Wainright with the cash in their hands, and their accounts not made out."

"Their accounts are ready for them, sir; and Jones wants three months' time."

"Well, he won't get it. I've waited on him over a year, and—"

"He has had bad luck lately," Jamie went on, calmly unmindful of the interruption. "Stove his scantling, and the fire got into his bark. I told him we would wait until he run his logs. We will finish our talk after supper, mother;" and the young man followed his father to the store.

Davy soon entered with Miriam. Both faces were eager and smiling.

"Oh, little mother, do say I may go with Davy! We'll have the nicest time—*do* say I can!" And the girl caught her mother in her arms, gave her a hug and a whirl, and seated her at the table.

"What a crazy creature she is!" exclaimed Davy. "Suppose she should get such a fit on when we were ten miles from anywhere! Don't think I'd better risk it, mother; say *no*, for mercy's sake!"

"And leave me alone with her?" Mrs. Morgan said, wiping the tears of laughter from her eyes. "I think I will say yes, and see if you can tame her."

"And you know all about it—Jamie has told you? Isn't it splendid? Davy says my new calico dress is plenty good enough, and I better take another, for fear it might rain—but it won't, I know—and I must make some biscuit and some ginger-snaps. But say, mother—" she lowered her voice, and a look of scorn curved her red lips—"Davy says I better walk over to Auntie Rodgers and wait for him there; because father will make such a time, if he knows I want to go, and—" A crimson flush swept from chin to brow.

Davy's voice broke in impatiently. "Mother, if we can have a little pleasure, do let us have it in peace. You know just what a row there would be about expense, and trouble, and my fooling away my time and not attending to business; and if I failed to collect a bad debt, it would be because I took Miriam. Now, it is easier to prevent evil than to cure it, you often say. Probably she won't be missed, for he is going to court, Thursday; and if she is, you can say she went over to Auntie Rodgers; but it isn't likely a question will be asked. Now mind, Miriam, if there is any trouble about it, you can't go;" and he hurried back to the store, where customers were waiting, for few would trade with Mr. Morgan while Davy was about. His jovial manner and hearty good-will attracted customers from far and near. His plan was carried out. The following morning Mr. Morgan mounted his horse and rode away, saying he would be home Saturday. For the remainder of the week Jamie and Jack were left alone in the store, and worked until late at night posting books and copying accounts. Saturday evening Davy drove up to the store door, and unloaded the merchandise he had collected—a bale of hides, two tubs of butter, a roll of home-made flannel, a pail of honey, a cheese, and a quantity of eggs—besides the notes and cash his pocket-book contained. A few minutes later Miriam entered the door, an anxious look dimming the brightness of her smile.

"Has father got back? Oh, we've had the *splendidest* time!" she said, between kisses, "and the hired girl came, and you got along just as well without me? That was all the worry I had; that and "—lowering her voice —"the fear that father might get back first; but Davy was sure he wouldn't. I never had such fun. We made believe we were gypsies and Irish emigrants, and Davy would say the drollest things; and I stayed all one day at Point Pleasant with a real nice lady, and she taught me a new kind of knitting with one needle with a hook on the end of it. She asked me if I wouldn't come there to school next winter, and board with her. Do you s'pose I can, mother?"

"Why, what a chatterbox my little girl is, and how sunburnt! I intend you shall spend this winter in school, my dear, but not so near home as that."

"Do you? Can I? Oh, I am so glad! Has father said I could?"

"I can't answer your questions now, my daughter. You will go to the best school we can find, but how or where I cannot tell. We must work and wait.

Before dark Mr. Morgan came, and was immediately shown the results of Davy's tour. He had gained a long-contested lawsuit, and this, with the collected debts, put him in good-humor with himself and the world. He retired early. Miriam went over to Bessie Morris's home to tell of her journey, and Mrs. Morgan sat upon the porch with her sons. Long and earnestly they talked of hopes, trials, desires, plans, and of Miriam.

"You are right, mother. Davy ought to go to school, but Mira must; and I see no other way than the one you propose of appealing to Uncle David. Your letter will awaken his interest in her, and I will write to-morrow, making myself personally responsible for the amount of tuition."

"But her clothes—there isn't a thing in the store fit for a nice dress, is there, Davy?"

"No; and no chance to get anything until I get the fall goods. She ought to be ready to go to Philadelphia with you, if she goes to school there. You don't think Aunt Clarissa would board her, do you?"

"'Friend, first thee tells a lie and then thee asks a question,' as the Quaker said. Why not, Davy?"

"Because a peevish, nervous invalid wouldn't have a wide-awake girl like Mira around. And her headaches and hysterics would kill a healthy person to hear of; though Aunt Clarissa thrives on them."

"Why, Davy, my visits there are always pleasant."

"They never lessen your hotel-bills, I notice; and if you don't want an explosion in the family, don't put a red-hot coal into a gas-bag! Now, there is a seminary within a day's journey of Philadelphia," Davy continued, "where Uncle Dave wanted me to go two years ago. He is acquainted with the preceptress, and said she was the loveliest and most accomplished lady and most earnest Christian he ever knew; he could not say enough in her praise. If he had a dozen children, he said he would send them all to Miss Caldwell to be educated."

"Is it an expensive school?" asked Mrs. Morgan.

"No; that was its chief recommendation, as far as I was concerned; for Uncle Dave did not know much about the school, except in Miss Caldwell's department. But he was dead sure everything was right where she ruled."

"Perhaps it would be right to speak of that school to him. A girl of Miriam's age needs some one to attend to her health, her dress, and associates, as much as to teach her book-knowledge."

"Oh, Uncle Dave will recommend his favorite, you'll see. But how about her clothes?"

"There is that wool delaine of mine—it's not at all soiled—I think that will make over nicely for a best dress; and with two good ginghams for every day, she will get along very well."

"A made-over dress for best!" exclaimed Davy, contemptuously, as Jamie said,

"But that's *your* best, mother."

"Yes, my son; but I can wear my old pongee a little longer."

Davy threw himself at her feet, and

laid his head in her lap. "You shall 'walk in silk attire' one of these days, you dear, generous little mother! And there is a remnant of blue in the store that will trim your fawn-colored delaine just gay. Oh, I guess we can fix Mira up in style, after all! She's the kind of a girl that looks pretty in everything. There she comes with Jack now."

"Don't say anything about it to her until we are sure she can go," said Jamie. And the conference ceased.

The semi-weekly mail carried the two letters to Mr. Walton's office, and as soon as possible the answers were returned. The school of which Davy had spoken was warmly recommended, and arrangements were immediately made for Miriam's entrance at the Ellensport Seminary in the fall. The preparations were kept secret from Mr. Morgan, in order to postpone and abbreviate the storm sure to come when their intentions for Miriam were revealed. She was to accompany Jamie to Philadelphia, where her uncle would take charge of and transfer her to the care of his friend, Miss Caldwell, to whom a letter had already been addressed by Mrs. Morgan, describing Miriam's disposition and desires. In return, came a long pleasant reply. "The Seminary," Miss Caldwell wrote, "was beautifully situated in sight and sound of the sea, with a grove of pines at its back. Although established a comparatively brief period, and having many difficulties to overcome on account of the prejudice existing against boarding-schools for the education of opposite sexes, yet so watchful was their government, so unceasing their care, and so perfect all the arrangements for instructing the youth of the land, that already three hundred young ladies and gentlemen were under their charge—even a larger number expected the coming year."

A month later brought the hour of parting. Miriam ran from house to house, laughing and crying, kissing and being kissed, the excitement subduing her grief, until the wagon which was to carry herself and Jamie to the station stood before the door. Jack was standing in the kitchen, and the affectionate girl threw herself into his arms.

"Oh, Jack, my dear, good Jack!" she sobbed, "how I shall miss you! You'll write me, won't you? And don't let mother work too hard—you can help her in so many ways;" and she darted off to find her mother, who was seeking the strength she needed beside the old arm-chair. She opened the door at Miriam's hasty tap, and clasped her daughter to her heart. Her peaceful face calmed the girl, who listened quietly to her parting counsel, and replied,

"I mean to be very good, mother; and I shall tell you all I do, think, or feel. Father was very angry when he went away; but I mean to improve so much that he can't help seeing you did right in sending me away." And she threw her arms once more around her mother's neck, and sobs choked the good-bye.

"Come, Mira, the wagon is waiting." (Davy quelled the tears with a forced laugh.) "Stop crying, for

Bruce is looking dangerous; he thinks somebody has hurt you."

The dog was growling viciously, as he stood by his mistress's side. "The dear old darling!" she said, giving his shaggy head a hug. "Don't you die while I'm gone, nor let bad dogs catch my rabbits. Now, let's go."

Davy sprang to the driver's seat, Jamie seated himself beside his sister, and they were gone. Two weeks later the mail-carrier brought this letter:

"MY OWN PRECIOUS MOTHER,— I think I am going to like it very much. I got here yesterday. Uncle Dave introduced me to the preceptress. She is lovely; she looks so sweet and gentle! The girls all like her. I know five of the girls, and there are one hundred and sixty. There are great long halls without any carpets, and we have to wear slippers. Uncle got me some. The rooms are on each side. They all have numbers on the doors. Mine is 87. The girl I room with is my *chum;* she is little, and real nice, and very polite, but I don't think she likes me. Uncle David got me a new dress—it is blue—and black velvet ribbon to trim it. Miss Caldwell is going to have it made. Give my love to the boys and to Bruce. Kiss Robin and Bessie for me. Give my love to Morris too. Please tell father I mean to learn enough to teach school and pay him back every cent. I do hope I will get a letter from you to-day. My chum is studying. She does sums with letters and figures mixed up. The recitation-rooms are very large. One has blackboards all around; another has maps. In one room there are pictures of the human body: one is a man with his skin off, and another of just the bones. I don't think that a bit nice. Chum says we have got to learn the names of all the veins, and muscles, and bones. Uncle is going to take me out riding, and Miss Caldwell too. Chum has such beautiful clothes. But my dress is real nice too. You were so good to give it me. No more at present from your very loving daughter,

"MIRIAM MORGAN.

"P.S.— There are five professors, and four lady teachers. This is the first letter I ever wrote.

"P.S.— My chum's name is Dora Montgomery.

"P.S.— I have been 'way up in the belfry and seen the ocean. It looked just like the sky, but through the telescope I could see ships. Uncle is going to take me there to-morrow. I am so glad."

But the next day brought a cold east wind and rain. Monday morning summoned Mr. Walton away, and the June roses were fading before Miriam's eyes were more than tantalized by sight of the ocean, whose deep, incessant roar suggested its fathomless depths and boundless extent to the earnest, restless heart of the girl, creating an intense longing for a nearer view of its foam-capped waves, and to hear more distinctly the solemn tones which seemed to syllable the yearning of the world.

CHAPTER XIV.

"Friend of my heart, and foremost of the list
Of those with whom I lived supremely blest;
Oft have we drained the fount of earthly love,
Though drinking deeply, thirsting still for more:
And when confinement's lingering hour was done
Our sports, our studies, and our souls were one."
BYRON.

MONTHS passed, and Miriam's frequent letters grew longer and less laconic. The seminary, a six-storied, hastily constructed brick building, erected between and joining a stone church and a wooden academy, was graphically described, and the peculiarities of each teacher portrayed —pen-and-ink portraits aiding the words; while the best qualities and weak points were depicted with a subtle insight of character unusual in one so inexperienced.

"I feel as though I were on another planet, mother dear; life is so different here. Instead of being awakened by the birds singing in the apple-trees or the men whistling on their way to the barn, I am roused by the ding-a-ling-clang of a big bell, passing my door as it goes up one side of the hall and down the other. I often lie still with my eyes shut, and imagine how that bell must look swinging itself along with such a deafening clangor, and if it weren't so dárk and cold I would get up some time and take a peep at it; but when I spoke of it, Chum said I was a goose—that it was only the watchman ringing the rising bell! Now, Chum is always up and dressed when the horrible thing goes by; so she must know. In fact, I'm not sure she sleeps at all; for she is at her desk writing when I close my eyes, and poring over a book when I open them. After the horrible noise has ceased outside, I hear her voice saying, 'You will be too late for prayers!' That made me jump at first; it sounded awful—as though the end of the world had come!—and I had a terrible dream about the rocks falling, and people rushing, when ding-dong! went the big chapel bell, and the doors were slamming, and the girls running down-stairs, and I *was* too late to get in the chapel that time; for the door is locked when the bell stops ringing. After prayers we have half an hour to put our rooms in order. Dora is so neat and orderly that she dreaded having a chum; but we agree in all our habits so far, and take turns in keeping our room in order, which is no easy matter, with all the litter of our sleeping, dressing, studying, and writing. Yesterday morning when I was getting my history lesson (it was about the Indian wars in 1684, when De Barre, the Governor of Canada, thought he could scare the chiefs into submission to the French), I could not make myself remember it; so I put some books in the middle of the floor for a camp-fire, and stood chairs around for the Indians, and a pillow for the Frenchman, and then making believe I was Garrongula, the chief of the Onondaga tribe, I 'walked five or six times around the circle,' just as he did, and then began his 'bold sarcastic speech.' I had got as far as 'Hear, Yonnondio! What I say is the voice of the Five Nations,' when, rat-tap-tap! came a knock at my door. I tried to pick up the books and the pillow and put back the chairs all at once, when the door opened, and there stood the preceptress and a lady and gentleman visitor. Miss Caldwell frowned, and the visitors stared. I could not say a word, but the preceptress said, 'I shall mark you for disorder, Miss Morgan,' and shut the door. I was afraid Chum would be awfully put out, but she only laughed, and said the teachers often showed her room because it looked the nicest; and she hoped this would put a stop to it.

"We have half an hour for breakfast, but generally get through in fifteen minutes. Then some of the girls take a walk; but it is awfully poky going down a back street with one teacher ahead and one behind us; so Chum and I run up to our room and go to studying. At eight o'clock the chapel bell rings; there are nine classes to recite then. In forty minutes it rings again, and there is a crowd going up and down stairs and in and out of recitation-rooms every forty minutes all day, or until five o'clock, when we all go to chapel for evening prayers. The roll is called; then one professor reads a chapter from the Bible; then we all stand up while another professor prays; then another reads a hymn, and one of the music-teachers plays it on the melodeon while we all sing. There is a chapel choir, and I am in it, and sit on the front seat with some gentlemen. There are a good many more gentlemen than ladies here, and some of them are real nice. All the faculties (oughtn't it to be written plural when there are nine of them? 'No,' Chum says)—well, all the faculty want every student to enter the course; that means, take up ever so many studies that I don't see a bit of sense in and haven't any use for; study all night and recite all day (as Chum does), and have headaches, and weak eyes, and no leisure to write letters, or take walks, or have a bit of fun; and in two or three years stand up on the stage in the chapel, with a face as white as one's dress, to receive a diploma. The graduating class for this year are horrid-looking frights; and Chum—she is in next year's class—looks almost as bad. She has thirteen studies: geology and geometry, and analogy and anatomy, and French and German and Latin: I can't begin to tell you all. She confesses 'she don't understand half she learns, and don't half learn what she recites.' I just say over the words—to think what they all mean would make me crazy! she said just now, when I asked her to explain this sentence which she had written: 'If the major premises be negative, and we draw a universal conclusion, the minor term which was undistributed in the minor premises (being the predicate of an affirmative proposition) will be distributed in the conclusion (being the subject of a universal); we would therefore have an illicit process of the minor term.' Now, what good will learning that do anybody? I would like to learn about flowers and plants; but it seems wicked to pull the lovely little things to pieces. I went into the botany class yesterday, and they had some prince's-pine and arbutus on the table. The sight and the smell made me think of home, and of Bruce and I hunting for blossoms before the snow was all off the ground, and how the sweet, precious, cunning little things peeped out at me from under their broad, rough leaves, and how I went down on my knees and put my hands under them to lift them out of their mossy bed, and could have cried for gladness at finding them. They seemed so cosy and comfortable, I could not bear to cut them off the vine; so I brought them home to you, bed and all. Do you remember?

"Probably I lost the first of the lesson thinking of that, and wishing I could have one little tiny flower to look in my face, and tell me about the woods, when the teacher called 'Miss Montgomery,' and handed her just the loveliest pink arbutus, asking her to give its analysis; and Chum just picked the dear little flower all to pieces, and said it was, '*Epigœa:* Suffruticose; corolla, hypocrateriform; anthers dehiscent.' And then a gentleman took the trailing moss you put around the looking-glass, and said it was, '*Chimaphila umbelleta:* Leaves cunate-lanceolate, serrate; flowers corymbose.' And a stem of winter-green, with only two little leaves and one berry, was '*Gaultheria:* Procumbose; pedicels bibracteolate, denticulate; leaves obovate mucronate, denticulate,' and ever so much more of it. I know you told me which is the cup and the crown, and the petals and stamens, and the names of almost every plant about home, and what they are good for; and I want to know about all flowers; but learning pages of names will not teach me. Chum's brother (who is 'way down in Texas) sent her some flowers in a paper, asking their names and medicinal qualities. She counted their leaves, and described their shape with a lot of long words, yet could not tell him anything he wanted to know. Now, I should think a description of a plant ought to make a name, and the name ought to tell one how it looks, or what it is for, as plain as *red raspberry*, or *catnip*, or *morning-glory;* and why couldn't it? Dora says if I will learn Latin I can understand it better; but how absurd to go to a dead language to learn about living things! I am very anxious to learn about the earth —how different kinds of rocks were made, and all that; but there are long lists of words again that mean nothing, and what is given as a fact in one geology is contradicted in another. What are the Exact Sciences, mother? Nothing seems exact but the multiplication-table. All there is to be gained by studying these books is learning what other people have thought, and then thinking it out for one's self.

"Dora and I have been talking while I have written, and she says our minds are supposed to be like the Indian's stomach her brother writes about. They starve for weeks, and then stuff and stuff to last for weeks to come. So she hopes all she is cramming into her mind will digest by-and-by, and make her brain stronger and wiser. Chum is very wise now; she knows about everything I ask her. She will be rich and famous some day, she says; and she writes stories and verses for the papers now, and gets money for them sometimes. Then she writes the best essays of anybody, and reads them on the stage before all the students, and a lot of down-town people.

"And now, O mother dear! I must tell you something that troubles me very much. I wrote about my having to write compositions. Well, I did not mind that; but I could not stand up before the preceptress and all my class and read them. If it had been anybody else's thoughts, I wouldn't mind it a bit. So I asked Jennie Purcell to exchange compositions with me, and she did. The next time she asked me if I wanted to trade again, and as I could not read hers easily, I copied it before I went into class. After reading, we laid them on Miss Caldwell's desk to be corrected. When she gathered them up, she said, 'Here is one without a signature; is it yours, Miss Morgan?' 'Yes,' I said, for it was the one I had just read. I wanted to explain, but couldn't before all the girls, and, too, I was afraid she would make me read my own next time. Well, in a few days Jennie was promoted to the public class, and so she came to me to write her essay. I did not feel right about it, but she said she had exchanged just to accommodate me, and my style was so different from hers that the preceptress would notice it immediately, and then she would be disgraced. I told her I would go to Miss Caldwell and explain, but she declared that would make it worst of all; for she would be put back in the composition class, and all the students would know about it; and then she cried, and said she never would try to do a kind thing again to please anyone; for folks that asked favors, and got other folks into disgrace, were just the ones that wouldn't turn their hand over to help them out. Of course I wrote her essay, and last Friday night she stood up in a pink lawn dress, and read it before an audience of over six hundred. It sounded very well, and they cheered her and threw bouquets. And now I know she will come to me for her next essay, and I will have to write it; but I shall never read another composition of hers as my own. Well, I must stop writing now, for the bell has rung for lights out. Chum always puts the extinguisher on her little fluid lamp the minute the bell rings; then she drops the curtain and lights it again. Lots of girls do that; they have to, if their lessons are perfect. And Chum takes some kind of medicine to make her sleep nights, and a few drops of the same stuff to keep her awake in the daytime. She says she is going to stop it as soon as she has caught up with her class; for though she is ahead of them all in belles-lettres, and has read 'most everything, she is away behind them in mathematics; for she is putting the three years' course into two years.

"*Tuesday Morning.*—I have just got the nicest letter from Uncle Dave—it came in one to Miss Caldwell—and says I may begin music-lessons right away. Oh, I am so glad! I wanted to ever so much, but it costs twelve dollars, so I didn't say anything about it. And our professor of vocal music says he will give me private lessons if I will assist him in teaching a primary class. Isn't everything just splendid! This letter is very long; I have been two weeks writing it; but, before closing, I must tell you about our darning society. You know we do our own mending every Saturday, and so I proposed our meeting in each other's rooms with our work, and having some fun over it. We organized last Saturday with three officers—president, monitor, and critic. Every member is to give us a story, a song, or an original conundrum or riddle; failing once, she is suspended; failing on the next attendance, expelled. They elected me president, though I voted for Dora; she was made critic, and Virginia Parry monitor. Virgie is a very dignified, lady-like girl, and she insists we shall sit straight while sewing, and not raise the roof when we laugh. Well, we had the jolliest fun. Chum told a story about 'her darter, Sally Jones's, settin' eout.' I shall coax her to tell it to you and the boys if she comes home with me next vacation; and I do hope she will, for she has never lived in the *real, sure enough* country, and it would do her good. Well, we just screamed with laughter, and our monitor rapped on the table, and called 'Miss President! Miss President!' and I tried to say, 'Order, ladies!' when Dora would make up the funniest face, and say something comical about the 'six cracked plates that were jest as good as new,' and we would all shout out again. In the midst of the fun Miss Caldwell rapped—I knew she would—but no one else heard her, and I opened the door quietly, and she stepped in. All sat on the floor in a circle around Chum, with their eyes on her; and if they saw the preceptress, they pretended not to, and Chum went right on with her story—and she is the greatest mimic I ever saw; she beats Davy all to pieces—and in a minute Miss Caldwell was holding on to her sides, and tears of laughter were running down her face, when Dora suddenly sprang to her feet, saying, 'Young ladies, I am surprised at such levity in the preceptress's presence!' She couldn't scold, of course, but wiped her eyes and said she hoped we wouldn't be rude, and suggested an unfurnished room in the attic as a place of future meeting. That was a good idea; so we have swept it, and brushed down the cobwebs, and are going up there next Saturday. Well, we had two or three more stories, and I sang a Scotch song I learned from Bessie, and we had some riddles to guess. All the stockings were mended after a fashion. When the first bell for supper rang, I had just got in a frolicking humor, but Dora was doleful as a gravestone. That is the only thing I don't like about Chum; sometimes she is gay and very happy, and sometimes silent and sad for days together. When she wants to talk, I let my tongue loose; and when she don't, and I can't keep still, I run away. I am in Miss Caldwell's parlor real often. She is just as sweet and good as anybody can be, though lots of the girls say she is cross, and too strict, because they are too lazy or ugly to do right. Now, mother dear, I shall have to put two stamps on this letter, and please don't let the boys open it in the store, but just read parts of it to them. Give my love to them all, and to Bruce too. From your daughter MIRIAM."

The next week brought a letter from Ellensport, addressed by a strange hand. It read:

"MY DEAR MRS. MORGAN,—Please do not be alarmed at what I am about to tell you. Your daughter has met with an accident, but the doctor says it is not serious. If she had not been so brave, so heroic, so unselfish, it would never have happened. She might have remained uninjured and unscarred, though probably our seminary building and all its contents would now be a smouldering ruin; and Heaven alone knows how many lives might have been devoured by the fiery element. But I will hasten to give particulars. Yesterday morning we arose as usual at 5 A.M. A lady student rooming next to Mira and me rapped on the wall to ask if we had any fluid; her lamp was empty, and they had no light. The morning was rainy, and their room is always rather dark. Mira took her lamp to them, and had just returned to finish dressing, when we heard a scream. Mira rushed into the room, which seemed all ablaze, and with her bare hands tore off the table-cover, which was on fire, and stamped out the flames in the carpet; and when the students, teachers, and watchman came running at the cry of 'Fire!' there was not even a spark to be seen. They scolded the girls for screaming, and praised Miss Purcell for putting out the fire; and then we all went down to breakfast. I thought Mira had gone too, and, as we do not sit at the same table, did not miss her. When I returned to my room, there stood my dear chum at the open window, her arms outstretched in the rain and wind, and sobbing so pitifully! Going to her, I saw her poor arms were burned and blistered to her elbows, and her hands in even a worse state. The matron soon came and dressed them in Indian-meal and molasses. This increased her suffering; but now she has oil and flour on them, which has eased the pain. She is very patient, though she can neither feed nor dress herself. She does not know I am writing this; but I thought you ought to know all about it, and what a brave, sensible daughter you have. Mira now sits in my little rocker with her arms on a pillow in her lap. I got excused from one recitation on plea of a headache, to sit by her and write this letter. She is a dear girl! I love her more than anybody living, unless it is my mamma and brother Bruce. She shall not lack for anything I can do, though I lose my standing in class. With respectful regards to my dear Mira's mother, I am yours truly,

"DORA MONTGOMERY."

A few days later a note from Miss Caldwell enclosed a line from Miriam's own hand, assuring her mother that already she was able to study, and the pain of the burn decreasing.

"The confusion was so great at the time of the accident"—the preceptress wrote—"that I understood Miss Morgan to be the cause of the conflagration, and that Miss Purcell extinguished it. It was so reported in the chapel, and the president censured Miss Morgan severely. Later, however, all was explained by Miss Montgomery, who is very enthusiastic in praise of her room-mate. The accident was caused by Miss Purcell's attempting to pour the burning-fluid from your daughter's lamp into her own while one was lighted; a thing not likely to again occur in the lives of any students here, nor in the history of this school."

Week followed week, and one by one the school duties were resumed; but the bandaged fingers could neither use slate and pencil nor practise the music-lessons just begun.

"Miss Caldwell told me to ask you to come to her parlor, Mira," her room-mate said one evening.

The girl raised herself from the bed wearily; "Anything gone wrong, Dora?"

"No, I think not; she looked perfectly radiant."

Miriam walked slowly down the hall, and tapped at the preceptress's door, then entered, saying, "Dora said"—gave a quick scream of delight, and was clasped, sobbing, in her uncle's arms.

"My precious little girl," he said, kissing her again and again, "I did not know you were so badly burned, or I would have come before. But don't cry now, when you are almost well; for I have a nice plan to propose to Miss Caldwell for your benefit. And to-morrow, if we can arrange it, we will take the long-deferred trip to the sea-shore."

It was soon arranged. Mr. Walton was to call with a carriage at eight o'clock the next morning for Miss Caldwell, Dora, and Miriam.

"I'm just as happy as I can be! But oh, if mother were only here!" she exclaimed.

Her uncle laughed. "Consistent mortal! perfectly happy, *but*— Your mother and I have had many a frolic on the sea-shore, Birdie," he said, putting his arms around her; "and if you write her of to-morrow's jaunt, it will undoubtedly recall a happy day she once spent with me at Cape May."

These poems were the outgrowth of the day's impressions:

The scent of roses fills the air,
And morning clouds a rose tint wear!

The breath of *this* year's rose I feel;
While *last* year's rose the clouds reveal.
The body clasped within my hand,
The spirit floats in bright cloud-land.
O earth so fair! O life so sweet!
O sunlit Ocean! thee we greet,
And claim a kinship now with thee,
In one glad song of ecstasy!

Lightly the bright waves kiss the shore,
Rippling with laughter evermore:
Tossing its gifts with proud disdain—
Yet 'neath its mirth, list its refrain!
Deep and sad is the Ocean's moan,
A lonely yearning, a solemn tone!
Bubbles reflect the sunbeam's ray
Wrought by the storm of yesterday:
While waves that shine upon the sands
Were floating ice in snow-bound lands.

My mirth thus on the surface lies,
Reflects the light of happy eyes,
Thoughts glide from cold to torrid zone,
And make their chill or warmth its own.
While 'neath my joy is hidden pain;
My gayest song a sad refrain.

The Ocean was out for a holiday,
 And so were we.
We love to leap, and dance, and play,
 And so does he.
We saw him beckoning foam-wreathed hands,
Then met him on the shining sands.
And, oh, a jolly time had we
Frolicking with the grand old sea!

A blue wave trimmed with silvery lace,
 Came up to me.
"Come, child," it said: I gave it chase
 In thoughtless glee.

It turned and quickly splashed my feet,
Gave me no time to make retreat,
Then rippled o'er with jollity:
This merriest, maddest, foam-capped sea.

"Take that," I said, throwing a rubber ball.
 It disappeared;
No mermaid brought it at my call;
 But, as I feared
My ball had found a watery grave,
Henceforth a toy in Nereid's cave,
It tossed and rolled it back to me:
The playful, tricksy, mirthful sea!

But hark ye! What means that deep, sullen roar?
 It comes more near!
And the waves look dark, and fierce, and cold,
 And the sky grows drear.
Oh, deep are the waters, and dark, and wide:
Strong and far-reaching its ceaseless tide!
Weak atoms beside it, frail mites are we:
I'm frightened at thoughts of the boundless sea!

One soon appeared in the poet's corner of a county newspaper—"Written expressly for the *Luminary*"—and the other was tucked away in a wooden box beneath all the clothing in Miriam's trunk.

"What do you keep in that box, Mira?" Dora inquired one day, when, suddenly entering the room, she found her arranging some faded flowers and scraps of paper.

"Bottled sunshine, Chum, for cloudy days," she said, closing the lid quickly, and putting the box away.

CHAPTER XV.

"Knowest thou Yesterday, its aims and reasons?
Workest thou well To-day for worthy things?
Then calmly wait To-morrow's hidden season,
And fear not thou what fate so'er it brings."
CARLYLE.

"NINE days, eleven hours, and thirty-five minutes to vacation! I'm the gladdest girl you ever did see, mother dear; for, after hesitating so long, Dora has consented to come home with me, and I'm just bubbling over with happiness. She is so intensely honorable that she insists I should know all about her past life before she would go to my home. Now, I do hate to know people's secrets! I feel as if carrying a key to their trunk; and if anything were lost, I might be thought the thief. Besides, I have thoughts *I* cannot tell, and I am perfectly willing *she* should. But when I saw she was unhappy about it, and said she never would enter our home until you knew all about her, I consented to listen; so here is my dear friend's sad history.

"Her father was an actor, and her mother ran away from home to marry him. She was disowned by all her friends; and when her father died, his property went to her brother, Dora's uncle. There were two children—my chum (Medora Melinda Montgomery), and a boy thirteen years older (Bruce Hamlet Henry Theodore Montgomery). All the children between them died when they were babies. Dora cannot remember her father, but she has his picture painted on ivory, and he looks very handsome, though his face does not seem strong and good. But Dora says he was *too good to live*, and so God took him. I think they were very poor while he lived, and Dora's mother was sick all the time. She says the first thing she remembers is the greenroom of a theatre, and her delight at the gay dresses of the actresses. She says their family would all have died had it not been for the kindness of the company her father belonged to. And after he died they supported them for a long time, her brother doing what he could at the theatre; and Dora, little thing as she was, they carried on the stage, in children's parts, several times. After a while, Mrs. Montgomery's brother, who was a widower and had no children, sent for her to come and live with him. He has educated Bruce for a civil engineer; and he is now surveying lands in Texas. Dora, he expects, will be a teacher, but she means to make money by writing books, and be independent of her uncle very soon. She is determined to graduate with honor, as a diploma does any one credit; and to write well one needs to know something about everything. There! now you know the whole of it; and I know it won't make one bit of difference with your love for her: you will pet her the more; for I don't think she ever had much petting. Uncle is coming for us, and we are going to stay a day or two in Philadelphia, and then 'Home, home! sweet, sweet home!'

"P.S.—Where is father? Is he willing I should have company? I do hope he will like Dora."

The day or two in Philadelphia lengthened into a week. Dora, accustomed from infancy to the whims of a querulous invalid, adapted herself to Mrs. Walton's fancy, coaxing her to join in their pleasures, or remaining at home to amuse her, leaving Mr. Walton free to accompany Miriam to evening entertainments.

"I have lived in the city all my life," she said, resisting Miriam's urgent invitations; "have seen both sides of stage life, and really prefer staying with Mrs. Walton."

No one guessed the earnest but futile attempts at serious conversation, or with what repugnance she resumed the reading of the French novel handed her; the sneering infidelity of this ailing woman being harder to endure than the morbid melancholy of her mother. But at last the visit was ended; and Miriam, with many new scenes and sensations to describe to the loved ones at home, resumed her journey, her uncle and Dora accompanying her. The Erie was still a single-track railroad, and accidents and detentions frequent. The setting sun gilded the river, and lingered on the vine-covered porch, where Mrs. Morgan stood waiting.

"Is the train so late to-night, Jamie, or am I very impatient?" she said, looking eagerly down the depot road.

"Both, mother. Davy went half an hour sooner than he need to. If the travellers are as hungry as I, I trust there's a bountiful supper."

"Oh, we have enough: fricasseed chicken, muffins, maple syrup, strawberries and cream, cottage-cheese— I haven't forgotten Miriam's favorites, nor brother David's either."

"Whew! I'm still more hungry! What sort of a girl do you think this friend of Miriam's is? She is too enthusiastic over her to suit me; I don't think I shall fancy her."

"Jamie, do you remember the young man who boarded here for a while when they were building the railroad? Theodore we called him."

"Yes; why?"

"I half believe, recalling several things he said, that he is— Oh, there they come! My precious daughter!"

Happy days followed. Mrs. Morgan often joined her brother in long drives about the country; and once the big hay-wagon carried the whole family, including Jack, to a lake four miles away, and the day was spent in fishing, picking berries, lounging in the shade, and cooking the perch and pickerel, gypsy fashion, for their picnic dinner.

"I feel twenty years younger for this visit," Mr. Walton said, on the evening of his departure.

"And I — oh, uncle, I feel older, wiser, better, for every hour I have spent with you! How lonely we will be without you!" And Miriam slipped her hand in his, as she joined in his walk up and down the room.

"Mira almost idolizes her uncle," Dora said, with a half-sigh. "Had my papa lived, I fancy he would have been like Mr. Walton. There is nothing can atone to a girl for a father's loss. She needs his loving counsel and protection more and more as she grows older."

"Cannot a mother's love make up the loss?"

"No, ma'am, I think not. It seems to me that boys need a mother's gentle restraint and caressing tenderness more than her daughters do. But every day I want my father! A woman sees life differently from a man. She must look at it through his eyes also, if she sees it rightly. I want my father's criticism in my writing; I want his advice in my plans; I need his influence with editors and publishers. But he is gone!"

"My dear child, did you never think how much this ideal father has helped you? I once had a sister several years older than myself: she died when I was a little girl, but I often heard of her goodness and beauty—how unselfish she was, and how patient during a long illness. And though I have always longed for her, I believe that sister has been a greater blessing to me than if she had lived."

"I do not understand that."

"Why, the sister I love and have always tried to imitate is something more than human: *she is perfect*. Had I known a fault in her character, she would have had less influence."

A long silence, in which the cricket's chirr and the far-away whippoorwill's song blended, but did not break. Dora drew her chair closer to Mrs. Morgan, and murmured, "Will we know our friends in heaven, do you think?"

"My child," she answered, "death has always been a very real thing to me. Nature often gives me warnings that her hold can be quickly broken; and I have often fancied what the spirit would feel when released from the body. Now we are bound by the laws of matter. We see a place where we wish to be: step by step, inch by inch, we go on until it is reached. But, freed from the body, the desire would take us there with one bound! So I think the freed spirit hovers an instant till a desire stronger than all others propels it to that object."

"I should fly to my father's arms!"

"Those who have friends in the spirit-land love them for some special quality. The mother loves her babe because it depends on her, and she has suffered for it. The child loves the mother because it trusts and needs her. We love our friends for their charity or sympathy. Now, all these qualities are the *God in us* going out to the *God in them;* and all these qualities diluted and perverted in us are perfect in Christ. If, then, our eyes have been opened, if we are justified by his love, our strongest desire is to him, always to him. And when we put off this body, oh, what bliss to see him as he is!" The thin hands clasped, the dark eyes closed, and the lips parted with a smile. A moonbeam struggling through vine-leaves rested on her face.

Mr. Walton and Miriam paused in their walk. "Mary," he said, softly.

Miriam sprang forward.

"Mother, mother! oh, forgive me!" as Mrs. Morgan started up. "I thought —I was afraid— Why, you looked like an angel! And you, Dora, do come out of that corner. I declare you look like a ghost in that white dress! Let's go to the store, and see what the boys are doing; and let Uncle David and mother have an old-fashion visit. Jack went to the depot this evening with a lumber-wagon; maybe the new goods have come. Oh, don't it seem good to be free to run out at night? I felt as though I should break every one of those exasperating rules that were tacked on every door —thirty-nine separate temptations to rebellion. I have wondered if Eve would ever have looked at that apple-tree, if there had been no 'Thou shalt not' pointing her to it. Oh, Dora, what do you say to going to the big picnic at Chehocton?"

"She-hawk-ton! What a funny name!"

"Yes, the Indians called it Shauwanetung—the two rivers made one. There is an Indian burying-ground there. But shall we go to the picnic?"

"Oh, Mira! don't let's go anywhere, or do anything, but read, and rest, and talk with your mother. And I would be so glad to learn cooking and baking. I never had any chance to learn before."

"That will suit me, for I have lots of sewing to do. Uncle says I can go back to school with you, and I'm so glad. What are those boys about?"

They paused before the open door of the store. Jamie and Jack were on their knees beside a box on the floor, and Davy held a lamp above them.

"What are they doing?" whispered Miriam.

"Hush! it can't be a secret with the door wide open. Let's keep quiet and watch them."

The boys slowly raised a dark shining box from the large wooden one on the floor.

"Oh, Dora! it looks like a little coffin."

"Hush! hush! I know what it is: it's a present for you. Now, don't let's spoil their fun, but run to Mr. Morris's for a little while." And, putting her arm around her, she drew her down the road.

"A present? How do you know? What is it?"

"Don't be so inquisitive; it's something real nice; and I'll give you lessons, and we'll practise duets and sing. There! what a ridiculous blunderer I am! But don't have hysterics over it; I declare if she isn't laughing and crying all together! Lunar rainbows trickling down her cheeks."

"Oh, Dora, is it a *melodeon*, do you think? I'm afraid you are mistaken."

"I know I am not; but you wait

and see. Don't spoil the giver's pleasure by showing you know all about it."

"It must be from uncle, and he has given me so much already. How can I ever repay him?"

"By just growing up the true, brave, energetic, thorough-bred lady he expects you to be. Did he ever tell you he knew my mamma when she was a young lady?"

"Why, no!"

"It was yesterday when we were out rowing, he and Davy and I, while you were getting supper. Some nonsense I said to Davy made him look at me curiously, and I feared he thought me rude; but he asked suddenly, 'What was your mother's maiden name?' 'Clara Lemar,' I answered. '*Then that's it,*' he said. 'Again and again it has seemed to me that I had known you before we met at Ellensport, and now it is explained. Child, I danced with your mother at the governor's ball in Richmond; called upon her, sent her bouquets, followed her to her father's plantation, and might have thrown hand, heart, and fortune at her feet, had not such a crowd of admirers surrounded her continually that I knew she would never condescend to accept the best I could offer. She was the handsomest, most fascinating woman I ever met. And a Mr. Montgomery won the prize! Was he a resident of Richmond?' Just fancy, Mira, how hard it was for me to hear and answer that! I only told him that my father was from New Orleans, and took mamma there; that her health failed, and she had been an invalid ever since I could remember. Then came another queer turn to the talk. Davy asked me if my brother Bruce (how absurd to hear you call that homely, cross dog, *Bruce!*), if he had—"

"Homely? Cross? Why, Dora Montgomery! he has the handsomest eyes, and he's just the best—"

"Well, there; I apologize! I respect his age if I cannot admire his beauty. But to proceed with my story—let's sit down on this log—Davy asked if my brother was not a civil engineer on this railroad. He said there was a young man named Theodore Montgomery boarded at your house for three or four months while they were building the road. I could not tell him, but I'm going to write Bruce about it. Wouldn't it be funny? But you're not half listening. Come, we'll walk home now."

As they reached the cottage, the sweet harmony of melodeon and violin wavered in the air.

"Oh, it is! it is!" And with a bound Miriam left her companion, hurried through the gate, rushed up the walk, and entered the room. The music ended with a crash of chords and loud laughter as she threw her arms around the musician's neck, crying, "Oh, you dear, blessed uncle! I wanted it more than anything else in the world. Oh, I'm glad as glad can be!"

"Well, well, child! I'm glad too; but you are choking and thanking the wrong man. This is the boys' gift."

"Oh, Jamie! Davy! I'm so grateful! and Jack"—with a timid, expectant tone—"was it Jack, too?"

"Yes, 'twas Jack's suggestion,"

Davy replied: "thoroughly selfish on his part, for he wanted an accompaniment to his violin. But you interrupted that schottische just as Jamie and I were going to take a turn. Now I'll resign him to you. Miss Dora, will you honor me for the next dance? Now go ahead, fiddler!"

Up and down, round and round whirled the two couples—faster and faster flew the violin-bow—laughing, panting, till snap! went a violin-string; and Jack stooped over Mr. Walton's shoulder, and whispered three words. "Better pass it off as your gift and save a storm," he added.

Mr. Walton looked perplexed, troubled, as he gazed searchingly into Jack's face. "Is it so bad as that?" he said.

Jack glanced out of the window, where a horseman was dismounting.

"What is the matter?" the dancers inquired. "Is your violin broken?"

"I don't believe I can play any more to-night," putting the violin into its case; "we'll finish that dance some other time. Isn't that somebody coming here?"

Miriam glanced through the window. "It is father!" she said, her face turning pale, as she went to her mother and put her hand in hers.

Davy caught up the violin and carried it up-stairs, whispering a sentence in his uncle's ear as he passed him.

Mr. Walton sprang up as Mr. Morgan entered. "Ah, how do you do, John? Come near missing me altogether, as I leave to-morrow. I brought your little girl back safe and well; wiser, and prettier too," as Miriam came shyly forward with outstretched hand, and raised her face to be kissed.

The father took the caress kindly, saying, "I see she is taller, and I guess she looks as well as most girls."

"And this," continued Mr. Walton, "is another one of my girls that I'll lend you until school begins—Miss Dora Montgomery, Miriam's roommate."

He shook hands with her. "Your cheeks are too thin and pale for a country girl. We'll try and fat you up if you stay here all summer. Wife, I haven't had any dinner or supper to-day. The jury was a set of fools; decided right contrary to evidence after being out three hours. Had no time to get anything to eat and get home to-night."

"Then you lost the suit?"

"Yes, it went against me this time; but I shall carry it up. What have you got there?" pointing to the melodeon.

"Why, the girls have taken music-lessons while at school, and I don't want them to forget what they know; so they have an instrument to practise on."

"Well, if it's yours, it can stay here; but I'm not going to have money wasted on such fol-de-rols! And I don't want you to put any nonsense into Miryum's head. She's got to settle down into a plain, practical housekeeper, like her mother, some day."

"But if she has talents for something higher, you have no objections to their development?"

"Something *higher!* There isn't anything higher than doing the duties of your position — the position one is born to fill. My children have their work planned before them every day; their business is to do it well. All this talk about talents and spheres is disgusting. Miryum, tell your mother to make some good, strong tea; my head aches. Davy, have you collected that note of Saul Perkins?"

"Yes, sir."

"Did I ever tell you that story about Squire Noyes preaching here, Walton?" settling himself in an easy-chair. "No? Well, it's a pretty good one. You see, when we first came here my wife was very anxious to have religious services every Sunday; and she fitted up one wing of the store for a school, and got me to read a sermon to the natives one Sunday morning. Then she tried an old Baptist elder from the cook-house; and finally Squire Noyes came to the rescue. My wife was hardly satisfied, but he was so zealous over the matter that he took it right out of her hands, and announced far and near that he would preach in her school-room the next Sunday. He was a regular horse-jockey, a pettifogger of a lawyer, a farmer, lumberman, speculator, justice of the peace, and a local preacher in the Methodist Church. He was on a sheep-buying tour all the week, and managed to advertise the meeting so thoroughly that the room was crowded, and the log fences and lumber piles were filled with his congregation, while over twenty babies were left here as their mothers went to meeting. Mary and the boys did most of the singing; he called upon me for the opening prayer; then got up and announced his text: 'Saul, Saul, why persecutest thou me?' He looked steadily at his congregation a minute, then read it again. 'Saul, Saul, why persecutest thou me?' Up jumped Saul Perkins, and yelled out, 'It's a blamed lie, Squire Noyes, an' you know it! I never prosecuted you nor any other man; an' *if you say it agin, I'll thrash ye!'*"

In the midst of the laughter which followed, Mrs. Morgan called her husband to supper.

"Your father will not fancy our music, Mira dear, so we will try and time our practice when he is too far away to be annoyed by it; and when we learn some of the songs I have in my trunk, he will enjoy it as much as anybody, you'll see," Dora said, caressingly. "Mr. Walton, do you think I can learn to cook and make pies, cake, and bread as nicely as Mira does?"

"No doubt of it. Do you intend trying?"

"Yes, sir. At uncle's there are twelve servants and a house-keeper. I always had a maid to do what I ought to have done for myself. I laugh whenever I think of my first attempts at sweeping my room at the Seminary. My ideal woman, Mr. Walton, is one who considers nothing useful beneath or beyond her ability."

"Good! Then you believe in woman's rights?"

"Certainly; whatever she has strength of body and mind to accomplish *thoroughly* is right for her to do."

"Good! and no woman is fit to preside over a house until she understands every branch of house-keeping. Now let us sing that grand old hymn,

"'Jesus, lover of my soul!
Let me to thy bosom fly.'

Jack, will you take the tenor? Dora, you sing alto; Jamie and Davy, bass; and Mira and I will carry the air."

A gentle prelude from the melodeon, then the voices blended in the supplication. Mrs. Morgan sat silent, with closed eyes, joining each petition with a fervor the younger people could not know. A few pages from Dora's letter to her brother tells the history of the following weeks:

"In this hollow 'mid the hills live the most charming people! My chum I have described to you; but she grows prettier every day—the purest complexion, flushing and paling into loveliest tints; long thick braids of nut-brown hair; perfect teeth; scarlet lips, just pouting for kisses; and eyes — oh, Bruce! I wish you could look into her eyes. Their color, like her complexion, varies with every change of thought; but they look so true and earnest and brave. But there! you will call this a lover's rhapsody, as you did before. I just wish you could see her! Her brother Jamie is a fine-looking man, rather quiet, and very good. Davy is more my style; no one can be sad or gloomy where he is. He is not as handsome as his brother; but his face is so sunny, and his eyes sparkle with fun; while Jamie's have a steady, intense light in them that is beyond my comprehension. They all have a timid or defiant manner toward their father. I have seen nothing so terrible in him; but he is a loud-spoken, positive kind of a man, who never acknowledges a fault in himself and sees no end of them in other people. I like to hear him tell stories, and it pleases Mira; so I often go to him when he sits smoking on the porch, and ask questions about the country and the people who were here when they came. He told me about a man I saw in the store to-day, a funny old chap, who talked rapidly and incessantly. Years ago he was on a raft going down the river, and saw a locomotive for the first time. As it puffed out great clouds of smoke and fire, he shouted, 'What's that?' 'The devil, Dick; he's after you,' said the men. Just then the whistle sounded, and Dick gave a yell and jumped into the river. The raft passed over him, and while the men were trying to save him, it struck a rock and stove all in pieces; but after the train passed, he swam ashore. The cars are still a great curiosity to the natives. Another funny story is of a man called K'neal. He has an enormous nasal appendage, out of all proportion to his face. He says the only objection he has to it is when he stoops to drink out of a spring—his nose riles the water! and these mountain springs are not shallow.

"I have quite a number of queer folks and strange incidents to weave into my stories. I like the place and people immensely. But Mira, though born and brought up here, has an intense dislike to the uncouth manners of the people. We were invited to Auntie Rodgers's, as they call Jack's mother, to spend the afternoon. We took our work and went over there about two o'clock. It was the richest kind of fun for me to get the old lady talking about old times. Her expressions are so quaint and original, and her piety so fervent and emphatic. But Mira was annoyed at something, and provoked at me for drawing the old lady out; for she knew I was just getting an odd character to imitate; so she found one of Jack's books, and sat under a tree near the house till Jack came.

"The old lady had reached the climax of her story when they entered, so she bustled about to get supper. And such a supper! There were 'meat victuals for the men folks,' eggs, bread, and biscuits and butter, honey and custard, raspberries, and two kinds of pie and three kinds of cake — I really don't know what else. The men *slooped* and *gulped* their food, and put their knives 'way into their mouths; and when one man picked his teeth with his fork, I saw Mira shudder; and after another had reached across her plate and with his own knife cut off a bit of butter, spread it on a slice of bread, took a huge bite, then, stretching out his coatless arm, sliced another bit, Mira leaned back in her chair with such a look of suffering on her face I felt sorry for her. Fortunately, the men folks were soon *gorged* — that really seems a most appropriate word — pushed back their chairs, and went away. Then Auntie Rodgers and I finished our tea at leisure, while Mira and Jack talked and sang together. His mother says 'Jack lots a powerful sight on Miryum;' that he 'sort o' took to her when she wa'n't knee-high to a grasshopper, and he don't seem to git over it a mite;' adding, 'Wall, my Jack's a powerful good boy, ef I dew say it!' I agree with her; he seems good, and is handsome: dark-blue eyes and jet-black hair, heavy side-whiskers, firm well-curved lips, and the whitest of white teeth. He is taller than Jamie or Davy, and, at first thought, finer-looking. He is treated like one of the family, and seems to take the same interest in the business. If Mira was not so fastidious, I might be a little anxious; but there is no man good enough for my Mira. I told Mrs. Morgan about her annoyance at Auntie Rodgers's table. 'Poor child!' she said, 'she cannot help it! These strong prejudices are inherited. She tries to overcome them, but she never will.'

"I have said nothing about Mira's mother, because I have no words to express my admiration or my love. Cultured, refined, with little adaptiveness, this life in the woods has been a daily martyrdom to her. She has told me of her efforts to make the cottage (which is the same cabin they first moved into, built over, and added to) the *home* she desired her children reared in. It would be comical, if not so pathetic, to hear of her labors. They painted the wood-work of the rooms with a mixture of blue clay and milk — before they could get white-lead — renewing when soiled or worn. She covered the ceiling overhead with white muslin, and made oil-cloth by painting canvas in a pattern of her own invention. Vines and shrubs surround the house, brought from the woods by her own hands. Two huge pine-trees clasp arms over the gate; a hemlock hedge surrounds the flower-garden; a rustic arbor, all overgrown with wild grapevine, is in the centre of one grass-plot, and a mound of flowers on the other side of the stone walk that leads to the door; a veranda runs across the front under the eaves, and an entry opens into two large square rooms. The one next the river has a striped carpet, a table, and some hanging shelves filled with books, a lounge, and chairs cushioned with crimson cloth. White-muslin curtains at the windows, and vines and pressed ferns are on the mantle and around the mirror, while little shelves holding vases of flowers are in the corners. The other room (whichever apartment we speak of, the other is distinguished as *the other room*) is carpeted with white sand; each alternate board has a wavy figure down its whole length made by Mrs. Morgan's broom. This carpet is taken up every morning; and as there is a wholesale store of it on the river beach, a new one every day is not considered extravagant.

"Mira teaches me to mix bread, work over butter, and make cake and pie; for I am resolved to learn every useful thing I can. Mrs. Morgan superintends our labors. There are also closets, a pantry, and a milk-room where the water runs around the pans of cream and jars of butter. A summer-kitchen has been added to the west end of the house, where all cooking and baking are done. A spring from the mountain brings water to the back door; and there it pours a steady stream from a wooden spout—so cool and refreshing. Since writing this, some remark of Mira's reminded me of a query of Davy's. He said there was once a young man here, whose name was Theodore Montgomery, and inquired if it was my brother.

"*Evening.*—Oh, my dear brother, how strange! Indeed truth *is* stranger than fiction! I have just returned from Mrs. Morgan's room, where I had been assisting with the week's mending. She told me of the Theodore she liked so much, and then put a book and a faded daguerrotype in my hand. I opened the red morocco case; and there was the same dear good-natured face mamma has in her locket and cries over so often. I could hardly believe my eyes! I opened the book—there was your name plain enough—'To my Kind Counsellor and Valued Friend, Mrs. J. Morgan, from B. H. H. T. Montgomery.' There could be no mistake! She put her arms around me and kissed me so lovingly, saying, 'The dear boy is in Texas, you said. How far away that seems! But I am very glad to know he lives, and is doing well.' Then she told me how much you helped her by your example in training her boys. You were 'always so neat and polite, so attentive to her wants, so graceful and well-bred.' Hasn't your right ear burned all this afternoon, I wonder? They are calling me to go boat-riding. Hoping to receive a letter from you before I leave here, I remain, your affectionate sister,

"DORA."

CHAPTER XVI.

*"Is it true, O God in heaven, that the strongest suffer most?
That the noblest wander farthest, and most hopelessly are lost?
That the highest type of nature is capacity for gain?
That the sadness of the singer makes the sweetness of the strain?"*
Author Unknown.

THE Christmas vacation was over; and from North and South, East and West, came the students of Ellensport Seminary.

"I'm heartily glad to begin study again, aren't you, Mira?" Dora said, as she was hanging her new dresses in the wardrobe.

"Yes; but I had a real good time at Virgie's home. It is a perfect curiosity shop from the parlors to the attic. The whole family are 'travellers and sojourners,' and several are sailors: their corals and shells and fossils are just wonderful! And they have cases of stuffed birds and animals, and specimens of fancy-work of Indians and Africans. Then everything has its story, from the anaconda coiled over Major Torry's desk to the pearl brooch at madam's throat. And there is a conservatory full of flowers, and a library full of books, and a bowling-alley, and ponies to ride. Virgie has her own carriage and ponies, and a footman in livery to ride behind on a gray pony. Oh, it was lovely! And they all invited me to come again, as if they really wanted me to. Did you enjoy the vacation? You look thinner and paler than when school closed. Now, Chum, you must not study so late at night: it is just killing you."

"Mira, this is my last year at school. I stand first in my class, and I wouldn't miss taking the honors for *anything*."

"Not even for health?"

"Oh, I'll get over this nervousness as soon as I have won the prize. The president says ours is the best class he has ever graduated."

"Yes; he made that same remark to last year's graduates, I remember. Probably they grow better and better till they die of it!"

"Miriam, you are very provoking."

"Forgive me, Dora. You know I wouldn't offend you for anything in the world; but to see you so sad and pale, in almost constant pain, and yet forcing yourself to work for what really doesn't seem to me worth winning — my dear chum, *I* get provoked too."

A laugh followed, that rippled over tears. "Kiss me, Mira. Now, let's each 'gang our ain gait,' as Bessie would say, and quietly submit to what we can't enjoy."

"Will you go on with French?"

"Yes; I intend to read 'Corinne,' though I'm sure our Yankee teachers' pronunciation would never be understood by a Parisian. I find I can read in the library from eight to ten, and then practise one hour and study until dinner. After dinner come recitations until prayers; then I put in another hour's practice. In the evening I mean to read poetry, saving the coarsest print for lamplight. Chemistry and German recite at the same bell this term. I'm sorry, for I wanted to begin German. Professor Clark advised me to give a half bell to each; but I don't enjoy half doing things, so I shall study chemistry. Are there many new students?"

"Several gentlemen—one real handsome one at my table; he looks like Jack. You needn't try to get him down to your section, though, as you did those interesting Barnhams."

"Now, Dora, you know I got Mr. Smith to ask them to come, because you made fun of them."

"Mira Morgan, we did not."

"Well, you got them to talking about *crops*, and the best way to *fat beef*, and then foppish Paul Percy would sneer. I saw one of your gentlemen hold his hand over Tom Burnham's head, as if to warm his fingers, and then frown as though he burned them. Tom can't help his hair being as red as a live coal, and he's a real good student; while that Paul Percy, with his superior smile and gold fob-chain, never recites well. Who will room with Jennie Purcell this term?"

"A new student—an awkward, sullen-faced country girl. She was dressed in homespun, or something equally ridiculous, and her face was red, and eyes swollen from crying."

"Poor thing! she is homesick. I know just how to sympathize with her."

"Yes, you can sympathize with every one. Jen' prefers an unsophisticated creature that will stare with admiration at her cheap jewellery and her great bundles of love-letters. By-the-way, that Jim M'Gowan was requested not to return to Ellensport Seminary, so that flirtation is ended. How such a sentimental piece as Jennie Purcell can write such spicy compositions is a mystery to me."

Miriam's face flushed crimson.

"You'll be in the public class this term. Your modesty and Miss Caldwell's clemency will avail no longer. But why do you look so conscience-smitten?"

"Because I *am*, Dora; I have written all Jennie Purcell's essays."

"Miriam Morgan! don't you know that is considered a very disgraceful thing to do?"

"Wait until you have heard the whole story."

"Now, I do not wish to be too severe a judge of Jennie," she said, when all was told. "She has not a fine sense of honor, and she is naturally very lazy. I see now I was foolish and did wrong; while she, in obliging me—"

"Mira, you are a goose!"

"Yes, Chum."

"The double-distilled quintessence of imbecility permeates the perspicaciousness by which your mentality is illuminated. I shall go to Miss Caldwell—"

"Oh, Chum, please don't!"

"And tell my *suspicions*. She will request Miss Purcell to write her next essay in her presence. Oh, Miss Caldwell has managed more difficult cases than this without any noise. You may as well begin to collect your thoughts for your essay. What will be the subject?"

"An address to this Old Friend," holding up a well-worn shoe. "It is an earth-worn traveller. Its sole has been bound to mine while climbing the rough steeps of life and passing through deep waters. Oft has it shielded me from unseen dangers. It knows the ways of the world; it has experienced the ups and downs of life. But the voice that once sounded through these classic halls is forever hushed! The *tongue* is silent; the *last tie* severed! Though mourning over its premature departure, I had no power to heel!"

"What pathos! Put that into rhyme, Mira; it will be capital."

The books were on the study table; the wax-candles, which Mr. Walton had substituted for the dangerous burning-fluid, were lighted, and Mira revelled in the fortunes of "The Faery Queen," while Dora puzzled over a problem in conic sections.

"Oh, Dora, just listen to one sentence! It is splendid! When Sir Arthur is—"

"Please don't bother me! 'There is a property of the above polynomial quotient which belongs exclusively to equations, containing only imaginary roots.' Oh, dear! I cannot get this lesson; and I wouldn't fail in a recitation now for the world! Oh, what shall I do!" And, rising, she went to the wardrobe and took a small bottle from the shelf.

"Chum, don't you think those drops do you more harm than good?"

"I suppose they would in time; but I shall stop using them as soon as my studies are finished."

"But you take them so much oftener than you did last year."

"I don't take the bitter stuff any oftener than I have to. Virgie Torry takes more opium in one day than I do in three."

"Poor Virgie! She told me she began it when she was suffering heart-sorrow, and could not sleep without an opiate. I think her parents sent her here to get her away from a lover. She corresponds with him, though."

"And it will end in an elopement probably: these quiet, dignified girls are so deep! Well, I wish I had no more pain in my head than I have in my heart. Yesterday the neuralgia came on earlier. I had been to the principal's room to see if the review of trigonometry was added to this term, and just as I came out I thought something struck me on this side of my head; I know I screamed or groaned. My head was numb for a second, and then, if it had been shattered into a million fragments I could not have been in more agony. How I got to my room I don't know; and if I had not had these drops, I should have died with the pain."

"But if you should take too much?"
"Oh, I shall not; I always drop it carefully in the spoon," and, picking up her book and slate, she again forced herself to study. But the pain in her left eye grew intolerable. She sprang suddenly from her chair, seized the bottle, and with shaking hand tried to pour out the desired quantity.

"Let me do it, Chum."

She raised the spoonful to her lips, shuddered, then swallowed it quickly, and staggered to the bed. "Don't bother me," she muttered; "let me sleep if I can."

The first dose had just taken effect, and in a moment she seemed sleeping, though her forehead was contracted with pain, and her face and eyes twitched constantly.

A half-hour passed. Miriam had removed the sleeper's shoes, unfastened her dress, bathed her face gently; but her breathing grew heavier—the eyeballs seemed dilated, and the eyelids were half open. The lips, dry and white, were parted in a ghastly smile; and her dark curling hair, moist with perspiration, clung to the livid face.

Miriam tried once more to rouse her, then ran quickly from the room. "Virgie may know what to do," she thought; "and the faculty will make a time if it is reported."

One glance at Dora's face, and Virgie said, "Open the windows, and raise her head. Now, keep quiet until I come back."

The minutes seemed hours until she returned. "Came within one of getting caught by the matron! But one of the dining-room girls has often given me cold coffee to drink at night, and I helped myself to salt and mustard. Now, raise her up. She's got to swallow this emetic, and when the opium is off her stomach we will make her drink the coffee."

An hour later, Dora sat in a rocker before the open window, the wintry air blowing full on her pallid face.

"She will be all right to-morrow, I think, though I cannot tell how much opium may be in her system. She may sink back in that stupor again. Dora," she cried, shaking the helpless body, "do wake up!"

"Oh, let me rest," she murmured, "*do let me rest!*"

"Had I not better call the preceptress?" Miriam asked, as they tried for the second time to make Dora walk across the room, and then bore her fainting to the bed, where her heavy breathing warned them she must be instantly roused.

"No, no! If we get tired out, I'll call Kate Hadley. In two hours more the danger will be over. If the story gets into the papers, as it will, if any but ourselves know it, the school's reputation would be injured, and then the faculty and board of managers would make an example of Dora."

Another hour of unceasing effort passed, and Virgie sank, half fainting, in a chair. "You may call Kate," she gasped.

Miriam's slippered feet ran noiselessly down the hall, up the stairway, and entered Miss Hadley's door. In five minutes she was back again. "I could not waken her," she said, "though I sprinkled water in her face, and shook her again and again. Oh, dear, she is dosed too! Well,

Dora must be made to waken herself. Here, Virgie, take this candle and wave it back and forth before her face; *close!* no matter if it burns her nose." Then, making a trumpet of her hands, Miriam put them to Dora's ear, and screamed, "*Fire! Fire!! Fire!!!*"

"Oh, oh!" cried Dora, "help—quick! The seminary's burning! Help! *Fire!*" She sprang up and leaned out of the window. "Are they all out? Where is Miss Caldwell?"

"She is safe, Dora, and so are you, now. Mira, dear child, don't cry! the danger is over. I don't believe you ever told a deliberate lie before, but you never did a better act. Dora, for seven hours you have been in the jaws of death! a disgusting, disgraceful death! Now rouse yourself and think of it.

"Mira, close the window and try to sleep until the prayer-bell rings. Dora will not need watching now; and I'll send the hall-maid to put your room in order."

Late that afternoon Virginia Torry sat by Dora's bedside. The two were earnestly talking.

"No one suspects what ailed you. Madam Ferris presumed you had brought a box of goodies from home. 'If the students would only confine themselves to the healthful diet of the institution!'" she said.

"Healthful food!" exclaimed Dora, indignantly. "The bread is made of musty flour—that is one of the matron's economies. The beef is tough, the potatoes watery, the butter strong; and that is all the variety we have. I hate to grumble at the board when we pay so little; but I'm sure it would cost no more to give us milk, rice, fish, and eggs, than the indigestible food we have now. Then, with fewer studies and more exercise, and more sleep, we might do ourselves justice, and the school credit. If we were not living such an unnatural life, we would not have these horrible cravings."

"Well, we cannot reform the system; but we can leave the school or conquer the habit here."

"Oh, I cannot leave without a diploma."

"You came very near leaving last night, Dora, in a most disgraceful manner. Fancy the newspaper paragraphs: the surmisings as to whether it was accidental, or deliberate suicide; the prying into your family affairs; suggestions of a fickle lover, a stern guardian, or—"

"Oh, stop, Virgie! Stop!"

"Dora, if Mira had not called me as soon as she did; if I had not known exactly what to do; if strength had not been given us to prevent your going into that stupor again, until you were roused by Mira's voice—Dora, scores of editors and reporters would now be sharpening their pencils to dishonor your name and vilify your friends."

"Oh, Virgie!" Tears trickled down the crimsoned cheeks.

"Darling, you think I am very cruel; but it is all true. Many times I have thought,

"'It were better not to be,
Life is so full of misery.'

But the horror and grief, perhaps disgrace and reproach, brought upon those I love—that deterred me. It is cowardly to escape from pain in that way."

"Virgie, do you think—"

"You intended suicide? No, Dora; but if you were found dead in your bed, many would believe it. Reasons enough for self-murder would be invented before your body was laid in its coffin."

"Oh, Virgie! oh, do stop!"

"Dora, these torturing words are like dagger-thrusts to me! But I solemnly make this vow, by all the strength of my nature, never, *never*, to touch or taste opium again—not in any form—not if I was told it would save my life! Dora, will you register your vow with mine?"

"I do mean to give up using it; I wouldn't be a slave to it as mamma is for anything! But, Virgie, I couldn't graduate if I stopped now."

An impatient movement made Dora look in her friend's face.

"You think I could?"

"No; but I think you are like a fly in a spider's web; the sooner you break loose the better! But I won't talk to you any more. Mira is coming; let her bathe your head, and you try to go to sleep."

A week later the school duties were resumed, reviews of the lessons lost during sickness being added to Dora's duties. The weather was intensely cold, and the furnaces put in the building during vacation sent more gas than heat to the students' rooms. Headaches, nausea, and rheumatic pains were constant complaints. But the energetic toiled on, and the indolent evaded duties and discipline, studied equivocation and sophistry, attended recitations only to exchange glances or *billets d'amour* with gentlemen of the same amount of intellect and ambition.

"Here's a letter for you, Mira," Dora said one evening, as she came wearily into the room with a pile of books on her arm. "If it is from Davy, do read it aloud, for I never needed a little nonsense more."

"It is Davy's writing:

"'New York City, January 18th.

"'MY OWN DEAR SISTER,—Do not be surprised at hearing (or reading) of my departure from the banks of the Delaware to seek banks of gold in parts unknown. You know I have always intended to seek my fortune somewhere out in the big world; and the time to cut loose has finally come. I never can amount to anything while I stay at home; would only be a machine to carry out father's plans, with just sense enough to obey orders; and I hate making money for money's sake! so I've made up my mind to pull out. Do you remember those words of Goethe's that Jack put to music? They are singing themselves in my ears all the time:

"'Keep not standing fixed and rooted,
   Briskly venture, briskly roam;
Head and hand, where'er thou foot it,
   And stout heart are still at home.
In each land the sun does visit
   We are gay, whate'er betide:
To give space for wandering is it
   That the world is made so wide."'

"'So I've decided to make a venture, and start on a roam that may carry me around the globe. Just think of the countries I shall see, and the adventures I shall have, and the stories I can tell you when I get back again! Won't it be jolly? I would like to be home when you and Miss D. come; for, of course, she will spend her vacation with you. I saw the happiest days of my life last summer; but they were too good to last, and I have wished a hundred times that I had gone away before; but that is folly. "What can't be cured must be endured." Jamie is the best fellow living, and nothing is too good for him. I don't intend to come back until I can see him married without feeling like a villain or a fool. I am writing in a great hurry, as one of the men of our expedition is waiting for me.

"'We leave New York in a few hours. I have written to mother and to Jamie, giving him all right, title, and interest in my share of the property. I've stood it just as long as I can; so don't feel badly about it, nor blame your affectionate brother,

"'DAVY.'"

"What can he mean? Has he really gone?"

The girls' faces were white with horror and surprise, as they stared at each other. Miriam glanced the pages over again to see if no word or line proclaimed it one of Davy's frequent jokes, then dropped the letter on the floor, and threw herself upon the bed. Not a tear came to her eyes; but sobs, deep and irrepressible, shook her form as she thought of the happy hours forever gone! of home without Davy's mirth and mischief; his frequent discontent, the inward rebelling at his father's arrogant voice and dictatorial manner; the evening talks with his mother, the wild fancies crushed, the desires repressed for mother's sake. What new experience, what added provocation, had made home unendurable? Little by little, words, acts, glances, like fragments of a melody, came to mind. "Dora has done it," she thought, and a feeling of resentment embittered the sorrow of her heart. "She likes Jamie best. Oh, my poor Davy!" And she buried her face in the pillows again.

Dora had picked up the letter Miriam threw down, and, with tear-filled eyes, read every word carefully. "And he thinks — oh, Davy! Davy! how could you? Jamie don't care for me, *not that way;* and he has gone, and I can never tell him! Oh, Davy! Davy!"

For a moment she rested her head on the table, and tears fell fast on the letter clasped in her hands. Then, rising, she went to the bed and knelt by Miriam's side: "Oh, Mira, darling! I did not know — he never said. Mira, I cannot be blamed!"

The tear-wet face was clasped to Miriam's; and with one long, fervent kiss, the girls' hearts were sealed in a new bond of sisterhood.

"Our impulsive, ambitious Davy needs the discipline he will get in wandering. Dora, my dear, sweet sister, God will keep him safely, and bring him back by-and-by." Then thoughts of the lonely home, of mother's sorrow, brought a rush of tears.

"Oh, how could he go without a

good-bye? or telling us where he was going? Oh, my darling Davy! where are you now?" And again she trembled with gasping sobs.

The prayer-bell rang, but they could not endure the curious eyes of students nor Miss Caldwell's kind inquiries. Soon the supper gong sounded through the halls. Miriam still lay, with closed eyes, upon the bed, and Dora sat by the window, gazing at the wintry sky, and wondering where, under its arching blue, Davy could be. An hour passed. The study bell resounded from the chapel tower, and she rose and lighted the candles. Mechanically the books for the evening study were arranged.

"Chum," she said, softly, "it is study hours now."

Miriam raised herself slowly. "Dora, I am going home!"

"Oh, Mira!"

"Yes, dear; mother needs me."

"But what will I do?"

"You may go with me."

"No, no I cannot do that: I must finish the course, and get my diploma. But oh, dear! how can I learn these lessons, now?"

"Maybe you are learning other lessons, Dora. Maybe the Master sees we need to learn patience and faith."

Her friend again bowed her head upon the table, and Miriam went quietly to Miss Caldwell's room.

"I was sorry to mark both you and Miss Montgomery for absence from chapel and dining-room to-day," the preceptress said. "But what is the matter? You have been crying?"

"I have sad news from home: my younger brother has never been satisfied to live among the mountains, and he has gone away to seek his fortune. Mother is very lonely, and I must go home."

"I am very sorry, Miriam."

"Yes 'm," choking back a sob; "but I must go!"

"You will return soon?"

"No, ma'am: my school-days are ended."

"Your uncle will not consent to that."

"I shall study all I can. My mother is not strong now: she needs me."

"Well, my dear child, you know best. Wherever you are, you will do your duty bravely and thoroughly; and whenever I can help you, let me know."

That night, Dora, under the influence of her usual opiate, slept soundly; but Miriam lay with open eyes, staring at the darkness and wishing for dawn. "Where is Davy now—just now?" was her only thought. Slowly the interior of her brain seemed expanding; slowly a pure white light illuminated the arched space as though her vision were in the centre, and, gazing into a limitless expanse, she saw vague outlines hovering; slowly they took shape. 'Twas a schooner with every sail reefed. Boats were floating beside it; a man swung himself from the schooner's side, dropped into the row-boat, and took the helm. He pushed his hat from his brow. *It was Davy!*

Miriam sprang up. "What have I seen?" she gasped. "Oh, is it a dream, or is it true?"

CHAPTER XVII.

"We live in deeds, not words; in thoughts, not breaths;
In actions, not in figures on a dial.
We should count time by heart-throbs.
He lives most who feels most, acts the noblest, lives the best."
OWEN MEREDITH.

"Richmond, Va., April 27th.

"MY DEAR MIRA,—It was no use. I tried to live without you; tried to continue my studies with aching head and lonely heart, but I could not! I lost my standing in the class, and consequently the honors. I was forced to drop some studies; and so my diploma was gone. I might still have graduated scientifically, but finally concluded to bring what remains of health and sight I still possessed back to my uncle's house and my mamma's home. Of course she cried over me, and uncle grumbled at my failure, though he declared it was what he expected all the time. How I have suffered in conquering the craving for opium no words can give you an idea; and now I am forced to keep it in sight, or the mania is intolerable.

"Maum Anna is the only one who seems really to sympathize with my disappointment in failing to graduate, or to be anxious about my health. She has nursed and doctored me, as she did all through my weakly childhood; and I am already stronger than when I came home. She has had bitter sorrow of late. Her Liza, who was my maid for years, has been sold South. Uncle said there was no use of so many servants about the house; so he traded her for a span of black ponies. I had taught her to read and write; so I console her mother with the thought of receiving a letter from her, and promising to buy her back, and give her free papers some day. My faithful, kind-hearted Liza! to think of her being abused makes my blood tingle with pain. Poor Maum Anna grieves sadly; Liza was all she had left. Since my health has improved, I have tried to get scholars to teach; but uncle was very indignant. None of his blood should descend to Yankee occupations, he said. I do not know what to do. If mamma needed me, of course it would be my duty and pleasure to stay with her. I was not a welcome child when first placed in her arms; and all my life have I heard regrets for my lack of beauty, reproofs for my irrepressible mimicry, and prophecies that fate was against me. Perhaps from sheer obstinacy I have lived on, determined to make my face grow beautiful *from within*, and conquer adverse fate wherever encountered! Failing to receive a diploma after toiling so long and hard is discouraging, certainly; and I returned completely disheartened. But uncle's 'I told you so,' and mamma's tearful allusion to *fate*, brought me to my feet again, and, aided by Maum Anna's tonics, I stand ready for battle once more.

"Now, my dear chum, *my adopted sister*, will you write to Mr. Walton, inquiring if there is any position in Philadelphia that I can fill; that is, any he can obtain for me without trouble. Perhaps you know of a country school I could get near you. I am willing to undertake anything that will pay for board and clothing, until I have experience enough in teaching to command a larger salary. I am writing a long story, for which I expect to be well paid. Give my best love to your good mother, and remember me to Jamie and Jack. Of course you will let me know as soon as you hear from Davy. Write immediately to your true friend,

"DORA MONTGOMERY."

Miriam read the letter aloud to her mother and Jamie. "There's no use in bothering uncle; he was talking to Miss Caldwell about her going to Philadelphia—I think he tried to get a position there for her—and I heard him say there were ten teachers to every situation. But you are a school director, Jamie; don't you know of an opening?"

"Yes; I have no teacher engaged for this district; but is Dora competent?"

"Competent? James Morgan, what a question!"

"Oh, I don't doubt she has enough book-larnin', as Bill would say, but that is only a part of the requirements for a public-school teacher. She must have firmness, tact, knowledge of child-nature, and a vast amount of self-control. You know I have quite set my heart on making this a model school. I have the house built to suit me without taxing the people; and now I propose to have a teacher who will carry out my methods."

"You dear old fellow! if that isn't just like you! You will reform the world, give you time enough."

"My will is a sufficient lever; but, like Archimedes, I have no fulcrum, sister;" and his face saddened. "Yet I will do all I can. That reminds me, Mira, will you take charge of the library Saturday night? The folks come from five miles around to get books, and I cannot leave the store, there are so many accounts to settle that evening."

"Of course I will, or anything else I can do to assist you. How does the temperance society flourish?"

"Good; nearly every man, woman, and child around here are members; but that reminds me, I must write to a lecturer to come next week—Friday. It is our anniversary, and we propose to have a cold-water convention, or oblation. It is Jane Rodgers's suggestion, or Mistress Kent's, I should say, and I promised to see it through."

"Which means you will do two-thirds of the work, brother."

"No; Jane always does her share,

and Jack will assist. I have some letters to write yet, so good-night."

"But, Jamie—"

"Oh yes; you wish to know what to write your friend. What do you think, mother?"

"I think Miriam better ask her to come and make us a visit, with an idea of taking the school if you find her fitted for it."

"Well, perhaps that is best; though it might be rather awkward to decline her services."

"And you ought to let her know the teachers board around."

"Oh, mother!"

"I would be glad to have her with us, daughter; but the salary is so small she cannot afford to pay for her board, and your father would not consent to her staying for less than two dollars a week."

A look of contempt and disappointment swept across Miriam's flushed face.

Jamie looked annoyed: "I will see that her salary is sufficient to pay for her board; and if you think she can adapt herself to the position, she shall have the school."

Miriam's arms were clasped around his neck.

"Thank you, dear," he said, giving kiss for kiss. "It seems like home to have you with us once more. Oh, tell Miss Dora I shall be in New York week after next, buying goods; if she will come to the Merchant's Hotel, I will be her escort to our home."

"That will be just splendid! I'll write to-morrow."

"Now, good-night, my sister; good-night, mother."

Tears filled the eyes of each as they parted. All thought of Davy, but none had courage to speak his name.

"Where is he? Why do we not hear?" was the burden of every heart.

The next day was cold and windy. A storm of mingled rain and sleet dashed against the windows, and the pine-trees waved their long arms in reckless defiance of the tempest. Jamie came from his room in the store to the early breakfast, looking sad and tired.

"You did not sleep well, my son?" his mother said, resting her hand tenderly on his forehead.

"No; and I have a long ride before me."

"Not to-day?"

"Yes, mother. Matthew Bryon is sick, and has sent for me."

"But you are half sick yourself!"

"No; only one-third," looking up with a smile that irradiated his face. "Don't worry about me, mother; I am only a little *under the weather*, and shall put on my oil-cloth suit before I ride out into it. Besides doctoring old Matt, I have collections to make before going to buy goods. Father will be away attending a lawsuit while I am in New York. I do wish he would stop litigation and attend to business!"

"Can Jack attend to the store?"

"Yes, he understands my system of book-keeping, and can keep the men's time; but he will need help to wait upon customers. Can you spare Miriam when trade is brisk?"

"Yes. Is this property nearly paid for, Jamie?"

"Hardly five hundred dollars back

now, mother. I can make half that in the store, and father ought to make the rest with his lumber, besides paying his lawyer's fees and costs of suits. You will be glad when it is paid, mother?"

"Yes, my son, for the place does not seem our own until there is no debt resting upon it."

"It is a grand estate! Look whichever way you will, the land is all ours; ride for miles up the creek, or down the river, it is all *ours!* But you do not look at all elated, mother?"

"My son, I remember '*The earth is the Lord's, and the fulness thereof.*' We are only his stewards, put here to dress and keep it. I never felt like saying one acre of land, one tree, one grass-blade, was mine!"

"Well, mother, when a man has worked with hand and brain for years to earn a thing; when he has put his strength and will into it, and the law at last proclaims it his, he is ready to believe he owns it. It is not land only that I glory in: we have the finest tannery within fifty miles; three saw-mills cutting lumber night and day; a store doing a flourishing trade; and a more intelligent, virtuous lot of workmen were never got together. I tell you, mother, it is something to be proud of!" And Jamie rose from the table with flushed face and eyes sparkling.

"'O my inheritance, how wide, how fair!
Time is my wide seed-field:
Of time I'm heir!'"

exclaimed Miriam, who had entered in time to hear Jamie's last words. "Are we rich, Jamie?"

"We will be, if I live ten years longer. But I must be off now! It will probably clear up by noon. I'll be home to supper."

"Jamie never cared for Dora, did he, mother?" Miriam stood by the window, watching her brother ride away into the pitiless storm.

"*Care for her?* He always seemed to enjoy her company."

"Yes; but he never thought of her as a wife?"

"No. Does she care for him in that way?"

"No, mother, I'm sure she never did; but Davy—Davy imagined they would be married! Let me show you his letter, mother. Dora always read Davy's letters, and she read this. Oh, how she cried! She loved him so; and he never told her how he felt!"

Tears were raining down the faces of the mother and sister, as they read the mistaken, misguided boy's last message.

"But he will come home, mother; he is out on the ocean now; but he will come back again!" Miriam's face was lighted with a glad smile, that shone strangely through her tears.

"Yes, my daughter; Davy is pure, brave, unselfish. God will lead and guide him, and I trust my family will all be united again. But your mother, Miriam, your mother is growing old."

A quick gasp, and Miriam gazed searchingly into her mother's eyes, while a look of horror and defiance crept over her face.

"Daughter, I am very weary of this earth-life. If it were not for my children, I should have asked my

Saviour to take me long ago. Duty and love have kept me so long; but a few short years will finish my work, and I can go home."

"*And leave me?* Oh, mother!"

"The Saviour who has kept me will keep you, my daughter. He has a work for you to do. While I can help you, I shall stay. But you must learn to go to him for strength, comfort, and counsel, my child. Your mother cannot lead you much farther; I do not even know your way, or your work, my darling. I have taught you to be faithful in that which is least, and I know you will be faithful to God's great trusts."

Miriam's head drooped lower and lower, until, slipping from the stool to the floor, she buried her face in her mother's lap. The thin, toil-hardened hands rested upon the glossy braids of hair. "My daughter, I have long desired an uninterrupted talk with you, and this stormy day has brought it. Do not think because I speak so seriously that death seems very near; it does not. I feel quite as well to-day as I have for months; and I may live on for years. But, daughter, you are a woman now, and must face life bravely without faltering, knowing your own powers, and realizing your responsibilities. I have always felt you had a mission in life different from most women. God has given you beauty and genius, Miriam, as he has given you feet and hands, that you might do the work that is before you. Bestowing his best gifts, he requires best work. Fit yourself for it, daughter; read the best words of the best authors; think often of Jesus Christ; the *best man;* study to make each act and desire what he will call *best*. Oh, daughter, when I look at you and think of life—its miseries, its disappointments, its regrets, its burdens and labors—I have felt as though I must take you in my arms and shield you, or carry you away from earth with me! But my Saviour has given me more trust in him. I see how every burden develops strength; the disappointments leave us wiser; the trials bring endurance and courage with them; and the spirit in us is purified, invigorated, glorified! It grows into a higher life even here, and made fit for heaven and God. Now, my daughter, go to your room and bathe your swollen eyes. We are alone for dinner; so the morning is yours for study, and practising music."

Miriam arose slowly, pressed one long, earnest kiss on her mother's lips, and went up-stairs.

By one of those climatic changes so common in the Northern States, the summer sun shone hot upon the earth before the winter's snows had gone. The mountain streams, released from icy fetters, came rushing down the hillsides, overflowing the mill-ponds, and endangering the dams. The river rose above its banks, and, surrounding the piles of lumber and bark, threatened to sweep all away.

Mr. Morgan was still from home. Jamie mounted the swiftest horse, and rode to the upper mill to remove the sluice-boards from the dams. Morris, with the tannery men, was removing leather from the drying-house to higher ground, when Jack ran from the store, shouting,

"Bill, send a man to row a boat. If those lumber-piles are not tied, they'll go off!"

"Can't help it; leather's worth more 'n lumber!" the answer came back on the south wind; and that instant a low seething roar was heard, and the brook grew smooth with its added power.

"The water's raising again. I'm afraid a dam's bursted! *Do send me some help!*"

"Can't spare a man; wish I had fifty more. Something's got to go!"

Jack caught up the coil of rafting rope, and ran to a boat tied below the mill, now some rods from the shore. Miriam, watching from her window, flew down the stairs, and never paused until, springing upon a slab, with a board for a paddle, she had pushed her craft beside his.

"Now, Jack, I'll row. You 'tend to the lumber. Can you tie that pile to this beech-tree? All right, that 'll hold! Now, Jack, the other!"

Soon the sawed lumber was secured; but huge logs came leaping over the dam, and floated by them down the river.

"If we could make a boom and save them. It's a blamed shame to lose them big rafting logs!" Jack exclaimed.

"Well, let's make one! There are bows and plugs in the shed; and *I can row!*"

Jack leaped to shore; was back again with pike-pole, auger, axe, plugs, and bows.

"Don't know as we can git it done quick enough to do any good; but ef the middle dam has broke, the logs will come down till morning. An' 't has! That's Long John's mark. He brands hisn" (letting the logs float by). "An' here's a Morgan" (catching the smooth pine stick); "I'll hitch this to the bank: it's a good one to begin on."

They worked until the sun sank behind the hill and the cold mist began to rise from the river. "Just a few more logs and we are done. We've saved a good many thousand feet of lumber, Miriam, but I'm afraid you'll be sick. Bill might 'a spared a man; but he's so mad about your father's going off, he'd let the lumber go to Guinea. A man couldn't done no better 'n *you* have, though, Miriam, *brave girl!* I—" He stopped suddenly. "Hand me the axe and a plug! Now here comes a sixteen-foot stick: row east a little—steady—so. Here she comes!" And the sharp pike descended in its side; and Miriam rowed back to the long line of logs that stretched across the mouth of the creek.

The last stick was fastened, and Jack, taking the rower's seat, pulled the boat to shore.

"The water's falling," Miriam said; "unless there is a dam undermined, there is not much damage done."

"Not more than a hundred dollars' worth of our lumber gone; but, unless the sawyer got off the slush-boards before Jamie got there, it will cost considerable to get that mill in order."

Miriam entered the house with wet feet and muddy skirts; but her face was flushed with triumph: "Did you see us, mother?"

"Yes, daughter; you did well. But bareheaded, and no shawl?"

"I could not row with a shawl,

mother, and I had not time to get my hat. *I just flew!*"

"I heard you. Here comes Jamie, wet, cold, and tired. Poor boy! he is doing the work of three men."

The mill was much injured, the dam gone, and several days were spent in obtaining a millwright, removing flood-trash, restoring order as fast as possible, and getting business to run smoothly before leaving to purchase the spring goods for the store. With pulse at fever-heat, a heavy pain in his head, and every bone and muscle filled with a burning ache, Jamie left home for a week's exhausting labor in the city.

"The smartest business man of his age I ever knew," an old merchant said as Jamie left his office.

"Not a more shrewd buyer in the market," another remarked, as he receipted the long bills of Morgan & Sons. "Nor a more honest man," he added, remembering how Jamie corrected an error which was in his own favor.

Night after night he dragged himself to his room, threw himself exhausted upon the bed, and, too tired to sleep, went over and over the transactions of the day; the business at the store, the tannery, the several mills; each creditor's account, circumstances, and intentions; the books needed in the library; the drugs used in his practice; the goods yet unpurchased; and, like a minor chord vibrating through every strain, thoughts of Davy, "*dear brother Davy.*"

"A lady to see you, sir," the clerk said, as the fifth day ended, and he wearily entered the office.

"There's some mistake, I think. I know no ladies here."

"She has just arrived, and asks for you; better go up to the parlor and see her."

"There's some mistake," he muttered, following the clerk to the parlor door.

"Jamie!" The glad voice recalled his consciousness.

"Dora!" The outstretched hands were clasped in his own.

The clerk smilingly withdrew. "Guess she is a relation or a sweetheart! Well, it's time somebody came to look after him; he's one of those fellows who put a week's work into a day, and die young. Hope the lady 'll take him home, or he'll be sick on our hands."

In a moment the parlor bell rang. The smiling clerk answered the summons.

"Is there an express train leaving on the New York and Erie Road to-night?"

"Yes 'm; one leaves in two hours."

"Very well. Is there a friend of Mr. Morgan's, or a physician, who can persuade him to go home with me on that train? He is ill, and should leave the city before he gets worse."

"Yes 'm; you are right. I will see that he has good advice immediately. And with your permission, miss, I will pack up his clothes."

"Thank you; and bring me his bill, and mine too, please; and have a carriage here in time.—Jamie," she said, returning to the sofa where he sat, "let's go home to-night. I am in such a hurry to see your mother and Mira."

"No; I'm not through buying goods yet; you must wait until I finish that bill of crockery, and buy some hardware. I have a list here," and he raised his hand to his pocket. It dropped languidly on his knee, and his head fell back. "Dora, go and call Davy. Tell him I wish to talk business. Tell him I need him, Dora."

With aching heart and tear-filled eyes, Dora turned to leave the room, as a tall, portly, gray-haired gentleman entered, bowed courteously, and then crossed the parlor to Jamie's side.

"Ah, Morgan, I'm sorry to see you ill," he said. "You are overworked. Better get home right away."

"I'm rather tired, doctor, that's all; haven't slept well in a long time. Give me something that will bring sleep, and I'll finish buying goods tomorrow, and then take a rest."

"Oh, let the goods go! Your brother will come down and finish."

"Davy is gone, doctor."

"Gone? Where?"

"I don't know; no one knows. He came to New York for father; put everything straight in the business, and then left for parts unknown."

"How? What! *not run away?*"

"He wrote me he did not like life on the Delaware; he never did; and he did not want to hear objections to his going, nor be coaxed out of it, as he had been before. So he went without our knowledge."

"Have you made inquiries?"

"I came immediately to New York, but could get no trace of him."

"Strange! Strange! He was a venturesome, impulsive young fellow. Perhaps — but it's hardly possible! Morgan, give me your address; I may want to write you."

Jamie took a card from his pocket.

"And now, Morgan, I want to see you on the night express for home. You will get there early in the morning, I suppose. The lady whom I met came for you, did she not?"

"Came for me? I don't know. Was it mother? Oh, pardon me, it was Dora. She is coming now. Miss Montgomery, my friend, Dr. Seymour!"

"You know Morgan's family, Miss Montgomery?"

"Oh yes, sir; I am on my way to his home now."

"Then, as his physician, I advise you to take him home to-night."

"If he will go?"

"He must go!"

"Will you not accompany us? There are no skilful physicians there in the woods."

"Unfortunately I cannot; my patients here would make an ado. But I will prepare a sedative, which you may give when the train starts. He will probably sleep until you get home. Telegraph for the best medical attendant to meet you; for I fear he will have a severe attack of brain-fever. You are all ready?"

"Yes, sir; and the carriage is at the door."

"Come, Morgan!"

Jamie rose wearily, accepted the proffered arm, and, with a dazed look and faltering step, walked down the stairs and into the carriage. Dr. Seymour seated himself by his side. The clerk placed a pillow in the carriage, and a small flask in Dora's hand.

"You will need these to-night," he said, "and I have put a light lunch in Morgan's bag. We shall be anxious to hear how you get home. Will you kindly drop a line to me or the proprietor?" slipping a card into her hand.

"I will, thank you. Good-bye."

He grasped Jamie's hand; but no notice was taken of the warm clasp or friendly farewell. They stopped for a moment at a drug-store, and then drove on. Rousing Jamie with difficulty, they assisted him into the ferry-boat, and with even greater difficulty into the car. Seats were turned and cushions arranged, that he might lie down.

"I will put a counter-irritant at the base of the brain, and give a stimulant. Nothing more can be done, until he is at home and in bed. Here are some written directions for you: follow them until you procure a physician."

A long, long, weary night followed, with restless tossing, feeble mutterings, and frequent calls for Davy. Little semblance of Jamie in the flushed face, blood-shot eyes, and uncombed hair falling over the forehead, as in the gray morning Mrs. Morgan and Jack entered the car. A hurried, grateful kiss on Dora's lips, and the mother clasped her first-born, best-loved child in her arms. He stared at her vacantly, then said, "There was an unsettled account that ought to be attended to immediately."

"Jamie," said Jack, "you are home now. Come, we must get off the cars." He closed his eyes, saying "he hoped Davy would come soon, for he must tell him something."

The conductor came. "Morgan, here's your station; can you walk?"

Jamie rose quietly. "Certainly; though I feel rather weak. — Jack, how are you? Where are you going? And mother, too?"

"Yes, my son, we came to meet you and Dora."

"Dora? Why, when did she come? Glad to see you, Dora. Are all well at home?"

Stepping unaided into the carriage, he sank back helplessly. When they reached the house, he could not be roused. He was carried to the bed Miriam had prepared in the parlor; and for forty-eight hours muttered and moaned, but never rested, never recognized a face or voice of those who watched over him day and night. His father came. Three physicians exercised all their wisdom and skill, but Jamie was no better. It was Sabbath morning: his mother sat beside him, his father stood near, and Miriam knelt upon the floor. He opened his eyes — those deep-azure eyes — and looked long and tenderly into his mother's face. "I'm going away, mother," he muttered, feebly. "Going out of this life into the other life. Don't be sorry: it is better so. Mira, all of my work that is worth doing I leave to you. My property I give to—father, do you hear?—I give my share to Miriam: let her carry out my plans. Davy will come by-and-by."

A long silence. Then, while the repressed sobs tore every heart with agony, he murmured again, "Tell all the folks good-bye. I love them all. Father, be patient, be gentle. Comfort each other: you will be lonely now. Mother, mother, we will meet soon!"

One quick, fluttering breath, and Jamie was gone!

Why attempt to describe the scene that followed—the bitter anguish, the unavailing regret? The father walked the floor, crying, "Oh, I put too much upon my boy! I ought to have done more myself. Oh, Jamie, my son, come back! *come back!*" While the mother, as pale as the dead in the next room, lay stunned and silent beneath the blow. Miriam moaned like one in physical pain: "Both gone! both my precious brothers gone! Oh, it cannot be true!"

Again and again she went into the parlor, raised the curtains, so that the sunlight might fall on the white face, folded back the sheet, and gazed long upon the clay that was no longer Jamie. Acquaintances, neighbors, uttered their well-meant words of consolation, but they fell on deafened ears. What mockery! how meaningless they seemed! The day for burying their dead came at last. Dressed in garments of mourning, they sat around the coffin. About them were Jamie's business associates from the city, neighbors who had known him from boyhood, workmen whom he had helped to live honest and pure, acquaintances from near and far—friends all of them, honoring, admiring, loving the intelligent, upright, enterprising man so unexpectedly taken away.

The burial-service was read; a hymn falteringly sung; then they carried him out into the spring sunshine, and one by one walked around his narrow bed to take a last look at the pale, peaceful face. A sleep most placid and profound had sealed those earnest eyes, closed the loving lips, stilled forever those active hands. It was not Jamie lying there! A long procession followed the body to its burial upon the hillside, beneath wide-arching trees. Apple-blossoms and fragrant ferns were showered upon the coffin as they lowered it into the grave; then the mourners turned away. Oh, the desolate house! the empty rooms! Oh, the anguish of folding away garments to be used no more! the weariness of every-day duties that will not be dismissed!

"Mister Morgan is completely broke down," the neighbors said, noticing his stooped form and whitening hair. But there was no relaxing of the stern face; no softening in the arrogant voice. Serving customers, inspecting leather, measuring lumber and in making bargains, there were the same keen glance and imperative tone. With his family he sat silent, unapproachable.

Mrs. Morgan arose from a sick-bed with a face so radiant with perfect peace, and eyes so expectant of bliss, that all seeing souls were gladdened. "Our Saviour has shown me *how right it is*, how best for all that Jamie should go," she said one day. "And I? I am only waiting."

One by one the duties of life were laid down; day by day she grew weaker.

"I do not mean to be an invalid, daughter. I had rather be found working when the Master calls me;

but as I have no strength for planning, nor earnest effort, let me keep my hands busy and be some help to you."

"Oh, the blessing of work!" Miriam exclaimed as she toiled in the kitchen from morning until night. "If the imperative needs of our bodies did not press us so closely, our hearts would break and our minds go wild.

"Dora," she said one day to the friend who did a sister's duties and received a sister's love — "Dora, I want to tell you all Jamie's plans for a school; and then, if you like, you can begin teaching in the new house. I know you have been anxious to talk about it, but I couldn't introduce the matter before."

The next Monday morning, the children were called together, and with earnest, tearful words the young teacher began her labors. That evening, at Mrs. Morgan's request, the melodeon was opened, and Jack joined them in an evening hymn. Then Miriam arose and accompanied her mother from the room.

Jack looked after them earnestly. "'Twon't never be the same here again," he said, "nor anywhere about this place. The business suffers; but that ain't the worst of it. The library 'sociation met t'other night, and the secretary tried to read some resolutions, but broke down; then, with sobbing you could hear all round the room, they voted on 'em, and went home. I locked the door, and *that is ended!* The temperance union was goin' to have a celebration, but of course they've giv' that up. There's four or five ol' soakers Jamie just hung on to an' kept up; *they'll go down now!* There'll be liquor sold here in less 'n a year, you'll see!"

"But can no one keep up these societies?"

"Mister Morgan can't; he don't see the necessity. I can't; it ain't in me. I can run the store, or a mill, or a raft; but I can't run a society! Missis Morgan sees the *why* of this affliction; but, to me, seems 's if the Lord had made a mistake."

CHAPTER XVIII.

"Sudden rest may fall on wearied sinews;
Workers drop and die—the work continues.
God names differently what we name *failing*;
In a glory mist His purpose veiling."

MISS MULOCK.

IN the quiet of a summer's evening Miriam wandered up the mountain path where she ran so gayly when a child, with Bruce, her faithful dog, by her side. "They are all gone now," she murmured, sadly. "My old playmate is dead long ago; Jamie safe in that far-off heaven! and Davy, oh, where is he?" She sank on the moss-covered ground, and buried her face in her hands. An approaching step startled her.

"Forgive me, Miriam, for following you," Jack said, "but here's a letter I want to show you, 'thout anybody's knowing it. One come a spell ago from the same person. 'Twas wrote to Jamie, but I opened an' answered it. Yesterday I got this. Maybe there hain't nothing in it — maybe there is! Thought you ought to know 'bout it anyhow."

The letter was from Dr. Seymour. After brief regrets at the sudden death of so useful and noble a man as his valued friend, he added, "The fact of David Morgan's departure about the time of the expedition's leaving New York (which I mentioned in my letter to his brother, and to which you replied), led me to think so adventurous and inexperienced a youth might have become inveigled into the secret and dangerous enterprise. In fact, from information I was already possessed of, I was aware that a young man answering his description had been induced to make one of the required number; though I was ignorant, and am still, of the youth's name or residence. The object of the expedition was to recover a large amount of gold buried in an island lying south of Cuba. Its amount and exact location are secrets in the possession of the leaders of the party, and no others. The money was recovered from a Spanish vessel wrecked on the coast years ago. That the effort to capture the treasure was discovered by the Cubans, and the Americans driven off or captured, I informed you in a previous letter. I have since learned that those in command of the schooner escaped, and probably sailed for South America or Mexico. If David Morgan was in this expedition, and escaped, you will undoubtedly hear from him in the course of a few months."

The vision of that winter's night came to Miriam's mind. "I do not know what to think, Jack. I feel as though it was true."

"So do I!" he exclaimed; "and yet it sounds like a made-up story: going off to look for buried gold."

"'A bank of gold!' Why, those were his very words! He was leaving the banks of the Delaware to seek a bank of gold. *And he was one of those going to shore!* Oh, if he was captured!"

"He wa'n't! I'm just dead-sure, Miriam, that he got away, an' is gone to some fureign country. All we've got to do is jist keep up our spirits an' wait patient till he gets home again. I'll bet he'll think there hain't no better place 'n this, after all."

The next mail brought a letter from Dora's brother, forwarded from Philadelphia: "That you should be forced to relinquish the coveted diploma is unfortunate, no doubt; but not half so bad, in my opinion, as the loss of your health. Go to the home in the Delaware hills immediately. In Mrs. Morgan's kindly care I shall feel safe about you; for her counsel, her presence even, will restore every good thing—hope, health, happiness. She was the ideal woman of my early manhood; and knowing one such woman lives in God's world has made much good seem possible to me, when I saw and heard nothing but evil. There is not a day of my eventful life—even though I had no conscious thought of Mrs. Morgan—

that has not been influenced by her counsel, blessed by her prayers. Her daughter may be beautiful, intelligent, all your partial affection describes her; but if she possesses one tithe the goodness of her mother, she is a girl worth a man's travelling three thousand miles to see, even if he had not the best sister in the world to attract him in the same direction. Briefly, if my next sale of stock equals my last—$6480, cash—I shall leave my ranch in the care of my partner and Antonio, to come North. A schooner is anchored across the bay, and I am going out with a boat-load of fresh vegetables and fruits to trade with her crew; possibly it may be an opportunity of sending this letter to you."

The schooner was not anchored, but aground on the treacherous, shifting sands of the bar; and the captain hailed Montgomery, as his boat appeared, for means of transportation to shore.

"Don't want none o' your gardensass," he yelled, in unmistakable Yankee accent. "Jest yeou pitch eout them thare greens, an' come 'ith yer boat to take us ashore!"

"Ay, ay!" Montgomery answered, and, unloading his cargo on the wharf by his boat-house, was soon beside the schooner.

"Where are your own boats?" he asked, as he caught the line thrown him.

"Los' 'em all but one; and that leaks. How much of a place you got 'ere?"

"Place? Why, there seems no end to it. Think of locating?"

"Wall, we ain't certing; we're looking 'round. Any Greasers here?"

"A few; we haven't been troubled with them, nor with Indians either."

"How long ye been 'ere?"

"Long enough to get five thousand head of cattle, and seven hundred sheep, a well-watered ranch, and comfortable cabin."

"How many is thare of ye?"

"Enough to protect our stock from thieving Mexicans or Comanches."

"Wall, we've got aground here, an' the tide won't lift us till arter midnight. Kin ye take us hum 'ith ye for supper; or ain't yer wife ready for comp'ny?" And the big, burly men about him laughed at their captain's joke.

One man stood alone — his broad-brimmed hat pulled low over his forehead, and his eyes fixed earnestly on the shore.

Giving a few orders to the crew, the captain swung himself into the boat. "Come, Delaware!" — the young man looked up — "a sniff of land breeze 'll hearten ye up; come ashore!"

Four other men sprang into the boat; and Montgomery rowed to land, and led the way to a log-cabin surrounded by a stockade fence. Two fierce-looking dogs sprang up; then, seeing their master, stopped at the gate-way, growling threateningly.

"Be quiet, Danger! Lie down, Cæsar! Enter, gentlemen, and welcome to Rancho Delaware! Antonio, what have we for supper?" A sallow-faced boy, with long black hair hanging to his shoulders, and deep-set, heavy-browed eyes, looked at the six strangers entering. "The schooner was aground; these men are come to eat with us. What have you?"

"Guajolote, tortillas, pulque."

"Good. Stir up a hoe-cake, and make some coffee! If you wish to take a look at the country, gentlemen, come up to my observatory."

He led the way up a ladder to the roof of the house. The outside logs had been carried up about three feet on each side above the nearly flat roof, forming an excellent breastwork, in case of an enemy's attack, and a convenient outlook for the fortification. "This was built when Texas was a republic, and every man had to defend his own castle. I have no idea we shall ever be attacked, but there is no harm in keeping ready for battle. With this glass," pulling a telescope from under a piece of awning, "I can recognize the face of a friend half a mile away, count my cattle scattered on the prairie, sight a sail five miles off, or gaze on the stars that shine on my old home. Sitting in this arm-chair of my own manufacture, or swinging in this hammock, I see visions, and dream dreams, as all lonely men do."

"Wall, Mister—"

"Montgomery."

"An' my name's Jones. Wall, Mister Montgomery, you've got the prettest-layin' farm I ever see anywhere. Them spots o' timber ain't wuth no great amount for lumber; but they set off the country mighty nice."

"Yes: those *mots*, as we call them, are more valuable than you think. Water and shade are found there, shelter from the summer sun and winter winds. But come, supper must be waiting us."

They seated themselves on the wooden benches around the bare table. "Roast turkey is not much of a treat to us, as game is very abundant," Montgomery said, pushing the platter toward the captain; "and torteelyas are rather too hot, with red pepper, for any but a Mexican's stomach. But this poolkä is a drink even a Yankee may delight in — cooling, exhilarating, and not intoxicating to any but the weakest heads. But here is coffee, if you prefer it. We have sugar, but no milk."

"An' thousands o' cows? How's that?"

"This is not a dairy-farm, you know. Sometimes the boys lasso a cow, tie, and milk her; but she doesn't give enough to pay for the trouble. One cannot have everything, and I am content to sacrifice milk and butter for fruits and game. The *garding sass* you despise, is my chief living. These cresses — you never saw their equal in size and crispness. Antonio, bring a basket of grapes. Sorry I have no cigars to offer; but I never smoke, and my partner, who uses tobacco enough for two, is out branding stock."

"Wall, you're the first man I ever met 'thout a woman 'at didn't smoke. There's a woman in it somehow, I'll bet!"

Montgomery looked annoyed. The youngest man of the party, who had spoken but seldom, was looking steadily into his face.

"Yes, I don't mind confessing that. When I was a few years younger than you, sir," returning the earnest look, "I was fortunate enough to meet one of those motherly women who are a blessing to the world. What I might have been but for her advice, I do not know. But her words ring in my ears whenever tempted to do a foolish thing, and they have kept me out of many a sin. Were any of you ever on the Delaware?"

A significant glance was exchanged. "We're from all over, Mister Montgomery. I come from little Rhody; Jim Mill's from England — he has traded with South Sea Islanders, and harpooned whales."

"I only asked because I lived there some months. I helped to build the New York and Erie Railroad. But come, let's go and look about the place. If any of you would like a ride, I can give you as good a mount as you'll find in the States."

The captain declined, saying they must get aboard soon; and, pocketing the money his host had declined taking, he warmly thanked Montgomery for his hospitality.

"I'm thinkin' of settling down som'ers for a spell. Settin' up a tradin'-post 'ith the Greasers an' you'uns; just enough to keep my schooner goin', an' maybe lay up a leetle. But I guess we'd do better to pint toward Mexico."

"Quite probably," Montgomery said; for he had no desire to see them settle nearer. ("That schooner is too slow a craft for a pirate, and too small for a slaver; but the crew might be anything," he thought, "except that boy, and he — how he got with such a low-down set is a mystery!") He watched them walking down the beach, the young man and the captain talking earnestly. Montgomery untied his boat and waited for them. While the rest were still talking, the young man walked hastily forward:

"Mr. Montgomery, if not asking too much, would you take me on board later in the evening? I have the captain's permission to stay on shore an hour or two, and accept your invitation for a canter over the prairies."

Montgomery looked keenly into the half-averted face. "If they meant rascality, they would have trusted it to a cooler head," he thought.—"I shall be glad to have your company, young man," he answered, pleasantly. "And as for the row, that will be no task at all."

The lighting-up of the youth's face, the joyous sparkle in his eye, gave assurance to Montgomery that no ill was intended, and that the pleasure given was tenfold greater than any inconvenience caused him. The captain uttered a few words in too low a voice for any but the ears intended. The young man's face paled, and a look of scorn and sorrow curved the lips just shaded by a brown mustache.

"He wants to get away from those villains, and, Heaven helping me, he shall!" Montgomery muttered, as, springing into the boat, he seized the oars, and calling them to "jump in," they were soon at the schooner's side.

"Bring that thare boy o' mine back 'fore the tide turns, mister. I was a tarnel fool for lettin' him stay; but he's be'n sick the hull v'yage, an' thinks a ride on a hoss 'll kindy put some heart in 'im. Bring 'im — " But Montgomery's rapid strokes had carried him beyond speaking distance.

The sunset had scarcely paled when silvery moonlight flooded the earth. The horses were eager for a gallop. The prairies stretched before them, smooth as a well-kept lawn. "Keep a stiff rein, and look out for rabbit burrows," Montgomery said, and away they flew.

Only once, a horse broke through the sod to his knees, and touched his nose to the ground. The rider threw himself back—the horse sprang—was up and away in an instant.

"Many a man gets pitched over his horse's head by those hidden rabbit-holes," Montgomery said, as they paused to breathe their horses on a rise of ground. "Was there ever a lovelier scene! That grimy old craft of yours is beautified by this light; and the Gulf seems a sparkling, quivering mass of silver. How fragrant the air is! Accustomed to flowers of every color and shade, I never had noticed what a variety could be found in a small space, until, trying to describe them to my sister, I concluded to send her specimens. It hardly seemed possible to her; but in a space not more than five feet square I found twenty-two varieties."

"Your sister is East."

"Yes: she has been at school for some years; but her home is in Virginia. I would be a happy man if I could have her with me; but this rude life, with only cow-boys for company, will never do for a lady. I hope to go home and see her soon. Why, what ails you, boy?"

His head had dropped forward, and his face was covered by his hands. Deep sobs seemed to shake his inmost soul. By a terrible effort he choked them down, brushed the tears from his face, and said, huskily, "Theo! don't you know me? I am Davy Morgan."

After the surprise, the joyful greeting, came a long earnest talk.

"I will never go on board that schooner again if I die for it! I cannot go back home to hear taunts and sneers, and be under orders all my days. And I would be watched by members of this gang, and the detectives too, whenever I went to the city. Until I have done something to be proud of—at least, until this affair has blown over, and I can go home unsuspected and independent—I shall not go at all. Just as much obliged for your offer, Theo, but I can't do it! You write to your sister, of course? And she is to be with Miriam this summer—is probably there now;" he swallowed hard, and pressed his hand to his brow. "Do not mention my name to her; do not let her know you have seen me."

"Is that treating your mother right? Think how she must be grieving—"

"Stop! haven't I thought of it when tossed up and down by that infernal old craft out there? Thought of it until it seemed my heart would burst! But what good would it do her to know I was a vagabond? What comfort to be told I was dodging the police, and a marked man among a gang of cut-throat robbers. When I am fairly out of this scrape, when I get into some honorable employment—then I will write to mother. But I had rather she would think me dead than know the truth!"

"Are not your fears exaggerating the real crime and danger? The hidden treasure is no doubt regarded as lawful spoil by the men; and though some of them are now captives in Cuba, I do not imagine the Spaniards will search for those who escaped: nor does it seem likely that our Government will trouble itself about the matter at all. The best thing for you to do is to go to Austin and get in some business. There are many things a strong fellow, educated as you have been, can turn his hand to. The horse you ride can carry you there in two days. You shall have a hundred dollars to start with. No, not a word! You shall not leave without it, and you can return it in your own time. Now we will ride back to my cabin and prepare for your journey."

"But the schooner—"

"Has floated off long ago. But did the captain tell the truth about the boats?"

"Yes, two were captured; the other got a hole knocked in her stern."

"Too leaky to trust on a smooth sea?"

"Yes; we had no way of getting to shore until you came and took us off."

"Then you are safe from them for the present: and as they intend to keep by the seaboard, you have only to stay inland. I have no idea they will trouble you. You do not know the exact location of the gold, and you have no information to give that does not implicate yourself as much as them; so why should they pursue you?"

Davy made no answer. They had reached the mound where they paused before. The Gulf of Mexico lay stretched out before them, with not a sail, not a boat in sight. The schooner had gone.

"They must have hoisted all sail, and swung off at the turn of the tide. Thank God, she's gone! and I pray I may never see the craft or crew again."

Without rousing his partner or Antonio, both being soundly asleep in their bunks, Montgomery fed the horse, packed the saddle-bags, folded and strapped two heavy blankets, put six Spanish doubloons and some silver coin in a leathern belt, which he forced Davy to wear underneath his garments.

"I had better give you a bill of sale for the horse, as he is well known in these parts; and I should hate to have you arrested for stealing him. You would be better off in the old schooner. These Texans are a rough lot; but just let them know a man means to deal fair, and live honest, and there's no kinder, nobler, more generous people on earth. Now, good-bye, Davy. Write to me whenever you get a chance to send a letter this way. I may get half of them, and that's a comfort. Oh, by-the-way, I was writing Dora when I discovered your sail; I thought it might be an opportunity of sending the letter to New Orleans. Now, will you mail it for me at Austin? I wish you would let me add a postscript, saying you are here. I really feel as though they ought to know, Davy. Well, well, we won't argue the matter; only, if you think better of it, you may slip in a line, or, better still, send a letter to your mother. Now, here is a chart of your way. The stars will guide you to-night, and to-morrow morning you will see the Colorado on your left—from there a plain trace will guide you to Austin. Put a line in the post-office announcing your arrival, and it will reach me after a while. Here are letters of introduction that will help you to work of some kind; you will not be particular. Now take care of yourself. Good-bye!"

The long, long journey was ended; and Davy rode up the wide sandy streets of Austin in the blaze of a mid-day sun, the reflected light from the white-rock buildings sending flashes of pain through his eyes. Dismounting at the post-office, he took the letter to Dora from his pocket. How he longed to write one word! Oh, to think of this paper being clasped in her hands, pressed to her lips! This little fragile thing—if it could speak, if it could tell them whose heart had kept it warm for more than forty hours of hard riding, and brief resting, across the wild, lonely country. For the terror of being pursued, the anxiety to find work and repay the debt to his friend, and be in a position to write to the loved ones at home—all this had spurred him on; and as he stood at the post-office door, with bridle-rein over his arm, the horse drooped his head wearily. Two men eyed him closely.

"That's so; that's ol' Blucher,

sure's a gun! An' he's be'n put through faster 'n an honest man ought to ride. Stranger," he said, coming up to Davy, who still stood gazing at the letter in his hand, "what 'll you take for that cowpony?"

Davy stared. "The horse? I don't care to sell him, thank you; at least, not until I'm sure I have no use for him. Can you tell me where I can find a gentleman named Lemar?"

"That's my name, stranger—Louis Lemar? Jess so; reckon I'm the man you're inquiring for."

"Are you a friend of Theodore Montgomery?"

"Wall, I'm all that, an' a little more. We're sort o' related. Did he send you to me?"

"Here's a letter he gave me for you;" and as Davy put it in his hand, he told a negro boy to hold his horse, and entered the post-office. A brief note to Montgomery was written, and, with Dora's letter, given to the clerk.

"So you are one of the family Bruce has told me about? And you've come to Texas to seek your fortune! I'm glad to know you, sir, glad to know you! This is Major Lally, Mister Morgan. An old soldier of '42. An'—he-he-he! ha-ha-ha!— why, he an' I took you for a horse-thief—fact, sir! he-he!"

The jolly red face of Colonel Lemar grew crimson as he laughed. "Now, you are coming right home with me, and make one of our family till you look about you. Here, you"—to the negro—"take that horse to my stables, and tell Tom I sent him. Major, come along, come along!"

But that gentleman excused himself, and Davy and his new friend walked up the street toward the Capitol. The stage dashed by them and stopped at the post-office. The mail-bags were thrown out, some passengers alighted. A thick letter addressed to Bruce T. Montgomery was added to the pile of papers and Davy's note. Ten days later it was opened at the Rancho Delaware. It was written by Dora in the first hours of their bereavement:

"Can you imagine how desolate the place seems with Davy gone and Jamie dead? If it were not for my school, and unceasing efforts to assist Mira, I could not stay here! Poor Mrs. Morgan sits by the window looking toward the store all day long. She sometimes walks to the gate and leans upon it, as though waiting for some one to come. Her hair has become perfectly white—a soft silvery white—and her eyes have such an expectant, trustful radiance in them, that her whole face seems beautified. Mr. Morgan is quite the same, only more silent and sad. Poor man, I do pity him! Dear Miriam bears all so bravely. She does nearly all the work of the house, has rearranged Jamie's library association, and hopes to again establish a temperance union; but several members have broken their pledge, and the others seem discouraged. Jack aids her all he can, but it is unpleasant to have their names continually associated. If Davy were only here! The business needs his attention, and the family need his company and care. Not one word have they heard from him, nor a trace of his whereabouts been found."

The next morning Montgomery started for Austin; but Davy had gone. "He got restless," Colonel Lemar explained, "an' thought he might find what he wanted farther west. Platte was going to San Antone—had a lot o' freight to take over. Morgan took a deck-passage on the driver's seat. He! he! he! Reckon he'll see Texas! ha! ha! ha! Gone as a freighter! What! bad news for him? Sorry, sorry! Nice fellow. Can't do anything for him till Platte comes back. Reckon Morgan will come back with him. Can't tell, though. Can't tell. May go on to Goliad."

Montgomery awaited Platte's return, but Davy was not with him. He had joined a party of Americans and Mexicans going to inspect some silver mines.

Three months passed.

Montgomery, with eye to his telescope, was standing upon the roof of his cabin, looking across the prairie.

The steady "lope" of an approaching horse brought news, or a friend. Either would be most welcome, for the steel-blue haze on the horizon's edge foretold a wet norther; and a three days' storm without occupation or company was a dreary prospect. "It is old Blucher!" and, hoping to meet Davy at the gate-way, he ran down-stairs.

A stranger swung himself off the horse. "How-de, capt'n? how-de? Brought some letters and documents to ye. Some's from Colonel Lemar, an' some's from a young fellow in San Antone de Bexar."

"David Morgan?"

"I reckon so. I was comin' to the capital, an' promised him I would drop down on ye, ef I could, an' tell you 'how-de' for him. He sent money to pay for yer horse; but the colonel said *he* had no use for the animile, an' Morgan hadn't had no good of him, so he reckoned I better carry him down yer, an' you could keep the money or the horse, or both, ef ye liked."

Davy's letter assured Montgomery of his health and increasing prosperity: "I have a small store—keep an assortment that suits señoritas, miners, cow-boys, and planters. Have, as I promised you, written mother, and hope their anxieties on my account are long since relieved. But I have received no reply from any member of the family, though I have since written to Jamie and Miriam."

A letter was written that evening while his guest was dozing by the fire, to be enclosed with the latest messages from Dora, urging Davy to go with him to the States. For Montgomery's preparations were all made, and he only waited his partner's return with a supply of provisions before starting on the journey. The rain poured in sheets, the wind and waves roared when morning came, and the traveller was storm-stayed for another day.

"I must get out o' this before sun up to-morrow," he said, after he and Montgomery had finished their stories of the war with Mexico and quarrels with the Greasers. "Let's have a game of seven-up."

"Very well; I've no objections to cards, but I never gamble."

"Do you mean you'll play 'thout a stake?"

"If you like."

"Why, I wouldn't play 'thout betting something on it, if no more 'n a glass of *aguardiente*."

"But I never bet, my friend; so I fear a game would be poor amusement. My library is limited, but here is a book that was given me by Morgan's mother years ago. Let me read a little from it:

"'O come, let us sing unto the Lord: let us make a joyful noise to the Rock of our salvation.

"'Let us come before his presence with thanksgiving, and make a joyful noise unto him with psalms.

"'For the Lord is a great God, and a great King above all gods.

"'In his hand are the deep places of the earth: the strength of the hills is his also.

"'The sea is his, and he made it: and his hands formed the dry land.

"'O come, let us worship and bow down: let us kneel before the Lord our maker.

"'For he is our God; and we are the people of his pasture, and the sheep of his hand.

"'To-day, if ye will hear his voice, harden not your heart.'

"Living alone as I do, with my sheep and cattle around me, I take great delight in reading of the old patriarchs and their pastoral lives. I fancy this country must be similar to Judea. Knowing that the strength and beauty of the earth is a part of the Life Eternal that made and keeps us, gives an added glory to the flower, and more grandeur to the ocean. When going among my flocks, driving them to green pastures and still waters, I am glad to know the Lord is *my* shepherd."

"Well, Montgomery, I haven't heard a man talk religion outside the pulpit since I left the States."

"Maybe so, stranger; I don't often talk of God; but somehow the deep voice of the waves makes me feel like it to-night. I have horses out there on the prairie who will not acknowledge me as their master, though they know I can bring them on their knees by a lasso whenever I choose. And they know too, or ought to know, that I do them good, and not harm, whenever I ride among them. Now, there's old Blucher; he was a wild horse on the prairie three years ago. Sired by one of those Kentucky bloods, brought to Texas by the Rangers (probably left riderless on some battle-field), Blucher was as much superior to the Indian ponies as you and I are to the Greasers. Well, how or when he strayed among my herds, I don't know; but he was soon leader, though he had to fight hard for it. But that horse kept unbranded for four years; he would dodge the lasso every time. Tom vowed he'd ride him down; and nearly knocked up the best cow-pony we had. But one day Blucher got trapped. Cantering along with his head up, and mane and tail flying, down he went in a ditch of black clay. I saw him with my telescope from the roof. I was on a pony, and after him in a flash. He jumped, and plunged, and struggled, but my lasso just settled down over his head, and I had him! He nearly choked to death before he would give up; and after he was tied and blindfolded, I found his shoulder was sprained. I corralled him—put a stockade around him, in fact, before I got through with my experiment—kept him blindfolded the first time I bathed him, and then rubbed and petted him—fed him sugar and bread, when he would take them from my hand—finally saddled and mounted him, and rode triumphantly to the cabin door. I never had a nobler beast under me, nor one who took more pride in his paces; and he is handsomer, more intelligent, and a happier horse than if he had never surrendered to a higher power."

"An' you think a man is just as much improved by owning God as his master?"

"More! Just as much more as he is greater than a brute, and the God who made him is higher, holier than we are."

They sat silent for a long time, facing the fire of muskeet roots and branches, which glowed beneath its many-hued flames, while the wind and rain whistled and beat against the log-cabin; and the waves moaned drearily on the shore. But their eyes and ears were closed to the sights around them. Their thoughts were of the past.

"Montgomery," the stranger said, suddenly, "I don't mind telling you there was a time when I felt as you do. But life's been rough on me. I'd got to thinking religion's all stuff an' blarney! I know better. I know you've spoke the truth; an', God helping me," he added, rising up, "I'll be a better man. Give us your hand, Montgomery! Now, good-night. The storm is dying out, an' I must be off by sun up."

Montgomery decided to wait until Davy could join him. In a few weeks the answer came. He was shocked, grieved beyond all power of expression at his brother's death, and longed to be at home to give what little comfort he could to his mother and sister: "But I could not fill Jamie's place. I should only be like a hired hand to my father, as I always was. To be tied down there seems just as irksome to me as ever. I should only go home to leave again; and if I lose the chance I have now of accumulating a fortune, I may never find as good a one. In a year I hope to go home with money enough to begin business in some Eastern city. Give them love — oh, how commonplace that sounds! I cannot put in words the longing I feel toward my mother and sister. To think of them in the lonely home brings unmanly tears to my eyes. Only a year, or perhaps eighteen months, I can be with them again!"

How unknown is the future! The messenger who brought the letter to Montgomery carried back another from Miriam. It was dated:

"Home, October 20th.

"MY DEAR AND ONLY BROTHER" (she wrote),—"Could you have seen the joy that one little sheet of paper gave, you could understand something of the agony of suspense we have endured. Thank God the message was delayed no longer! It was morning when it came; father was in Philadelphia; Dora had gone to her school; mother was sitting in her usual place by the window in the easy-chair Jamie bought for her a year ago; and which you remember she laughingly told you she would use when she was old. Poor mother; it was not time, but trouble, that brought old age! Jack brought the letter to me tremblingly. I put it in her hands. Such a light came into her face!

"'It's from Davy! my precious boy! O God, I thank thee!' She held it clasped in her hands, and tears fell from her closed eyes. Then she handed it to me: 'Read it, Miriam. Stay, Jack'—for he was quietly leaving the room—and I read your message. 'It was not all we would be glad to know,' she said, 'but so much is a great blessing.' Again she closed her eyes, and we knew that she was praying for you, with the letter folded in her hands. Jack has had letters from a friend of our dear Jamie, telling about a secret expedition that left New York the same time you did, and we have felt for several reasons that you were in it. Your half-revealed wanderings confirm it. So, in the evening after Dora had again read your letter to mother, I brought Dr. Seymour's letters and read and explained them.

"Dora was much affected; but dear mother was perfectly calm. She always had a subtle insight into her children's hearts that no experience of theirs seemed to astonish or overwhelm. Dora laid her head on the arm of the big chair, and mother's hand rested on her curls. 'It is all right, dear,' she said; 'trust our Saviour—it is all right. Davy will come back again with all his best qualities improved. He needed the discipline. Oh, my boy, my boy!' she moaned, 'you will never see mother again!'

"That night she rested quietly, though I do not think she slept. She rose as usual in the morning, and walked to her chair. All day her eyes seemed following me, instead of gazing out of the window, as was her habit. Often I stooped to kiss the face so like an angel's, and yet so like our mother's face. She always gave me some sweet word for each caress— 'Faithful daughter,' 'Precious child.' After a little I saw her eyes were closed, and I thought her sleeping. Dora came from school, and I motioned her to be quiet. The setting sun sent a ray of light to linger on her lovely face. I leaned over her to touch my lips to her snowy hair. Oh, Davy! my darling brother! how can I tell you? There was nothing left us but the cold form! *Mother had gone home to God.*"

CHAPTER XIX.

"But love is never lost, though hearts run waste:
'Tis sorrow makes the chastened heart a seer.
The deepest dark reveals the starriest hope,
And faith can trust her heaven behind the veil.
GERALD MASSEY.

"It really seems, Mira, as if the summer, with Theo's visit, were a dream, and only this snow-shrouded earth and cold fierce winds were the reality."

The girls were decorating the little school-house for a Christmas festival.

"There were some days of last summer so full of heart-pain and loneliness that it is very real to me, Dora."

"Ah yes, I know. But even yet it seems, when I walk home from school, as though I should see your mother's face at the window. Reason with myself, chide myself as I may, I still feel disappointed when I come up the path and her calm, sweet smile does not greet me."

Tears fell on the ferns Miriam was grouping. "Only one thing reconciles me, Dora: she was tired of earth and wanted to go."

There was a long pause, broken only by the crackling of the fire and the moaning of the wind.

"You have substantial proof that your brother's coming was no dream, Dora."

"Yes; a bank-book and my dear good Liza. Wasn't it the luckiest thing that he stopped at St. Louis and attended that slave-auction? And it was strange she had persisted in retaining her old name when she changed masters. It was the name—Liza Lemar—attracted Theo's attention; but she recognized him instantly. Theo said he would have parted with watch and coat rather than refuse to buy her and her babies when she pleaded so pitifully. But say, Mira, honestly now, does she work enough to pay for keeping herself and her two pickaninnies? She never did anything but wait on table and dress me at uncle's, and she has been a field-hand ever since; and that Jerry is a precocious little imp. It was a perfect imposition in Theo bringing them here."

"I do not complain. Liza is forgetful, but grateful; more respectful than a white servant, and quite as intelligent. I do not expect to get all the cardinal virtues to live with me for their board and clothes. Jerry is more amusing than a menagerie of monkeys and kittens combined, and

Elsa is as pretty as a doll. I am satisfied with my bargain, and so is father since Liza has taught Jerry to bring him his pipe and slippers whenever he sits down in his easy-chair. Last night, while you were at Bessie's, he taught Jerry to sing 'Yankee Doodle,' and actually took little Elsa on his knee."

"I am delighted if your father finds amusement in Liza's encumbrances. Do you know, Mira, I feel very sorry for your father? Jack says there are notes for over four thousand dollars falling due next month; and he doesn't know where a dollar of it is coming from."

"Dora, I have heard that story ever since I was born! The boys never proposed any pleasure involving a dollar's expenditure, but the debts of thousands were opposed. Mother never suggested an improvement which would save her strength or add to her comfort, but the protested notes or threatened mortgages loomed in view."

"But the notes Jack mentioned were chiefly endorsements, where Mr. Morgan, with the kindliest motives, had gone security for his friends."

"When a man endorses a note, he knows what it means. If his friend is so hard pressed that he must borrow, and his credit requires bracing by another's credit, what reason has the man for thinking his friend will be able to pay the note when due? He seldom asks; he only hopes. Yet when forced to meet it, he grumbles and growls as if, by his signature, he had not agreed to do this very thing. I tell you, Dora, this credit system of doing business is disgusting and dangerous—a series of frauds which often deceive the deceivers."

"But how can it be avoided?"

"By four letters: C, A, S, H."

"But if you could not get cash?"

"Then I would take its equivalent. For instance, when I took lumber or leather to market, I would return with goods for the store, hides for the tannery, or comforts for home, in their place."

"And if a friend asked you to endorse a note for him?"

"I would answer, 'My friend, by putting my name here I promise to pay for you so much money. You do not ask it as a gift, so what will you give me as a full equivalent?'"

"An equivalent? that means a mortgage or something, I suppose."

"No: real estate might depreciate, so that I would lose my money; then I could not pay my obligations, and other people would suffer; or perhaps I could not sell the property at all. He must give me a cash equivalent for the note."

"And if he said, 'What you require would give to me now the needed amount?'"

"I would answer, 'Friend, that is also my opinion!'"

Both girls laughed as they tacked the wreaths of colored mosses and paper vases of pressed ferns upon the white walls.

"Maybe you would not find it so easy to transact business in that way as you fancy, Mira."

"Perhaps not; I would like to try it. But this I do know, Dora: if a woman took such risks in her household duties, the cloth for every garment would fall short in the cutting, and not a meal would be ready in time."

"That may be all true. I never gave it a thought before, innocently supposing men knew how to manage their affairs in a sensible way. But, unreasonable as it may be, Mira, I am sorry for your father; he looks so care-worn, and seems so lonely."

"Dora, my dear sister, please do not misunderstand me: I pity my father from my inmost heart—pity him for giving pecuniary credit to strangers, and denying affection's credit to his family; pity him most of all because he would indignantly spurn the sympathy his soul craves! My father has a strong, self-reliant nature, and has battled with adverse circumstances all his life. Not one desire, not one ambition, has been satisfied; and now, when age and sorrow are weakening his body, his spirit faces and fights the obstacles just as defiantly as ever."

"You mean as *bravely* as ever."

"Yes, it is brave; though I cannot help seeing how easily many obstacles might have been removed; how difficulties were at first only trifles; how a kindly word might have transformed a malicious enemy into a valuable friend; in short, how much strength and skill have been wasted, how much energy and intellect misdirected: and where arrogance failed, gentleness might have won. His unyielding spirit must need this discipline. I do not think the Master has allowed him, or us through him, to suffer too much. And yet, Dora, the object of my father's coming into this wilderness, away from all culture and comradeship—the object for which he has worked and worried a score of years—is slipping from his grasp, and may never be attained."

"What do you mean?"

"This property, which was almost free from debt when Jamie left us, is now badly involved; to what extent I do not know, nor whether father has any plans for releasing it."

"My poor Mira! I did not know the trouble was so serious."

"It is not the loss of the property I mind, so much as the suspense and the forced inaction. If father would give me a share of the labors and responsibilities of the business, I know I could save him some care and many dollars. But to be forced to idly wait and wonder and dread—this is misery!"

The last festoon of evergreen was arranged, and the girls stepped to the entrance to view the effect.

"Now fancy the gift-tree in the centre of the platform, with the little candles Bessie's making, all ablaze, and the little lace bags full of candy, and apples and strings of pop-corn loading the branches. What a jolly time those urchins of mine will have!"

"What is your programme for Christmas-eve?"

"Oh, we are to have a chorus from the school, and a speech from Squire Noyes—don't raise your eyebrows so—of course we must have a speech; the American mind ever demands a speech, and who so able to gratify both juvenile and masculine tastes as the I-flatter-myself squire? Then

Jack has promised a song, after which a few remarks from Miss Morgan will be in order. No? Well, then, little Sammy Jenkins will recite ' 'Twas the night before Christmas.' That is too funny for anything! He jumbles and stumbles over the lines at racing speed, never stopping to pick up the dropped words or catch his breath, making the most absurd gestures and funniest grimaces."

"But why haven't you taught him to say it properly?"

"Oh, he learned it at home, and I dare not interfere with Polly's teaching. Sam taught the gesticulations, I think. The boy is a perfect personification of Puck. After that performance, the goodies will be distributed to all, and my special gifts to the scholars; then another chorus and dismissal. Mira, I do believe it is raining again."

"I hope not. It's an old saying that if the river shuts up before Christmas 'twill break up before New-year's; but the weather has been so intensely cold, the ice must be very thick, and the river is very low."

"Jack says a rise in the branches would cause a break-up here without much rain. Just look what a quantity of logs are on the bank, and the board-yard is almost full. What *immense* loads of lumber those teams are drawing!"

They stood by the window, looking at the dull gray sky, black mountains, and white valley, with snow-roofed buildings and snow-walled paths. Some men unloading sleighs of scantling, and adding it to the piles on the river-bank, the blanketed teams stamping restlessly in the snow—these were the only signs of life. The south wind blew in fitful puffs as the girls walked homeward, and the gray light of evening settled down in the little valley. A crimson radiance swept across the road from the doorway of the blacksmith-shop; and Jack was lighting the lamps in the store as they passed by.

"Let's go in for a moment," said Dora.

"You may; and get the mail if we have any. I must hurry home and get supper."

A half-hour later Dora and Jack entered. "No more customers to-night," he said, shaking the rain-drops from his coat. "'Twill take the ice out if it rains a day or two longer. I doubled the ropes on them maple rafts this afternoon, though your father thought it was nonsense. He don't think the ice will go out; but Long John does, and he's the surest weather prophet I know of. Supper? Yes, your father heard the bell, but he is posting books. Let's go and try that new music till he comes."

The songs were sung, the supper eaten and cleared away; but Jack lingered by the fireside, now and then throwing a stick on the blazing embers and watching the sparks fly up the wide chimney. Dora had excused herself and gone to her room. Mr. Morgan wound up the clock, set back the chairs, and entered his bedroom, closing the door emphatically. Yet Jack did not go. Miriam's needle flew in and out of the canvas she was embroidering. The rain dashed against the windows, the wind whistled and moaned at the doors. Jack leaned back in his chair and looked long and tenderly at the fair, earnest face before him.

"Miriam"—the dark eyes looked inquiringly into his—"Miriam, it was just twenty-two years ago today that your mother put you in my arms. I was a shy, awkward boy, an' you was the prettiest baby ever was! You looked up in my face an' laughed jest the sweetest little gurgle of a laugh, an' I could 'ave gone down on my knees an' worshipped ye then; you seemed so sort o' holy! Well, Miriam, you know how it's been ever sence. W'en you got big enough to go to school, I drawed ye on my hand-sled. I learned ye to skate, an' ride horseback, an' drive; I whittled out playthings an' tended your flowers; I done everything I could to make you happy. No, don't interrupt me, *please, Miriam!* Don't think I'm mentioning this 'cause I feel 's if you owed me anything! Heaven knows I've been paid a hundred-fold by seeing one glad smile in your eyes; an' when you used to come an' nestle your little hand in mine, an' raise them moist rosy lips for a kiss—why, Miriam, I'd resk my life—*my soul*—for your sake. Oh, don't go 'way! Miriam, for once, *only this once*, listen to me! An' then I'll go 'way, where you'll never see nor hear from me again; or I'll stay an' work on an' keep silent, jest as you say. Miriam, 'tain't much I ask."

She stood before him, flushed, tearful, half yielding, half turned away. "Oh, Jack! oh, my dear, good friend! I know what you would tell me; but can't you see, don't you feel, what I *must* answer?" And her hands covered the crimson face as she sank on the stool at his feet.

"No, Miriam; you don't know all I have to tell you. 'Tain't only to say *I love you!* Every act, an' word, an' look, has told ye that sence you can remember, an' yet ye can't know what it means! Nobody does, 'nless they've seen the sunshine glorified, an' the hull earth look radiant when a woman smiled, an' the earth an' the air seem to lose their brightness when she went away. Oh, Miriam, you don't know nothin' 'bout a man's love! No other woman has ever attracted me for a moment. You have stood in the place of God to me; my judge, my lawgiver! Anything that could debase me in your sight, I have turned from with loathing; anything that would make you think well of me, I have tried with all my might to be and do. An' what for, Miriam? I knew you only thought of me as a friend—a sort of adopted brother; I knew you was my superior in every way, an' wa'n't in no way adapted to me nor my life. Yet, Miriam, jest so long as you loved nobody any better; so long as you come to me for help or for counsel now an' then—so long as you *needed* me, Miriam—why, I was willing to stay and work on right here."

"Then why have you spoken now? Oh, Jack! understanding it all so well, why give us both this suffering?"

"Because I had to: your father told me to speak! His business is in a bad condition. He needs a junior partner to manage the mills. He told me to marry his daughter an' take a third interest in the business.

"Don't move away from me, Miriam! I told him we did not care for each other in that way. He said he knew I had no bad habits, was industrious, honest, and so on, an' that you liked nobody any better. You was a good housekeeper, and I liked you better 'n anybody else. Said he felt anxious to have you settled. He would build a house for you and furnish it. The partnership would begin in January; our marriage be in the spring."

Miriam rose and walked to the fireplace, resting her head against the mantel. Jack stood with fingers tightly clasped, and his pale face twitching with suppressed pain.

"I see what you hate to say, Miriam. It hurts you to think of me as your husband! Be as kind as I could, as wise as I could, 'twouldn't satisfy you, an' thinkin' you ough' to love me more 'n you could would make you unhappy, maybe, an' both of us miserable.

"Well, I won't say no more, *never!* We'll let things be as they have been. I will do my best in the store, an' help your father all I can. Good-night, Miriam. Don't let this trouble you; you are just the same to me you've always been."

He opened the door. A gust of rain and wind swept in.

"Hark! What's that? Not the ice? It is! *The ice is going out!*"

He rushed out into the darkness —ran up the road—across the bridge —and was rapping at Bill Morris's door as Miriam awakened her father.

"It can't be the ice!" Mr. Morgan exclaimed. "It is the wind you hear."

But a louder roar and a crash like a falling forest answered him.

"*It is going!* and twenty thousand feet of lumber will go with it. Good heavens! haven't I anybody to help me?"

He rushed from the house, without hat or coat, wildly shouting, "Bill! Jack! Help here!"

The wind tossed his appeal to the clouds. The roar from the maddened river grew louder.

Crash! crash! came the ice against the shore; the trees shivered and fell; the piles of lumber heaved slowly upward, slid downward, and were borne away. Huge logs reared themselves like trees, leaned shoreward imploringly, then plunged desperately beneath the crowding cakes of ice, and were carried on.

"Bill! Jack!"—the frenzied man ran on—"the ice is going out! All hands help!"

"Yes, sir; we're coming!" two voices answered, as Bill crossed the bridge — already upheaved by the flood—with a boat-hook in one hand and a lantern in the other; and Jack ran from the store with a coil of rope on either arm. The rain had ceased, and the clouds were rolling and tossing as the moonlight struggled through.

"Father, father!"—it was Miriam's voice—"here's your coat and hat; let me help you."

She put the unresisting arm in the

sleeve. "Now the other, so; and here's the lantern, father."

He took it mechanically from her hand, gazing steadily out on the mass of rolling ice as it ground the timber to atoms and shook the ground beneath his feet. The men were running from one point to another, yelling directions which no one heeded, striving to rescue some lumber from the general ruin. In vain! The cables snapped like cords. The rafts floated away on the swelling waters, and the ice-blocks leaped upon them, tore them stick from stick, whirled and tossed them, and bore them away. The frantic bellowing of a calf, the cackle of hens, and a black mass floating by, told them Long John had lost his barn. Now a haystack, now a raft, now a boat went by. The ice reared itself block on block, the blue edges glistening in the moonlight, till they overtopped the highest bank; then fell with a deafening crash and a roar that seemed to shake the sky. Then came a pause and a swift surge backward of the angry waters.

"*It's damming up!*" Big Bill yelled. "Now we'll get drownded clean out."

The men left the lumber and ran to the tannery and mill.

"It's no use," muttered Mr. Morgan, as he tried to follow them. "It will all go! Wife, sons, all are gone! Everything's gone."

"I'm here, father; you have me." Miriam's arm was around him, Miriam's face close to his. He did not hear her; he did not think of her.

"Please come to the house, father! There are enough men here now. You are all wet and shivering with cold."

He pushed her aside impatiently. "Go 'way, go 'way! This is no place for a girl. Go pack up your clothes: the house may go before morning."

He walked toward the mill, but the bridge had gone. The water already surrounded the tannery, and logs and ice were floating up the valley, borne upon the resistless current of backwater. Then came a low rumbling and a crash, as though the foundations of the earth were rent asunder; one surging, seething moan, and the black waters sucked in every floating thing and rushed away into the mighty river. Every man stared breathlessly at the two buildings: were they undermined? and would they fall? Old Mose's voice shouted a reply, half drowned by the roar of waters:

"That tha-ur mill won't go. Got a good foundation; laid it myself. An' the tannery won't go nuther: there hain't no current agin it neow."

"I apprehend little further danger," Squire Noyes said to Miriam and Dora, as with hands clasped they stared in agony at the destruction around them.

"Oh, if the mill and tannery are not ruined, we may make up the loss; but see those scantling rafts, Dora! all broken into kindling-wood. The labor of months past, the hope for years to come, all destroyed in an hour! Oh, it is terrible!"

The overstrained nerves began to yield. Miriam trembled like a tree shaken by the wind. Dora's tears, repressed for a moment by the agony of increased terror, began to flow again. "Oh me! oh me!" she sobbed. "It is too awful! Everything will have to be sold—there's no lumber to pay the debts—oh, what shall we do?"

"Dora"—it was Jack's voice, and Jack's face—white and aged since she saw it by the evening fire-light—looked sternly into hers—"you'd better go to the house an' have Liza build a fire and get dry clothes ready for Miriam. She'll come when she sees the buildings are safe." He took the unresisting hand in his, and Miriam followed him up the road, while Dora hurried to the house, crying as she ran.

"The store ain't touched by th' water, Miriam, nor the house nuther; the vats is overflowed to th' tan'ry, and maybe some leather spoilt in th' dryin'-house; but the buildings is all right. Bill and Sam got over the bridge jest as it went off. Lucky they did, for they can get the flood-trash out th' mill: no knowing when they'd a' got over now, fur every stick o' th' bridge went, an' th' boats are all gone. Guess I can make a float an' pole up to the bark-sheds, an' see how much damage is done around there: the flat is washed out some, I s'pose. Them two maple rafts that I put more ropes on didn't go; they was shoved up on the eddy lot, an' are all covered up by cakes of ice. Guess when the water's gone down we can pick up a lot o' lumber worth rafting over. Things ain't half so bad as they might be."

A grateful glance was reward enough for his attempt at consolation.

"I will have breakfast ready soon," Miriam said, as Jack left her at the gate. "Have the men who worked all night come in."

The crimson light of sunrise tinged the sky and rested on the eastern hills; the snow-capped rocks glittered like masses of gold. Brighter, fairer grew the morning, while a mist covered the narrowing river, concealing the ruin night and rain had wrought. Slowly the white vapor rose, the gilded hills, the radiant sky vanished; only the faint outlines of home were visible beneath a dull gray sky.

"How like my life!" Miriam sighed, wearily, as she turned away and entered the house.

* * * * * *

The Christmas holidays were over. The mill had been repaired, and workmen were busy restoring bridges, tannery vats, mill-dams, and shops. The monotonous, never-completed labors of house and store went on as usual; and the school resumed its daily sessions.

One sunlit evening, Dora, walking homeward, stopped at the post-office for the mail. Several papers for herself and a letter for Mira were given her.

"It is from Miss Caldwell," she said to Jack. "I'm so glad she has written at last! We have not heard a word from her since she left the old Sem and went to Philadelphia."

Miriam read its contents with surprise. "Dora, she is going West as a missionary to the Indians! Did you ever hear anything so strange? With her culture and refinement, her horror of anything rude or vulgar, and her utter ignorance of uncivilized customs; why, one-half her salary would support a more efficient missionary than she will make, and—"

"Oh, read the letter to me, and moralize afterward."

"'My dear Miriam,—Circumstances which I may never be able to explain, make it necessary for me to leave my pleasant school and all the associations which have made this the happiest year of my life. I would be glad to leave my dearly loved pupils in charge of some one I know and can trust. I have thought of Dora Montgomery. If she is with you and is willing to take my position, ask her to come on at once, that I may give her some aid in adopting my methods, which are very successful and highly commended. It will be a consolation to me, in my exile, to know that one of my most esteemed young ladies of the past, which contrasted with—'

("Something has been erased. How different this letter appears from her usual elegant chirography! I cannot understand it."

"Well, read on; maybe I can.")

"'You will pardon my evident haste when I tell you I am preparing to go to the Western wilds as a missionary to the Sioux Indians. My intentions are as yet kept a secret from my friends and pupils. When a substitute is found for my school and my preparations are completed, then I will declare my purpose. Let me hear from you by return mail. I trust Dora will accept the situation; she cannot obtain one more lucrative or pleasant. With love to you, my dear Miriam, I must close. We may never meet again in this life, but I pray we may see each other in that far-off heaven where the wicked cease from troubling and the weary are at rest. Your attached friend,

"'Anna Caldwell.'"

"She does not say one word about terms or the number of her pupils," said Dora. "Our methodical preceptress is excessively flustrated about something. What's that about the wicked ceasing? Somebody's troubling the dear little soul. Oh, say, Mira, didn't our uncle Walton get that school for her?"

"Yes; that is, he engaged and furnished her school-room, and by his influence obtained the larger portion of the scholars: you know he thinks she has no equal as a teacher. But what do you say to her proposal?"

"What shall I say, Mira?"

"I do not want to prevent your getting a larger salary, or having more congenial society than these woods can furnish, but oh, my sister, it will be very hard to let you go!"

Dora threw her arms around Mira's neck and kissed her lips.

"That settles it, you blessed old darling! I was awfully afraid you wanted to get rid of me. No, indeed! Miss Caldwell will have to hunt another substitute. But what in the world makes her leave so desirable a situation, do you suppose? Is Mrs. Walton—"

"What, Dora?"

"No matter; it is none of my business, anyway. But I don't believe it is love for Poor Lo takes her into the wilderness. I will write to her this evening."

"Dora, you know our brothers say they are coming home soon?"

"Yes."

"How the pleasure of their coming would be spoiled if you were not here!"

"Mira, my sister, I don't want to go. I would rather teach these eager-faced, wide-awake urchins than the most refined and fashionable children in the land. I would not exchange my home here among the hills for any city boarding-house; and, *ma chère belle sœur*, you know there is no society in the world so delightful to me as your own. So let's write our regrets to Miss Caldwell, wishing her all the success possible in her new sphere, and—then don't let's say another word about it."

The lamps were lighted, the curtains drawn, and again the little household settled down to the routine of fireside pleasures and daily duties.

CHAPTER XX.

"So long! I announce a life that shall be
Copious, vehement, spiritual, bold.
And I announce an old age that shall
Lightly and joyfully meet its translation."
WALT WHITMAN.

"THREE years and a half since Theo was here, is it not? a brief, sad visit! And now we are going to have both our brothers near us for good and all! It really seems too good to be true, doesn't it, Dora? I expect Davy will be changed considerably by four years on the frontier."

"Yes; 'bearded like a pard,' no doubt."

"And sunbrowned. But his eyes—they will be unaltered—such laughing, sparkling eyes Davy has! But I suspect he will find us changed, too. And poor father! always so strong and active, to see him sit there helplessly waiting for some one's hands and feet to serve him! Don't you think, Dora, that he can speak more distinctly than when he was first paralyzed?"

"I do not know. This morning he told Jack to have the deed of the Wharton place recorded immediately. Jack said, 'Yes, sir,' as he always does; but I felt sure he did not know one word your father said; so I followed him out and explained. It happened to be something of importance, and your father seemed so pleased at being understood."

"Then, really, I suppose he is no better. What a mercy he can speak at all! If he had been picked up dead when he fell in the store, our whole property might have been wasted in settling false claims and debts long since paid. I have compelled men to give me receipts for money paid years ago, and collected debts Jack said were outlawed. How provoked Davy would be to look over Jack's ledger! There are accounts running into hundreds of dollars against men who own nothing—not even the clothes they wear—men who are never honest till they *must* be, and whom Davy never trusted to a dime's worth of anything. But father, for all he seemed so stern, could never refuse a skilful pleader. He often reminded me of the unjust judge: 'Because this woman troubleth me,' the request was granted. Yesterday Jack received a new set of books, and a list of names not to be recorded."

"But what will these people do?"

"Learn to be honest, I hope. Do with less, and earn enough to pay for it. It is a sin to reduce laborers to paupers. In this lumbering country, where labor is fluctuating, there is a constant tendency to overwork and idleness. Between the rafting seasons there are lands to clear, and fields and gardens to till. Both stock and dairy farms are needed here, and employment and wages are abundant to those who desire them. But this credit system, once introduced, has spread like a weed, destroying the industry and independence of a naturally honest people."

"What did Jack mean by saying you could soon own all the land around you?"

"That we might sell goods to these men until every acre they now own was covered with debt, and sheriff sales had reduced them to beggary. But by insisting upon monthly settlements, the honest will be made frugal, and the dishonest restrained."

"Maybe they will take their custom elsewhere, my far-seeing, self-sacrificing merchant!"

"Perhaps so; but I hope to show them the mutual benefit of independence. How it degrades these free-hearted, free-spoken lumbermen to fawn around a rich man begging his favor! They should be as self-reliant as these hills—as unflinching in their integrity as these rocks!"

"You wax eloquent, *ma belle*. How your eyes shine, O champion of liberty! I could fancy you leading an armed host on to victory."

"I can only fancy myself stimulating the self-respect and encouraging the ambition of a few laborers; but in these stalwart, loud-voiced men and women, I see courage, energy, intelligence, which, developed, will be a power in the land for good; if repressed, will be idleness, despondency, and poverty: if misdirected, will grow into recklessness, craftiness, and misery."

"And that is why you will not sell your inheritance, and go where you would find more congenial associates?"

"Yes. You remember Jamie's last words; his work and his lands seem an equal heritage to me."

A sudden silence fell between them, and the southern breeze filled the room with the fragrance of spring flowers.

"Dora, what day do you think our boys will come? Did the postscript, which slipped away so mysteriously, say nothing more definite? Ah, if Davy could see that blush!"

"What a tease you can be, Mira! I believe all the stories Davy writes of your mischief when a child. No; you are as well informed of their plans as I. They are coming from Galveston to New York by steamer."

"They may telegraph their arrival."

"No; they will just walk in some evening when my flowers are all faded, the larder empty, and our work scattered about."

"There is only one way to prevent, Dora. I will keep the larder supplied; you replenish the vases every day; and we will keep our rooms in order."

"'A second Solomon! O wise young judge, how I do honor thee!'"

"I have made the proposal to Bessie's cousin. She comes Monday."

"I am glad of that. You have been kitchen-maid long enough, considering you are an heiress. Morris says you are worth four hundred thousand dollars."

"*Me?* If *I* am not worth more than units and ciphers can express, I am poor indeed! But money is power, and I am glad to possess it. I see so much good to be accomplished by it."

"A new house built, for instance."

"Yes, if it can be done without destroying this room. These walls—this furniture—are more sacred to me than church or cathedral. Jack has a plan to submit to our boys when they come. I would not like large rooms. I should be lonely in them when Davy takes you away, as I presume he will. And yet I want a large space that can be brilliantly lighted and warmed with open fires, to entertain large companies—the workmen and their families occasionally, and other parties when I choose. Then, when Davy and his wife, and Theodore and his wife come to see me, I want nice, well-furnished rooms for them."

"Theo's wife, Mira?"

"And so I shall need a spacious mansion," Miriam continued, with heightened color, "and several rooms with movable partitions, sliding doors, Japanese screens, or something of that kind. Davy may have some new ideas."

"What has become of the merchant with a Hebrew countenance who was to come here this spring? I hear nothing more about him."

"He was shown the plans for our new store, informed that the timber was at the mill, and the carpenters coming next week."

"And did that scare him off?"

"That, and the announcement that the stock would be double the present amount, and the store would be opened with a new name."

"What—Miriam Morgan?"

"No: Rodgers & Morgan."

"Jack?"

"Of course."

"Well, indeed!"

"It is time his services were appreciated. He could have received double the salary father has given him by going to the city; but he stayed here because we needed him. Hereafter it shall be for his interest to stay."

"That will make his mother happy. But if he asks to be partner in a wider sense—a nearer connection?"

"Dora, Jack and I understand each other. We settled that long ago. We tried to be as brother and sister; but the feeling lacked something and possessed something not belonging to that relation. Now we are *friends* in the truest sense of that word."

"An unsatisfactory relation."

"To some people, in most circumstances, but the best possible to us. Think, Dora; I could not marry Jack. Good as we know he is, his very goodness would weary me, it is so commonplace. His inelegance, which I do not mind' in Jack, would annoy and disgust me in a husband. The rare, gentle caresses he gives me are very sweet. If more frequent, or more fervent, they would fill me with loathing. And he—he would find himself illy mated to my flights of fancy, my luxurious tastes, my earnest beliefs."

"But if you meet some one just adapted to your views of life—one who could sympathize with your poetic fancies?"

"I never have. I do not think I ever will. You are thinking of your brother, Dora. Oh, you thought yourself very sly! Now, sister dear, I admire Theo very much; I enjoy his society; we have many ideas and aspirations in common; but if he should ask me to be his wife, I would wish we had never met! Dora, I have my own life to live, unfettered by any promise that could bind my future. I have my own duties to perform, unhindered by any human. A man who would enter my life to obey my will and carry out my plans, I *would* not marry; and one who has his own ideas and purposes to develop, I *could* not marry. So you see, dear, I am to round and perfect my life into a symmetrical whole: while you, poor deluded creature, are satisfied to become the better half of a real human man. Now I must go and decoct some dainties for the larder, and leave you to decorate the rooms."

The next day brought the travellers. The welcome the girls gave was intended to recompense them for long-missed caresses, and atone for the mother's kisses they would never again know. Mr. Morgan's feeble intellect recognized them both, and he tried to utter some word of welcome, but his palsied tongue gave only a low, inarticulate sound, and his hand could not return their greeting.

"How long has father been in this deplorable condition?" Davy inquired.

"Almost two years. I wrote to you of it."

"The letter was never received. Both your letters and Dora's have spoken of him as an invalid, but I had no idea he could be so helpless. What caused it?"

"He had worked and worried more than usual; many debts pressed him heavily, and collections were hard to make. He was settling a long-standing account with some men in the store; some entries were disputed, and he became very much excited; began to stammer and falter in his speech, then dropped helplessly to the floor. We thought he was dead when they brought him in; but day by day he has improved, until he is what you now see him—a restless soul, with a feeble mind in a helpless body."

"Will he never get well?"

"No; the physicians say he will never get better. They think he had a slight attack some time ago. Now he is only waiting the third and last, which is to set him free."

"And you, dear sister, have all this to bear!"

She looked up with a calm smile on her fair face. "It is a part of my heritage, Davy."

"And is he patient?"

"Usually; with that repressed, regretful look on his face that makes me long to tell him the past is all forgiven; that his liabilities are discharged, his credit redeemed, and his chief ambition gratified. Oh, how I wish he could feel the love and sympathy I have longed all my life to give him! But if our affection is desired or reciprocated, we can never know it now."

"Did not the loss of Jamie and mother soften him?"

"Not outwardly. The tears, which should have fallen, seemed to congeal in his heart. Suffering irritated him; when thwarted, he grew defiant. His thoughts, ambitions, affections, seemed all absorbed in the one desire to get property."

"Yes, and his daily demand was always *my will be done*. Yet he used to talk of slaving himself to death *for his family*, when an hour's participation in our sports, any appreciation of our desires and pleasures, would have been worth more to us than all the forests and farms in the county. I suppose he excused himself to his reason and conscience by thinking of the good the money would do us in our old age. He was putting us through purgatory that we might enjoy heaven; which sounds orthodox."

They talked of the condition of the property, of which Davy steadily refused a share. Of the needed improvements in mills and on farms.

"I am running the tannery on half-time now," Miriam said, "as leather is falling. But all of the best hands are kept; having comfortable houses and large gardens rent free, with opportunities of doing odd jobs about the home farm. Have you noticed the new street?"

"Yes; how the place has improved! Do you rent those Gothic cottages?"

"They belong to the tannery. I noticed some of the little houses in the Row were neatly kept, with an attempt at flower-culture before the door. So I had a new street laid out farther up the hill, and the first cottage was built at a venture. Roberts was directed to move in; and while the place was neatly kept, and his work satisfactory, the house and lot were free of rent. Then another, as pretty and convenient, but slightly different in appearance, was built, and Henderson moved in. The men understood it was a reward of merit, and the Row began to improve in appearance; rubbish disappeared, and by the time my six cottages were occupied the twenty little houses in the Row were vastly improved. Then I began to help them, and the women and children were delighted. For a month the bell for quitting work rang at five instead of six o'clock, and, through the long summer evenings, hammers and saws, whitewash and paint-brushes, were kept busy. Every house has now a summer kitchen and wood-house; nearly all have a porch and blinds; and each one has a white fence enclosing a garden, two shade-trees, and some flowers. Morris declares the men finished off more first-class leather that month than ever before; though he grumbled considerably over that lost hour when I gave the order."

"Does the reading-room still exist?"

"There are two. One has daily and local papers, with agricultural journals and popular magazines: this is self-supporting. The other has religious and scientific journals, maps, charts, and desks for writing. Our old picnic-ground has been cleared, and named Our Park. There the women bring their children and work; the boys and girls play, and their mothers gossip over their sewing."

"A real Arcadia, Miriam."

"Not at all. These people have little resemblance to the half-clad shepherds playing on their lutes. Do not think they have become angelic. They have their quarrels and prejudices. Jack's patience is often exhausted by their unreasonable demands; and the children vex Dora's righteous soul from day to day."

"Morris has charge of the tannery?"

"Yes; and Sam Jenkins of the mill. They each own their houses and four acres of land around them. Jane Rodgers's husband is team-boss, and her mother lives with them. But I see father is getting tired, and Jack has come to put him to bed."

The paralytic's chair was wheeled from the room, and the brothers and sisters gathered around the melodeon. Jack soon joined them, and his violin gave a prelude to each verse of Miriam's song.

"Home once more!
Welcome back to tree-crowned mountains,
Welcome to their pure sweet fountains,
Home once more.
Welcome to the fragrant wildwood
Where we wandered in our childhood
As of yore. Home once more.

"Just the same
Rolls the deep, transparent river;
On its waves the moonbeams quiver
Just the same.
Crickets chirr, and whippoorwill,
Calling from the distant hill,
Are in name just the same.

"Yet, how changed!
In the old familiar places
We see not the loving faces.
We are changed;
And with sad and weary yearning,
Life's hard lessons we are learning—
Oh how strange seems the change!

"Where are they
Who once shared in all our gladness?—
Counselled us in all our sadness?
Where are they?
While each heart in praise rejoices,
We are listening for their voices.
Tell me, pray—where are they?

"All are here.
Not in shadows of the room,
Not in chilling midnight gloom,
Are they here;
But in words our hearts still cherish,
Deeds which nevermore shall perish,
They are here, ever near."

The sweet thrilling voice ceased suddenly. Then the fingers glided over the keys, and the violin caught up the strain,

"Home, sweet home."

Other old favorites followed, until the clock on the mantel told them it was time for retiring.

"Can I have my old quarters in the store?" Davy asked.

"Yes: Dora and I have prepared it for both you and Theo, if you prefer it."

"You know *I* would: I haven't slept in the house since I outgrew my trundle-bed."

"It will seem much more like old times to me also," said Theodore.

Good-night kisses were exchanged, and the three young men left the house, Montgomery accompanying Davy to the room he and Jamie had occupied since boyhood. None of their old treasures had been removed. "Ah, here is my old rifle, and there is my Minerva," pointing to an owl perched above the mirror. "I took that bird from its nest and tamed it, so 'twould come to me when I called its name. How mother has laughed when seeing me stand on the gate-post, with a string of fish in my hand, yelling 'Minerva! Minerva!' She told me whenever I worked as hard, and called as earnestly for wisdom, I would become an astonishingly learned man. My owl died at last: so I tried taxidermy on her, and put her over the looking-glass. And here are Jamie's books. How near he seems!—as if he might enter the room this moment, with the old greeting and cheering smile. With father's quick temper born in both, we never quarrelled but once. Then we each wanted the same thing, and from words came to blows. I had just raised my fist to strike back, when some one caught my hand. It was mother. Oh my, how she looked! Pale, stern, with such a grieved expression in her eyes, she led us to her room, and, kneeling down with Jamie on one side and I on the other, she prayed. I shall remember that prayer if I forget my name! We were both crying when she rose. Then she made us shake hands with each other, and ask forgiveness. That was pretty severe. I remember Jamie hung back a little, but finally he got it out: 'I'm sorry, Dave; pl-please for-gim-me.' Of course I could say it after him; and then we had to kiss each other. That was a hard one for me.

I thought kissing rather unmanly at any time; but to be forced to kiss my brother when I was mad at him—for neither of us was quite conquered—that was rough. But we had to do it; and the instant our lips touched, why, I loved Jamie as I never had before! He should have my top and marbles, and everything he wanted; and we ran off together the two happiest boys in the country. We had many a disagreement after that, as boys will; but never again did he give me an unkind word. Oh, Jamie! oh, mother!"

Davy threw himself on the bed, and turned his face to the wall. A long silence, in which each thought the other sleeping, was broken by a muttered exclamation from Montgomery:

"If I only could; but it's no use!"

"Could what, Theo?"

"Oh, you are awake, Davy? I was thinking of your sister. If I could only win her, life would be worth living; but there's no use trying!"

"She likes you, Theo."

"Yes; I presume she likes a dozen just as well! She seems to have no thought of marriage."

"The fact is, Theo, she is too busy to think of lovers; and she never felt a lack of love."

"Dora told me she had received many offers of marriage, but declined them all. She said men were continually mistaking her courteous, confidential manner for love, and her earnest sympathy for a special preference; not seeing her in general society enough to know it was Miriam's way. The homage of many is worth more to her than the devotion of one."

"Don't get bitter, Theo. You know nothing would suit me better than to see Miriam your wife; but—" "I understand; you do not give me much hope. Well, I shall not make a fool of myself by whining. We will be the best of friends always. I will win and hold the first place in her esteem; and if she ever marries, I am confident the happy man will be Theodore Montgomery."

"Good. Hurrah for you! Now let's sleep on that resolution."

The following days were spent inspecting the tannery and mills, sanctioning Miriam's improvements, and suggesting further alterations, wandering through the woods and up the brook, hunting, fishing, picnicing day after day.

"Davy," said Miriam, one evening, after Jack's designs for the new house had been discussed and approved, "I want you and Dora married here. This is the bride's home. Her mamma is too much of an invalid to care for the ceremony, and her Uncle Lemar can come here if he will. Now wait until you are established in business with Uncle Dave, and my mansion is ready for guests, and we will have a grand wedding."

He looked at Dora.

"I think that a good plan, Davy."

"But it will be a year — maybe two!"

"And am I not worth working and waiting for so long?"

"That settles it, I suppose, and dooms Uncle Dave and I to months of loneliness. When did Aunt Clarissa die?"

"She has been dead to all society for years. No one but her nurse and physician were allowed to approach her for months. About five months ago she breathed her last."

"Where is Miss Caldwell?"

"She went West two years ago as a missionary to the Indians; and we have not heard a word from her since. I fear the rough life has proved too much for her delicate form."

"There you are mistaken. Frontier life develops and hardens delicate people, if there is any *vim* and *grit* in them; and Miss Caldwell has both, with a keen insight into human nature, and some faculty of adapting herself to circumstances. She never had half a chance to develop her good qualities among a set of school-girls."

"Well, I'm sure we exercised her tact and patience to the utmost," said Dora; "but you speak as though you knew her."

"I do, by good report. About ten leagues from San Antone is a temporary mission for a tribe of Comanches. A lady has charge, and I am certain it is our Miss Caldwell. I will ask Uncle Dave."

"He does not know, Davy. He wrote to Miriam asking her address."

"Then she determined to bury herself, did she? I fancy I can see through that. Poor Uncle Dave! poor, conscientious little teacher! But that will come out right, I'm sure it will. I'm provoked at myself for never riding over to the Mission. Captain Hyde did frequently, and was always talking of Miss Caldwell. Though I recognized the name, and the captain's description reminded me of her, yet I did not suppose it could be your preceptress. Now, however, I am sure it is. Here's a romance for your next novel, Dora. Sequel: uncle leaves me in charge of business, and goes to the South-west for his health. He is captured by the Indians; they tear off his garments, discover a gold trinket suspended from his neck; they break it open, and are appalled by the face of their teacher —their angel—looking reproachfully into their eyes; they prostrate themselves before their captive; they re-robe him; they convey him to the Mission and present him as a free-will offering to their adored missionary. That is so like the Indians—of a romance!"

"The plot does very well so far; but I see no need of introducing the hero's business partner into the romance," said Dora, laughingly.

"No, Davy," added Miriam, "you should be satisfied to live in Dora's history. How perfectly delightful it will be if our hopes are realized—you and uncle settled in Philadelphia, and Fred and Theo in New York! I can spend a part of each winter with you, and you will all come here for the summer. You can treat me to opera, concert, lecture, and drama, and I will supply you with butter, berries, and game. Jack, show Theo your designs for the church. You know the site, Theo?"

"Yes; it was to that point I carried Birdie Thistledown once upon a time. Just there she sprang from my arms and flew away. This front is grand, Jack. I did not suspect you of being an architect."

"Oh, I'm a jack-of-all-trades and master o' none. Mis' Morgan used to be always talking 'bout having a church here, an' I began to sketch plans for her. Every time I went down the river I'd go and see some cathedral or big building, an' study up their 'coustics an' arkytexyer. Las' spring Fred an' me went up the North River a ways, an' see a church they're puttin' up, to cost more 'n a hundred thousand dollars. An' 'twon't be so pretty as ours, after all. Mister Morgan is agoin' to furnish a memorial window, an' Fred says he'll send us the pulpit an' altar. Now, you'd better give us the carpet and cushions."

"Jack," Miriam said, quickly, coming to the table, "will you see Sam Jenkins about those shade-trees? I want them set out this fall—maples from Morris's house to the end of the Row, and pines the entire length of Cottage Avenue. Can you think how pretty our village will be, Theo, with the vivid coloring of the maples on the lower road overlapping the evergreens higher up the hill, and the houses through the trees?"

"Yes, Miriam, it is a beautiful place; but, with all your improvements, it cannot be more charming than when I first saw it."

"No, I do not expect that. No landscape could be lovelier than the view from that hillside. I remember standing there, with Bruce by my side, long years ago, and thinking what a delight that scene must give its Creator."

They walked to the window facing the moonlit valley. "I cannot make the scene more beautiful than when you first saw it. To make beauty keep pace with utility is a constant study. How strange seems the law which destroys the lower to build the higher! To create, we must destroy. Our stone-quarry has ruined that lovely cascade; our lumber trade is ruining our forests. Art and science are built on the ruins of nature, and yet they perpetuate nature in more effective forms."

"How?—here, I mean—how does your mill and tannery, destroying so much loveliness, serve to perpetuate or elevate nature?"

"This little valley is a small bit of God's manufactory, Theodore; and these men and their labor resemble artists and art—as the iron ore resembles the engine. Yet because we are, they are."

"*We!* How you identify yourself with your surroundings! I never thought so imaginative a child could become so practical a woman."

"Nor I, Theo; but in accepting the inevitable, I strive constantly to make the *best* of it, which means much to me, infusing the ideal into the real. So, while these people are practical plodders, they may become earnest thinkers. Each human is a trinity, Theodore. We have the physical, intellectual, and spiritual natures combined. Each of us is stronger in one than the others. As some seeds develop roots before expanding into leaves or blossoms, so most people expand their consciousness from the lower nature into the higher. Bessie's little Mary is a child whose spiritual nature seems out of all proportion to her physical and mental. She cannot reason; she only feels. Already she sees visions and dreams dreams. She must take deeper root, or earth cannot hold her long."

"Do you regard such a being as the highest order of creation?"

"The highest is the most useful. The being best fitted to its sphere, most in harmony with its surroundings, must be the highest, I think. In that sense little Mary is certainly not the best type of our species. Yet she is necessary to counterbalance the physical in her parents. Have you seen Big Bill walk about the place with that child in his arms?"

"Several times. What a contrast she is to the big, burly fellow. He is very tender of her."

"She teaches him many things. The shrewd, sagacious fellow never noticed the difference between the rustle of the oak and the whisper of the hemlock, never saw the mimic forests among mosses, or the down on a butterfly, till she discovered them. The Lord's earth is lovelier since this gentle interpreter came to their home."

"What do you think of the evolution theory, Mira?"

"I see how things are *evolved*—the higher from the lower; and I see how things are *involved*—the higher into the lower. Science goes up step by step, tracing the development of nature to its source. Revelation shows the spirit infused downward, step by step, into the lowest forms of existence: the development of the mineral into the vegetable kingdom, the growth of the vegetable into the animal kingdom. This is no myth to me; for as I take the tiniest grass-blade or frailest insect in my hand, I see vitality, and trace it back to God. Begin with this triune being, man," she continued, smiling up in his face, "in whom the Creator breathed eternal life, and trace the flow of the infinite downward; or begin with the zoophyte, and trace the development upward, what difference in the conclusions? We only trace two sides of an oblong circle."

"Then our failing to comprehend the subject is caused by believing too little, not too much."

"I think so. Many things ceased to be mysteries to me when I dropped the leading-strings of prejudice, and walked on untrammelled. My reason rules my intellectual nature, but my spiritual is guided by faith; so I believe what I cannot understand."

"You always used to demand the what and why of everything," said Theodore.

"Yes; and was a great annoyance to every teacher but my mother, who always encouraged my inquiries. She taught me how the sensations which enter the five gates leading to the mind are transformed into thoughts; and I have since learned how they travel through the avenues of the mind out into the highways of one's spiritual nature, on, on beyond our power of speech. Then, when fretted by the limits of expression, I console myself with the surety of stepping out of the physical into the celestial body by-and-by."

"Do you ever wish to die, Mira?"

"No; I love this life. It is grand, glorious!"

"Do you remember those inspiring words of Mary Howitt's:

"'Oh, how I long to die!
To be among the stars, the glorious stars!
To have no bounds to knowledge;
To drink deep of crystal fountains;
To be among the good, the wise, the glorified.'

How often I have repeated those lines when lying upon my hammock facing a Southern sky!"

"They are beautiful; but I would alter the first line:

"'Oh how I long to *live* and *grow* among the stars!'

Death, decay, are repugnant to me. I am only reconciled to their necessity by seeing how quickly the vitality of the living transforms the dead atoms into new forms. But see! Jack has fallen asleep on the lounge, and Dora and Davy have left us. Metaphysics are uninteresting to them."

She drew back the muslin curtains, and the moonlight and vine shadows played upon the floor.

"See, Theo, how lovingly the light rests upon that hillside and glistens on that marble column! All around are the dark, still woods; but that little spot is not gloomy. Ah! what a transition that monument records! Death is swallowed up in victory."

"Are you reconciled to everything, Mira?"

"I can trust where I cannot comprehend, Theo! But my life seems natural, harmonious. Their work is now mine; and each day brings strength, zeal, courage, content. I am fitted to my work, and my work fits itself to me. Jack!"—she crossed the room and laid her hand on his shoulder—"Jack, you know you have to start on a collecting tour early to-morrow morning. Did Mose bring any plugs and bows to-day?"

"Yes," Jack answered, rubbing his eyes and yawning. "He brought about a hunderd, and got a sack of flour and a chunk of pork. Said ef I'd let him have a pair o' boots he'd pay for 'em in honey: he'd lined a bee-tree lately. I told him he promised to pay for the hat he had on with eels, but he went an' sold all his fish to the depot! An' he was goin' to give us maple-sugar for his coat, but he never has. He is the laziest coon ever was. Do you remember him, Montgomery?"

"Perfectly. Davy and I stopped him once in the road with a bundle of grubs on his shoulder, and got him to talking of his last bear-hunt; and he actually stood there thirty-five minutes talking, with that load on his back: forgot all about it. After he brought them to the store, we put the bundle on the scales, and it weighed two hundred and fifteen pounds. Say, Davy, do you remember that?"

"Of course I do," Davy answered, from the veranda, leaning in the low window. "Mose is one of the strongest men along the river; he can follow a deer for a week, carrying his gun and a pack of provisions through laurel-thickets and underbrush; but to think of hoeing potatoes or piling lumber tires him. Dora has four of his children in her school, and she says they are right smart children. I reckon the new stock is improved."

Jack gathered up his books and plans, and bade them good-night. Davy and Theodore followed, and the white mists of night rose from the placid river and enfolded Woodbine Cottage.

Another week brought the day of parting. The brothers were to enter new scenes of business and the sisters continue the routine of their varied duties.

"Only one more meal together before Thanksgiving-day," Miriam said, as, after breakfast, they gathered on the veranda. "Liza, wheel father's chair to the sunny side of the house, and take care of him until we come home. Now, Davy, let us go up to the cemetery."

They walked arm-in-arm up the hillside, Dora and her brother following, until they paused beside the flower-clad graves. Across the valley, on the opposite hillside, were the two lines of cottages. The Gothic fronts of the upper tier harmonized with the rocky mountain at their rear, and the white-and-green prettiness of the lower row blended with the colors of field and brook.

Beside the mill were piles of lumber; the pond was filled with logs; and the low buzz of the saw, and briskly stepping men, showed business was progressing there. Teams drawing heavy loads of bark were entering the tannery-yard; a cloud of smoke from the tall chimney soared away into the blue sky; through the open door of the store Jack's assistant could be seen displaying gay prints to some girlish customers; down the winding road and across the brook came Mrs. Rodgers, the only unchanged figure in the scene.

"She is going to sit with father," said Miriam. "Though she cannot understand what he tries to tell her, he seems to enjoy her presence. *Poor father!*"

For a long time they sat silent beside the low mounds which covered their dead, looking at the vine-wreathed cottage below them, and thinking of their past.

"Mira," said Davy at last, drawing a blank-book from his pocket, " may I read these verses which you sent me after Jamie died? Theo would like to hear them, and they seem very appropriate to this place and time."

"You may; but first let me tell you how they were written, and why I have never been sure whether the lines are original or remembered. I am not an habitual somnambulist; but Dora could tell you of my solving a mathematical problem once in my sleep that our entire class failed on the day before. Another time I finished an essay with a verse I was incapable of composing when awake. I only mention these incidents as facts. Some day I shall know the subtle influences which caused them. After Jamie had gone, my mind was restless and excited; I slept little, and then heavily. One morning this poem lay upon my table. Dora said I arose and, without lighting the lamp, sat for a long time, with my portfolio in my lap and my head resting on one hand, apparently writing."

"Have you offered them for publication?"

"No, Davy; such thoughts seem sacred to myself and my best friends. You may read them to us, if you will."

And while the sounds of industry in the valley below mingled with the whisper of the pine-trees around them, and the blue waters of the Delaware flowed calmly and swiftly by, Davy read these lines:

"PASSING AWAY.

"O River of Time, how ceaselessly
Thou flowest on to the boundless sea!
Whether upon thy glittering tide
The sweet spring blossoms drop and glide,
Or whether the fierce winds lash thy waves,
And dead leaves fall to their watery graves;
Whether we wake, or whether we sleep,
Thou hasteth on to Eternity's deep.

"With sunshine and shadow life's sweet May,
My childhood, silently floated away.
The summer rose is in its prime,
And youth floats by on the stream of time.
The hours, whether sunny or overcast,
Are flitting away to the changeless past;
But I mark their flight by a smile of cheer,
And not by a sigh or a falling tear.

"So often, so sadly, we hear men say
'Passing away! still passing away!'
That the words have gathered a pensive tone—
With a shade of sadness not their own.
And I long to recall these words again
From their minor key on the lips of men;
And make the refrain of my gladdest lay—
Passing away! ever passing away!

"For what is transient and what will last?
What maketh its grave in the growing past?
And what lives on in the deathless spheres
Where naught corrupts by the rust of years?
Doth Time, who gathers our fairest flowers,
Uproot no weeds in this world of ours?
What rises victorious o'er dull decay?
And what is that which is passing away?

"The year is flying. The hours flit by
Like morning clouds in a breezy sky.
But Time is a drop in the boundless sea
Of an infinite Eternity!
As our seas are spanned by the arching skies,
'Neath the presence of God that ocean lies;
And though tides may fall in life's shallow bay,
Eternity never can ebb away."

THE END.

www.ingramcontent.com/pod-product-compliance
Lightning Source LLC
Chambersburg PA
CBHW022115160426
43197CB00009B/1040